THE SOCIAL EDUCATION
OF THE ADOLESCENT

THE SOCIAL EDUCATION
OF THE ADOLESCENT

Bernard D. Davies M.A.

*Senior Lecturer in Social Studies at Chorley College
of Education, Lancashire;
formerly Lecturer and Tutor at the National College
for the Training of Youth Leaders, Leicester*

Alan Gibson M.A.

*Head of the Youth Service Information Centre;
formerly Lecturer and Tutor at the National College
for the Training of Youth Leaders, Leicester*

UNIVERSITY OF LONDON PRESS LTD

University of London Press Ltd
St Paul's House, Warwick Lane, London EC4

Copyright © 1967 Bernard D. Davies and Alan Gibson

Printed and bound in Great Britain by
C. Tinling and Co. Ltd, Liverpool, London and Prescot

Contents

Acknowledgments

We wish to acknowledge our debt to the members of the National College for the Training of Youth Leaders for four stimulating and happy years of discussion and learning; and to thank, as well as our wives, Bill and Nessie Bayley, Maurice Craft, Jalna Hanmer, Islwyn Jones, Jim Leighton, Dennis Raymond, Stanley Rowe, Lola Selby, Edward Sidebottom and Alan Wheelhouse for their invaluable help and comments while this book was in draft form. For the views expressed, however, and for their inadequacies, we remain entirely responsible.

B.D.D.
A.G.

Preface

Subject as hereinafter provided, it shall be the duty of every local education authority to secure the provision for their area of adequate facilities for further education . . . [including] . . . leisure-time occupation . . . for any persons over compulsory school age who are able and willing to profit by the facilities provided for that purpose . . . [and] . . . to secure that the facilities for primary, secondary and further education provided for their area include adequate facilities for recreation and social and physical training . . . [having] regard to the expediency of cooperating with any voluntary societies or bodies whose objects include the provision of facilities or the organization of activities of a similar character.   THE EDUCATION ACT (1944)

. . . boys and girls alike . . . are subject to . . . all that April weather of the soul which marks the time of adolescence. Coming to terms with one's new self is a difficult and lengthy process, complicated by the fact that sexual maturity precedes by several years emotional and social maturity.   THE CROWTHER REPORT (1959)

These girls and boys must somehow be made much more active partners in their own education.   THE NEWSOM REPORT (1963)

They need to develop a sense of responsibility for their work and towards other people, and to begin to arrive at some code of moral and social behaviour which is self-imposed.   THE NEWSOM REPORT (1963)

As young adults, they will have to begin to learn how to manage more complex human relations, with their fellows, of the same and of the opposite sex, with older people, in their private lives and in their future jobs. They will need guidance on social manners, in every sense.

THE NEWSOM REPORT (1963)

There can be no simple transmitting of *a priori* values, because to the expanding energies and enquiries of adolescence most values are not *a priori*.   THE ALBEMARLE REPORT (1960)

The Youth Service . . . provides for the continued social and informal education of young people in terms most likely to bring them to maturity, those of responsible personal choice. It is now an accepted commonplace in education that the infant learns by play . . . but re-creation can be as educative to the adolescent as play is to the infant . . .

THE ALBEMARLE REPORT (1960)

Chapter 1

Social Education

Current Attitudes

The purpose of this book is to re-examine the ways in which young people are helped to develop socially during their leisure time. Its focus, therefore, is on adults, on the relationships which they deliberately form with the young in a variety of informal educational settings, and on the use which is made of these relationships. There are of course many other kinds of relationship which prepare the young for life in our society: indeed all adults who come into contact with young people, and especially parents and those who make their contacts in the more formal settings at school and at work, will make their contribution. However the adult who meets adolescents while they are at leisure has a crucial influence on their development, since it is then that a young man or woman is examining most closely the structure and content of his social environment. At a time when a growing human being achieves the independence to explore the opportunities, interests and forms of relationship of a wider society, his experiences will have a most powerful influence on the quality and nature of the rest of his life.

Many of the adults fulfilling these vital roles are to be found in entertainment and leisure-servicing industries whose context is plainly commercial and who may therefore find the philosophy and assumptions of much of what follows inappropriate to their setting (though it is hoped that this will not be true of all of them). It is principally for the many others, however, who are to be found in schools, colleges, youth organizations and welfare agencies, that this book is intended. Included among them will be many teachers and some social workers and ministers as well as youth leaders, wardens and thousands of 'part-time' youth workers. Whatever they are called, however, they stand in a common relationship to society and its adolescent generation, and each of them is for all or part of his working day a 'social educator'. For it matters little whether they undertake extra-curricular and non-syllabus work in schools or colleges, or whether they are available one night a week or two weeks a year, or every day of their working life; it is of no account whether they wear distinctive clothing or not; it makes no difference whether they receive payment or lose heavily from their personal pocket – for the adolescent they have the same role to play. For through their practice the young person will experience situations which foster his developing personality, elicit responses to a whole range of relationships and introduce interests and concerns which will give substance and breadth to his life.

Widespread and influential as the work of such adults is, however, the processes which it involves are often only incompletely understood. This is not altogether surprising, perhaps, since it is often very difficult to define the content of social education, to establish recognizable criteria for its evaluation and to demonstrate its achievements. For, by its very nature, it deals with experiences, emotions and ideas which 'normal' adults meet daily but which they do not commonly separate out of the fabric of their lives for discussion, dissection and onward transmission to the young. In other words, they do not necessarily recognize it as the subject of an educational process, or as calling upon 'skills' which at some time in the past they have had to 'learn'.

As envisaged in this book, in fact, social education's prime concern is with any young person's meetings with others, with his capacity in these meetings to accept others and be accepted by them, and about the common interests around which these meetings may revolve. Social education is thus concerned with a young person's ability to communicate, perceive and cope with the ideas, thoughts and opinions, the motives and the emotions inherent in such meetings and interests. It is about the interaction of human beings, about their friendships and enmities, about the ways in which these are deepened and extended, and about their consequences. Its product therefore is any individual's increased consciousness of himself – of his values, aptitudes and untapped resources, and of the relevance of these to others. It enhances the individual's understanding of how to form mutually satisfying relationships, and so involves a search by the adult for ways of helping a young person to discover how to contribute to as well as take from his association with others.

Social education cannot go on in detachment as an intellectual exercise. It demands young people's *involvement* in the relevant situations and inter-relationships, it demands that they know first-hand and feel personally how common interests and shared activities bring and keep people together and what causes them to drift apart. It recognizes that young people will discover for themselves the values implicit in the relationships which form as a result of these human contacts and that they will experience directly the conflicts and strains and the effort, as well as the opportunities and satisfactions, which are created by them. The human processes, which are generated automatically whenever people gather, irrespective of their stated purpose or immediate task, thus constitute the content of social education.

Of course, such lessons are also learned in many other forms of education, at home, and elsewhere; but then they are usually an incidental by-product of other intentions, and the effect of people's involvement in these processes – on their own feelings, inner responses and private thoughts – is usually below the level of conscious awareness. Social educational provision sets out deliberately to provide settings in which these 'lessons' of human association may be learned. But this learning, available and necessary to people simply by the fact of their meeting and attempting to communicate, has major results which are not measurable by external examination and cannot easily be demonstrated. A young person may grow in self-sufficiency and self-assurance because he has tested his social skills and knows that he can now meet others on more equal terms, because he is clearer about what he believes to be right and good in his life, or because he has discovered unexpected talent in himself. It may be difficult for others to gain a full understanding of what this means, *because* it is not measurable and because its most important meaning and value are intimate and personal to the adolescent himself.

Needs and Opportunities in Adolescence

It is possible to argue, of course, that, though there is a need for some young people to receive social education in our society, by adolescence this need has passed completely, or, if it still exists, it can be fulfilled as and when necessary without adults making any special effort to be helpful. Certainly the need to foster the social development of younger children is now widely admitted, since it is recognized that the very young must learn basic social skills from those around them. Indeed we now know that the most essential elements of social intercourse, and especially the ability to communicate in words *and* through feelings, are learned in childhood at home and elsewhere. Nor can that learning simply be left to chance, since a child's ability later in life to relate to others fully and in mutually satisfying ways will depend almost entirely on whether he (or she) gains or is taught a large number of social skills in early years. The very capacity to *feel*, which is so basic to any fruitful human process, to love and hate, to acknowledge that there is good and bad, to enjoy and dislike is not just born in a child but has to be acquired through having contact with other human beings, young *and* old.

Among those responsible for the education of young children, it is now also recognized that 'play' for a child provides unique opportunities for this social learning to go on, since it is not an escape from reality but a deep immersion in the experiences and issues which are most significant for the child's life and growth. In any effort to extend not only social but also practical and apparently academic knowledge, therefore, a great deal of the education of young children is today conducted through 'play' situations. The child's informal 'leisure' contacts with his contemporaries, when understood and carefully encouraged and fostered by adults, are seen as an indispensable medium for developing his personality generally.

However, as the child grows older, the educational potentiality of these relationships is recognized less and less. 'Play-time' comes to be seen increasingly as little more than a break from 'work', and the activities associated with play are less and less valued as a means of development and of increasing understanding and knowledge. At the same time, in spheres where deliberate efforts to educate the child *are* made, the need to acquire *social* skills receives less and less emphasis as the demand that he learn more practical and academic skills grows. Deliberately provided opportunities to grow and develop socially become less and less in evidence under the pressure of other learning. By the time the child reaches adolescence the 'play' periods of his life in which social education goes on most naturally and fruitfully, have been relegated to an insignificant status in comparison to the academic and the practical.

And yet adolescence is a stage of development when opportunities for social education need to be as rich and varied as those which were offered in infancy. For, as a result of the changes which occur at puberty, young people come to perceive much of the world afresh, more critically, more independently, through their own eyes rather than through the eyes of those who have nurtured them. Many long-held assumptions about social behaviour, many well-tried habits and customs which have always helped them hitherto are subject to scrutiny and perhaps actually discarded. Moreover, not only do young people at adolescence look upon others differently: others gradually come to look upon them in different ways, too. Adults, as well as their contemporaries, begin to make new demands on them, expect them to take up new roles, assume they will carry new responsibilities and fulfil new functions, just as much in the social as in the intellectual and vocational spheres of their lives.

Thus, in adolescence, there is a new and pressing need to help young people develop socially. However, there is more than this: there is also a major – perhaps the *last* major – opportunity for this to be attempted. For, firstly, though most young people by the time they reach their teens are already well set in many of their ways, hardened against any radical reorientation of personality, the turbulence of adolescence disturbs the patterns of behaviour more deeply than is likely again in the lives of most people. Indeed, if their education is imaginatively conducted in adolescence, it can turn to the advantage of both the individual and society this period of great openness of mind, of enquiry, of willingness to experiment. The adolescent's readiness to enjoy and deliberately to search for wide social contacts and stimulating social experiences is a human asset too little exploited except in the expensive provision for the social dimension of full-time higher education. There is a second reason why adolescence offers a special and perhaps the final opportunity for real social education: there is still plenty of time to play, long periods of unstructured non-work time which is not yet filled by the private and domestic responsibilities which marriage will bring to most adults. If their leisure is again regarded, therefore, not as a peripheral and largely unimportant area of their lives but as fertile ground for their further social growth, the new needs and the final opportunities which adolescence presents might bear the fruits they promise in personal richness and communal vitality.

Youth Work, Schools, and Social Education

The most easily identified attempts to achieve such social educational aims are to be found today in youth work, which provides the starting-point of many of the arguments of this book and the objective of many of its suggestions. But many other areas of the education system have set out, and are increasingly setting out, to offer social educational experiences to the adolescent. Schools and colleges, though mainly concerned to offer academic and vocational education, are growing more and more aware of the personal and social skills needed for effective participation in our society. The intellectual and technical competence aimed at by most of our educational institutions is certainly required in a complex and changing society: but that society is now widely recognized also as making searching demands on young people's social poise, on their capacity for making *sense* of their environment, and on their ability to make effective and rewarding personal relationships.

The Albemarle and Newsom Reports gave expression to this growing appreciation that adolescents should receive more help and encouragement in the social – which does not mean purely sociable – areas of their lives. In particular, the Newsom Report's recommendation that there be an extension of the school day seems to be impelling the schools still further to supplement formal and vocational teaching with efforts to help young people grow socially. So, too, do its suggestions that some adults be included in the 'teaching' programme primarily for their experience of the working world and that more school-time be spent outside the school campus. Some of the problems and concerns traditionally associated with youth work are therefore being faced extensively in schools, and to some extent in industry also as some employers undertake social educational responsibilities for selected employees. Thus, teachers and others, as they accept roles as social educators, may reasonably expect to be able to benefit from the experience of youth work. The schools in particular are increasingly adopting the habits which have been sanctioned by time and practice in youth organizations. Where they offer a third session of extra-curricular activity or when colleges of further education offer non-vocational courses to day-release students, it is not surprising that they turn to the approaches of the Youth Service.

Yet what youth work offers, though still containing a great deal that is of undoubted value, is today no longer automatically appropriate and may well need reassessment. Youth work's formative period was between about 1870 and 1910, and what was acceptable and (often accidentally, perhaps) beneficial to the young of an earlier age cannot be taken unquestioningly to be relevant today. For youth work has for some years been uncertain of itself and its future, and has been unenthusiastic about modifying its traditional practices and deepest assumptions. If teachers and others look to the Youth Service for well-evaluated experience and methods, therefore, they have good reason to be sceptical of a great deal of what they find. A social situation so radically changed from that obtaining for most of the history of the Youth Service, coupled with the wider range of agencies offering social educational experience to adolescents, make a critical re-examination essential.

For example, an underlying assumption in the philosophy or ethos of youth work has been that it is in some way – social, moral or spiritual – the rescue of one large section of the population by another much smaller group. This is clearly not an operation acceptable in an emancipated age, and as technical and educational advance releases still more of people's individual and independent talents it is likely to become even less so. It is increasingly inappropriate to build social education around models conceived by tightly-knit and influential groups of adults who then attempt to fashion the young in such images. Such elitism may continue to be tenable in academic and technical education where a definable corpus of knowledge, skill or accumulated experience can be identified for transmission to the beginner. But the substance of social education is not amenable to such treatment. In a society which is expecting more and more of *individuals* and which is removing more and more of the props of time-hallowed custom, no particular elite among adults (or young people) can hope to be authors of the *social* expertise needed by young people in general. Indeed, even if a consensus of opinion among adults as a whole were attainable, it could not be used as a 'teaching' syllabus. For what adults can tell the young about how to behave in social situations, what to believe, what is expected of them, and so on, is today very much less than what the young actually need to know of these things and what they must experience for themselves. The lessons of social behaviour and moves cannot be predigested, preordained and authorized, and they cannot be worked into a 'programme' or 'scheme' and become communicable thereby from one group or generation to another.

Truly helpful social education must of course balance individual self-expression with the encouragement of a degree of conformity. To some extent it will need to prepare young people for the parts they are obliged to play in society, for the proper and inevitable demands to be 'loyal', 'responsible', 'respectful' and especially 'law-abiding'. It must to this extent therefore be about young people's adjustment, their adherence, their familiarity with the conventional wisdom. But social education in general has loaded the scales too heavily in this direction in the past with

B

its prepared schemes and carefully worked-out programmes of development for young people. Its emphasis now must shift if it is to meet contemporary needs. It must become more and more concerned with the part young people have the ability to play in society – provided that their individuality, their very personal talents, feelings, beliefs and values are given fuller expression. Even though this lays 'society' open to greater risks and discomfort, social education must make its focus what is *individually* fulfilling and *contributive* out of all the things which are not socially unacceptable, rather than being mainly about what is socially *determined*, or socially *desirable*, or socially *expected*.

If a rethinking of underlying assumptions is important, a close scrutiny of method is crucial. Social educators must evaluate afresh the place in their work of adventure training, of badge-schemes, of arts and drama competitions, of single-sex activity, and the rest. For such externally imposed solutions to young people's needs, because they are so encumbered by artificially constructed models, either ignore the real situation of any particular adolescent or touch it only accidentally and peripherally. In fact, the comprehensively programmed courses and schemes, worked out by adults and made available to young people without reference to the individual, are the epitome of our traditional social educational attitudes and ought not to be extended any further until it has been established that they offer what is now most urgently required. Moreover, since practitioners can now look to theoretical frameworks whose source is more objective and reliable, there seems to be even more reason to question fundamentally much of what is now simply accepted and valued because it is there.

Thus, although this book continually finds evidence and support in the best past practice of youth workers, it does not concentrate on what is particular about the settings in which any given adults work. It attempts, rather, to discuss and evaluate the relationships between adults and young people *wherever* the social education of the latter takes place, regardless of the administrative structure to which the young people come or the administratively convenient label attached to the adults. This approach is exemplified in the use of the generic terms 'social educator' and 'client' to describe all those adults and adolescents, whatever their formal designation, who are involved in this sector of education.

Indeed, throughout this book it is assumed that social education cannot be, as so much youth work has tended to be since its inception, an agglomeration of sectional attempts to achieve limited objectives with those young people who happen to be able to identify with them. It is seen as essential, in fact, that the social education of the adolescent become an effort of the whole community to serve all its young unselectively. This may or may not require radically new institutional forms. What is clear, however, is that for the adults carrying out the work the objectives will be less clear-cut and the pattern of work less definitively laid down than in the past, so that social educators have a right to expect a theoretical framework which is distinct and appropriate to their contemporary functions. It is to the discussion and establishment of such a framework that this book is intended as a contribution.

Thus in the ensuing chapters an attempt is made, first, to examine critically the historical and sociological bases of social education, its purpose and the language in which its methods are conceived and discussed. A positive search is then made for a body of working principles and understanding which might guide and illuminate the social educator's practice, for a conscious discipline which might underpin this practice and for an appropriate form of training which might prepare adults for it. Throughout, three fundamental assumptions are made about such practice. One is that its aim should be less to secure the conformity of young people to the existing norms in society, and more to develop individual talent and potentiality. A second is that adults, in their contacts with young people through this practice, should consider the nature and content of the human processes which are set in motion rather than just the tasks through which these processes are expressed. And the third assumption is that the adults involved in this practice should be guided by a sensitive appreciation of the actual young people they meet and not by reference to their own models of what young people ought to be.

Chapter 2

A Historical Perspective

The Bases of Modern Youth Work

Youth work in Britain, in the form which is taken for granted today, is at most eighty or ninety years old. It emerged during the last two or three decades of the nineteenth century and the first decade of the twentieth. Almost all the major youth organizations and the most familiar types of units of work, with their characteristic methods and statements of purpose, date from this period. The first boys' clubs were being founded in the 1870s, the Boys' Brigade came in 1883, girls' clubs and the youth work of the settlements around the same time, the Boy Scouts in 1907 and the Girl Guides very soon afterwards. The Y.W.C.A. was established in 1877 by the amalgamation of two smaller bodies while by the 1880s the Y.M.C.A., which had already been in existence for nearly half a century, was extending its work among boys and eventually opened definite Boys' Departments. A period of thirty or forty years, therefore, fashioned what were to become the most distinctive features of youth work, for they were to a large extent accepted and taken over in later decades even by statutory youth centres and clubs.

That this occurred when it did, and during such a comparatively short period, cannot be dismissed as entirely fortuitous. Indeed, if youth work's origins are examined carefully, it is clear that they were closely related to and dependent on much broader and deeper processes affecting and moving British society in the late nineteenth and early twentieth centuries. Youth work must be explained above all in terms of the intellectual climate, class structure and material conditions which then existed.

To do this is not easy. A considerable effort of imagination is called for in order to see outside what now exists and to project oneself into the immediate and often pressing circumstances which caused youth work's founders to act as they did. Eighty or ninety years ago approaches may well have been available which had much to offer the young people of the day but which have since disappeared from view because they failed to gain the support of those influential and socially prominent adults who have for so long attracted most attention from historians. Such unorthodox forms of action are now often difficult to recognize as 'youth work', so firmly does the usual connotation of the phrase rule our perception. Again, much work which has emerged only subsequently may potentially have had far greater meaning for its time than longer-established forms, and yet it often received much less attention or less ready recognition as legitimate youth work. It is tempting from the vantage point of the present, in fact, to treat the growth and permanence of youth work in its current form as inevitable, even to judge that it was the only possible provision which could have taken root and succeeded as a means of social education during young people's leisure hours. It is tempting to assume that it is the inescapable conclusion of what was initiated in the past and to embrace its philosophy as received dogma with an obvious, universal and timeless relevance to young people's social growth.

Such a view however lacks a historical perspective, since in certain important ways it is incomplete and distorting. For not all that was done by the 'pioneers' was far-sighted: some of it at least seems to have depended on contrivance and opportunism. At times their actions seem much less the result of an inspired grasp of the eternal and the universal than of an accidental stumbling on incompletely worked-out expedients. Frequently they were pushed on, not only by altruism and generosity, but also by fear, self-defence and self-interest. Individuals joined the band of providers also because the activity of providing was itself moderately pleasant and satisfying. However, as so often happens once the organization was founded, to extend and strengthen it developed into ends in themselves, so that it became extremely difficult to re-examine fundamentally whether the provision being made was supplying what was needed. In any case 'needs' could hardly be objectively defined in the absence of a discipline rooted in the human sciences. Instead they were subjectively evoked, and projected on to potential clients who could clearly be seen to have *some* need or other, though not necessarily ones that could be met by what was being offered. Much that the pioneers did, therefore, has in the long term narrowed down the views of what social education might aspire to, and consequently limited its aims and scope unnecessarily. The achievement of the pioneers certainly needs to be acknowledged, but it must nevertheless be analysed and if possible judged objectively.

Stripped of all but its essentials, what occurred at that time? What were the common basic features of those movements which today help to make up what is called 'youth work'? Fundamental to them was a number of men and women of wealth, influence and some awareness of the society around them, who voluntarily joined together with the intention of creating a new type of institution. The main aim of this was to provide social educational opportunities for a group of people defined by age and social group – for working-class adolescents. The organizations thus formed were endowed with certain ideal purposes set mainly by the providers' own social, political and religious codes or derived simply from the only sources of guidance readily available to them, their own personal experiences. However, because they were intended to operate during the users' leisure hours, a variety of more or less informal approaches and programmes was adopted.

Beneath this amalgam of aims and responses lay a number of unquestioned assumptions. It was for example virtually taken for granted, firstly, that 'leisure' existed, making available to people a period of 'non-compulsory work-time' which they could dispose of at their own discretion, for purposes of relaxation and pleasure; and secondly, that in order to provide for the 'leisure' of young people it was necessary *deliberately* to create new social institutions. It was clearly assumed too that such action should and could be taken privately – voluntarily – by members of society who were moved to act either as individuals or in concert, but that it should not be attempted by statutorily created or directed authorities. In the conditions of the time, this inevitably meant that those who took such action were people whose adult status and social background placed them outside the section of the population for whom provision was being made. Nonetheless, it was concluded by such people that it was possible, necessary and acceptable for them to define a purpose which could be made meaningful for those using the new institutions.

Of course, not all of these assumptions were new in the 1870s. Many had been formulated and accepted much earlier. Undoubtedly there already existed a belief in voluntary action, in provision by a privileged social group and in the explicit statement of an ideal purpose.

Yet the *total* effect of youth work, when it first appeared, represented something original. Some of its assumptions at least were novel – that, for example, leisure existed in sufficient quantity to justify some effort to provide deliberately for it, and that adolescents shared in it so that, to cater for their use of it, informal educational methods needed to be worked out and adopted. Under the stimulus of change and innovation older ideas and habits were incorporated, often given new emphasis and shape and fused with fresh thinking and responses. Within the space of a comparatively short time a type of educational action was evolved whose overall form, function and impact was distinctive.

If present-day social education is to be more fully understood and perhaps reinterpreted for our own age, it seems important to keep separate these strands of youth work and to see why they have been so influential on our attitudes to social education generally. In particular, this means examining the factors in the past which have helped to shape our current conception of youth work, and assessing which of these factors really apply today. A fuller historical perspective might do much, in fact, to broaden our perception of how the young can be served in their leisure, and an attempt is made in this chapter to offer such a per-spective. What is presented is not a simple factual account but an inter-pretation which deliberately emphasizes aspects of the whole picture to which other interpretations have understandably given less attention. For, when seen from within an organization, motives and attitudes form a pattern which constitutes only one dimension of the whole. When looked at in the context of social and educational history generally, when com-pared with what has occurred in other youth organizations or in institu-tions concerned with adult education, those same motives and attitudes can be seen as forming quite another pattern in a different dimension.

It is this other pattern which this chapter is concerned to indicate. The aim is to illuminate the present situation more clearly by examining it in these broader, historical dimensions. Unfortunately, very little empirical research into the origins of youth work has yet been attempted; what follows, therefore, can only be a hypothesis based on the general features of social and educational history. It is a hypothesis which urgently needs to be tested by research if social education is to gain that unifying sense of future purpose which depends upon an accurate perception of past history.

The Solutions of an Agrarian Society

Modern youth work is a phenomenon of industrial society. Although one is not the 'result' of the other in any simple sense, educational-recreational institutions for the socially immature came into existence because of the special conditions and requirements of an urban and mechanized way of life. Neither the Boys' Brigade nor a village youth club would have been possible in Britain before the nineteenth century. While conditions remained predominantly agrarian, they were not needed to help the young prepare for adult roles.

This is not to say that all that is now attempted through youth work was ignored. It is true that distinct institutions to encompass all of it were not deliberately provided. As we shall see in more detail below, the provision which was made was not perfect, and often it was not even minimally adequate. Nevertheless action was taken, frequently through the community, to protect, regulate and even enlighten and develop the young when they were not at work. The family has always been an important educator in this sense, of course, and in pre-industrial society the family's functions were certainly different from, and in some respects more extensive than, those of today. (This is of course not the same as saying the family was 'stronger', a controversy which involves some evaluation rather than mere description of the family's role and so is one which is not relevant here.) In particular, its control of its younger members was more comprehensive and might continue longer in certain areas of their lives.

> . . . the working-class family, whether engaged in agriculture or in domestic industry, was the closely knit social and economic unit. Both men and women shared the productive tasks of the family and children were put to work at an early age, so that there was a definite division of labour within the family in the context of which the 'socialization' of the child – including such education, moral or otherwise, as may have been available – took place. Furthermore, such a family, in a community which lacked extensive geographical movement, would have its being within a particular locality and within a stable and extensive body of wider kinsfolk.[1]

Within the values, relationships and activities of such an institution and such a community, many of the functions of modern youth work, where they were required, would be exercised.

Moreover the influence of the family, theoretically at least, was exercised not only over those who were members of it by reason of their birth but also often over many others. It is for example impossible at times to distinguish where, in pre-industrial society, the family ends and the institution of apprenticeship begins. The role of the master and that of the father were often confused in people's minds in the way that an employer's role could not be confused with that of the head of the family today. Often the master was expected to feed, clothe and educate his apprentices as if they were sons, while they in turn were not allowed to marry and were kept wholly dependent until they were twenty-one. The rights and the powers of the master, at least on paper, were extensive, and terms of indenture often specifically forbade apprentices from frequenting ale-houses, brothels and other 'dangerous' places of amusement. What is more, the community, often through the Poor Law machinery, made some effort to ensure that masters fulfilled their obligations and clearly intended that some provision should be made for the education and supervised relaxation of children, including those in their teens.

Much of this provision, of course, existed only in theory or was actually used as a means of exploitation rather than protection and education. Very many of the families which depended for their livelihood on agriculture knew very little security and were often extremely unstable, while the apprenticeship system often worked against the interests of the young and could become a form of slavery which harmed children disastrously. Even according to the comparatively undemanding standards of the time, there were great gaps between the ideal and the reality of what was actually provided.

Indeed, in comparison with a later, predominantly industrial age, what is most striking about the agrarian period is how limited and ineffective were the ruling group's efforts to guide and control the social education of the children of the population at large. Important attempts were of course made to impart approved values, habits and beliefs, especially through the churches. However, the threat to the established order from the under-privileged was relatively weak, with the result that urgent and determined action to influence and regulate their children's upbringing was rarely required. Nor was consciousness of youthful suffering and waste an especially powerful motive. Thus, both the humanitarianism and the deep apprehension which were later to bring action from those with power and vested interests were usually lacking in a less complex, predominantly agrarian society.

In a discussion of the provision made in agrarian Britain for the social education of young people, two other contrasts with a more predominantly industrial era must be noted. One is the absence of any special emphasis on the virtues of 'voluntary' effort, in particular as a means of solving social problems. Certainly, during many periods before industrialization, resort was readily made to statutory authorities and extensive powers were given to Justices of the Peace and Poor Law overseers to act directly to influence the position and development of the young in certain circumstances. Again, in practice these powers frequently had only limited effects, but their existence illustrates that no special need was felt to rely upon the voluntary combination and private initiative of those with wealth and power in preference to official action.

The other contrast lies in the assumptions which were made about the existence and use of leisure. It is true that 'amusements' were available before the nineteenth century – taverns, fairs and sports of various kinds provided some relief from everyday toil. Moreover, patterns of work were often indisciplined by the standards of today: where recognized holidays and festivals were not immediately available to offer a break from labour, resort was often made to absenteeism. Yet agrarian Britain was not notable for its light-heartedness and gaiety, or its regular indulgence in pleasure. On the contrary, leisure was a scarce commodity. A small class had a great deal of it, but the vast majority of the population worked long hours, often six days a week. Even in 'good times' they could expect no regular daily or weekly break from labour for mere enjoyment or personal improvement, while during one of the intermittent crises of subsistence their very survival would be threatened. If people's basic needs were to be satisfied, the economy just could not afford to release too many of them too often.

In the absence of long periods of leisure, it was unnecessary deliberately to create institutions to cater for people's pleasure and informal education. The young – certainly by the time they were in their teens – were likely to be as fully occupied as anyone else. In any case, no particular social significance was attached to their teenage state. For it was not until much later that the gap between their physical and emotional or social maturity became wide enough to have important social implications, or that differences of adolescents from both children and adults were acknowledged in industrial legislation. Thus youth organizations catering specifically for those in their teens would have been completely irrelevant. However much the dominant elite might have wished to influence those 'below' them, and however much it may have been moved to action by young people's personal needs for social education, it had very little opportunity to cater for them through their amusements.

The Expansion of Leisure

The Britain of 1860 was a very different place from that of 1660 or even 1760. Industrialism, in some respects rapidly and radically, in others more gradually and imperceptibly, had altered the face of the country and profoundly modified the nature of society. Many of the institutions, for example, which previously had protected and controlled the young disappeared or acquired vastly different functions. The family, though not necessarily 'weaker', was much affected by the demand that many more fathers *and* mothers go *out* to work and obey the rigid discipline of the factory bell. The non-vocational obligations of a master to his apprentice were increasingly ignored: indeed many of the industrialists used the traditional apprenticeship system simply to recruit cheap labour until in 1814 the legal requirement to serve as an apprentice to a trade was ended altogether. The Poor Law altered too, and in 1834 almost entirely lost whatever concern for education and communal care had remained so that overwhelmingly its emphases came to be deterrence and punishment.

Indeed the changes which occurred in these decades had their impact in almost every area of life, and were often less obvious and material in their consequences than those which created the factories and produced the Poor Law Amendment Act. Among these less sensational results was undoubtedly the appearance from the middle of the century of an increasing amount of spare productive capacity in the economy, which made it both possible and necessary to release some of the young members of the labour force into full-time education and to reduce the working hours of others. Some of the latter found that in practice this meant that they were either unemployed or under-employed, but for many it did bring significantly long and regular periods of non-compulsory work time which they could use at their own discretion, for pleasure or relief. Leisure had appeared to an extent unknown in the past. Some of it was unwanted, but much of it was welcome and was accompanied by a rather greater financial power to use it for enjoyment and self-improvement. Although, as we have seen, time for amusement in an agrarian society had not been very great, it is possible to discern that the uses of what was available underwent considerable change as industrial and urban conditions spread. Though some of the traditional forms of amusement survived and contributed to the growth of new ones in the nineteenth century, many of them – like the vigorous sports, for example – depended so heavily on the proximity of open air and the ready availability of common land and playgrounds that they weakened or died out altogether as more and more of the population moved into towns and took up work in factories. Others of them were positively discouraged or banned because of their detrimental effect on discipline and effort at work or because they offended the susceptibilities of the ruling groups. Hence, for example, the disappearance of many of the ancient holidays and festivals, and the attacks by the Society for the Suppression of Vice on 'the twopenny hops, the ginger-bread fairs and the obscene pictures'.

It was in these non-material areas of life – in the hardening of patterns of work, in the sharpening of discipline, in the simultaneous loss of opportunities for releasing pent-up tension and frustration – that the impact of industrialism was felt most strongly. The 'Coketowns' were unprecedented in their intense concern for work and production, and in this sense if in no other the quality of urban life was felt by many to be a decline from previous agrarian standards. As long as the hours worked in the cities totalled at least sixty-five a week and often seventy-five, increased opportunities for relaxation obviously did not exist.

This situation changed only gradually, and even then not mainly out of intention, but incidentally, as a result of economic development and the creation of spare productive capacity. The reduction of working hours, first of women and children, and then of men too, and the establishment of free and compulsory education are only two of the signs. There are other equally clear ones: the gradual enforcement after 1850 of a half-day holiday in more and more trades; the Bank Holiday Act of 1871 which restored some of the ancient festivals abolished earlier in the century; and the slow spread of annual holidays with pay.

Provision for leisure and opportunities to be entertained and to gain relaxation also increased. Cheap day railway excursions date from this period; so too do Thomas Cook's tours and the growth of watering places like Blackpool, which attained borough status in 1876. The popularity of mass audience sports like soccer and cricket grew too: Test matches and F.A. Cup ties were first played in the 1870s and newspapers began to carry much fuller reports on sport in general about the same time. The fact that there was so much commercial involvement in these developments only confirms that leisure time, and the financial power to use it for pleasure, were available to enough people in sufficient quantity to justify extended interest in its use.

Commercial groups were not the only ones to see this. Educators too showed early on that they had recognized it, and began to adapt their approaches accordingly. While the main adult educational task had been seen to be the teaching of basic skills, and while most of those being taught had been earnest working-men anxious for self-improvement and with few opportunities and little desire to be distracted, quite formal approaches had persisted. From the start, however, these had left untouched most of the men and women whom the ruling groups would have liked to influence. As more people acquired regular time off work which could be spent in a much wider variety of non-educational activities, the pressure mounted to make the appeal of part-time educational facilities broader and more attractive.

Both content and method were therefore modified. There was, for example, a movement from teaching 'pure science' to offering 'useful knowledge' and then to 'countering the temptation to sensual indulgences'. As early as the middle of the century many of the mechanics' institutes were seen to have quite legitimate recreational and general cultural functions. There was here a response to new and wider leisure opportunities which was eventually to influence and merge with the more clear-cut efforts to cater specifically for the leisure of the adolescent. Informal social education began to acquire institutional expression.

The concern about how those in their teens were using their leisure became particularly strong only when they began to gain a noticeably large share of it. Early on only young children were released from labour for longer periods: by the 1870s they were being protected and instructed continuously by being kept at school. Women also benefited considerably, but as their 'spare' time was usually amply absorbed in rearing a family and managing a home they presented no special problem. Only when adolescents were singled out for consideration by the laws which reduced working hours could there grow up a danger that a substantial portion of the working class would be left without protection or supervision during their new-found freedom. If the growth of leisure represented a problem after the 1870s, adolescent leisure represented a special problem which needed to be tackled urgently. Faced with such a need – and such a threat – that part of Victorian society which was actively concerned reacted in predictable ways.

The 'Voluntary Principle' and the Provision for Adolescent Leisure

Though writers and politicians repeatedly extolled the virtues of individual effort and freedom from official restraint and interference, these extreme liberal ideas of the nineteenth century were often ignored or contradicted in practice. Out of necessity, governments frequently took direct action, and 'collectivist' solutions were invoked even before the middle of the century. The attempt to regulate working hours and conditions is an example.

Nonetheless, the Victorian faith in laissez-faire did have significant practical effects and in particular meant that official action as a method of coping with current problems was adopted with reluctance. The liberal and individualist emphasis of fashionable thought enabled enterprising businessmen to rationalize their drive – and their ruthlessness – very successfully. For those with vision and energy, economic success was there for the taking. The regulations and business customs which had survived from earlier ages in the guilds, the apprenticeship laws, the laws against geographical mobility and the 'artificial' control of wages and prices all threatened to limit the achievement of the ambitious. The latter wanted to be encouraged, given their heads, not restricted. Liberated from obstructions, left free to use the new power and the new machinery, they could make fortunes. The liberal social and economic thinking of their time was their justification.

The result was that among such people there existed a deep and persistent suspicion of direct government action. Wherever possible they resisted or tried to contain official 'intervention'. They fought this in the first half of the century even in areas where some people felt the need for action to be urgent. In some spheres, in education for example, this action was gradually taken, though often only indirectly and almost in disguise; but in other spheres governments were allowed to play no direct part until after the end of the nineteenth century. Into the last category fell the provision then being made for the social educational needs of adolescents in their leisure. Here, any government action, any obvious tampering by statutory authorities with the private lives of individuals, was held to be unthinkable.

Thus, those who had any awareness of the 'problem' which was emerging and who, whether for selfish or compassionate reasons, wished to do something to solve it, could not or would not turn to 'the State'. Other potential solutions lay open to them, however. They might, for example, await some commercial impulse – count upon the profit motive eventually to stimulate society into providing adequate facilities for the leisure of those in their teens. Another alternative was for those in need, or in this case their parents, to be allowed and encouraged to solve their own problems by mutual aid and cooperation. Yet neither of these solutions was adopted. Instead, men and women with power and a social conscience chose to act themselves and by their own private efforts attempted to fill what gaps they could.

Youth work thus came to be the voluntary effort of groups of people outside the class and the age-group in need. Other possible solutions were rejected. Commercial enterprise was unacceptable as a mode of offering leisure opportunities to those in their teens, although in many other spheres it was considered to contain its own virtues because it developed effort and self-reliance. Nor was any serious consideration or support given to the possibility that the young – certainly those of seventeen or eighteen or over – might be able to organize themselves. Those who *were* taking action clearly wanted to achieve something which, they believed, only they were capable of providing.

In important ways it is undoubtedly true that they and only they *saw* the need, felt their consciences being stirred and had the wealth and influence necessary to relieve the distress, the poverty and the waste which so limited the adolescent's use of leisure. Their altruism and their power together often offered the only practical solution to the problem.

> The working classes had no distinctive educational ideology of their own, and when the remnants of the popular culture of an earlier, rural England had been set aside as of no account, there was no alternative but to accept the instruction offered in the middle-class Sunday and day schools.[2]

– and later and in a different context, in the middle-class youth organizations. Yet it was also true that the making of provision was helpful to the providers themselves as well. For it did something to salve any guilt surrounding the methods which ensured their commercial success, and something too to compensate for the impersonality or even inhumanity of some of their everyday working procedures. There was therefore strong compulsion on them to ignore other possible solutions to young people's social needs and to become involved themselves. Yet it is at least an open and historically unexplored question whether or not these other solutions might have succeeded. In itself commercial enterprise was not necessarily incompatible with opportunities for adolescent social development, and offered some outlets which might have been viewed less suspiciously and so used more fully. And working-class mutual aid, to which the middle class, with their own devotion to self-help, might have been expected to give more support, would seem in retrospect to have had even more chance of success. Other countries certainly have found it possible for provision to be made for adolescents comparatively independently of adult 'leadership'. In this country, too, many spontaneous youth groups have emerged but have only irregularly received official support or been acknowledged as 'real' youth work. Moreover, if one takes into account the vast amount of working-class mutual aid which has prospered in other spheres, it would seem to have been at least a possibility that in the past the adults of a community might more often have made adequate provision for their own young people. If the 'lower orders' in Britain were capable of sponsoring insurance societies, co-operative movements and, most significantly of all in this context, working-men's clubs, it is not clear why many more of them could not have provided social and recreational clubs for their own young people.

Some possible reasons for the refusal to adopt these solutions can be discerned. Much working-class mutual aid and spontaneous adolescent activity proved unstable and short-lived. Even more, commercial enterprise in the nineteenth century was seen as irresponsible and incapable of providing for an immature section of the population. These, however, in themselves do not provide a complete explanation. For the providers of the most characteristic youth work facilities were concerned with imparting lessons which to them were essential if serious dangers were to be removed or contained. Without doubt they were altruistic: they opposed other possible types of provision and offered their own because with deep sincerity they believed this was by far the best thing for the young. But the motivation of many of them cannot have been so simple or unmixed. Many of them clearly viewed both working-class self-help and even, ironically, the commercial enterprise which had helped to make them rich, as potentially dangerous to their own class if given encouragement in the field of social education. And so they refused to use the opportunities it might offer. They seem to have been at least as much concerned to prevent themselves from being harmed as they were to do good to others. Their motives were not all disinterested because, in a very human and justifiable way, they were afraid and on the defensive.

Of course, the famous pioneers of youth work articulated and publicized their altruistic intentions effectively and in very direct and uncomplicated ways. Indeed the ability to communicate ideals and convictions was perhaps the most important attribute of men like Baden-Powell, William Smith, and of the boys' club workers Charles Russell and T. H. Pelham. Because their statements were so well expressed they have survived. Often they were the only ones which were in writing and so at all widely available. What these figures believed has thus come to dominate our historical interpretations and has also frequently over-simplified them.

For there must have been many others involved in youth work who did not make their interest or intention so clear or easily available to posterity. Many adults must have worked diligently in youth organiza-tions or contributed money and yet said little, if anything, about their aims or reasons. If this large body of anonymous supporters could be considered, the mixture and complexity of motives would almost certainly grow. For it is unlikely that all of them were primarily intent on founding something permanent or nation-wide. Many of those who are now seen as early pioneers must have been concerned, as are many social educators today, to overcome problems and head off dangers which were urgent and very threatening. Many must have reacted spontaneously to issues which were localized and immediate. They must have faced requirements which seemed to them to be transient, and whose very transience may indeed have been the result of their own successful actions. It seems inevitable that the aims of many of these early pioneers were, as now, largely emotional, non-intellectual and unverbalized, affected often unconsciously by the unquestioned and self-interested assumptions and values of their class and by the events of their time.

Such an interpretation cannot be put forward with finality as the only one which explains adequately what occurred almost a century ago. But it may do something to clarify why these early providers refused to accept either unregulated commercial enterprise or working-class mutual aid as a legitimate basis for young people's leisure-time social education. It also may account very largely for the fact that those who did eventually take the initiative invariably acted voluntarily and often in concert.

Where short-term and self-interested aims did exist among early youth workers they are by their very nature difficult to discern and to establish convincingly. Some evidence of their existence can be gained from a closer examination and more critical interpretation of the statements made by the more vocal pioneers. Much more, however, can be derived by considering these statements, and the actions which followed them, within the context of their society and their time, especially against the background of pressures – social, economic, political and religious – which must have impinged upon and moved many of those who, as

C

thinking members of society, played active parts in early social education. Both of these sources of evidence and suggestion need to be used if a more complete picture is to be gained of the feelings, hopes and fears of the pioneers of youth work.

The Impetus of Fear

In part, the reaction of those who were concerned about the use of adolescent leisure was undoubtedly a disinterested one. For many of them the motive-force was a genuine and unadulterated humanitarianism and generosity. Because others were in need they wished to help. There is no need to doubt the sincerity of the founders of Ardwick Lads' Club, Manchester, for example, who wrote: 'It [was] incumbent on us, fortunately placed as we are, to do something to help those who had to spend their lives in the mean and sordid districts and slums of our city.' Nor that of the Salford Lads' Club, part of whose purpose was 'to brighten young lives'. The compassion and sympathy of so much of this early youth work is unmistakable. It came, at least in part, out of a powerful social conscience and a deeply felt religious conviction that those with privileges could not just leave others to suffer.

There were signs, however, that not all those involved saw their task so simply. For many there were, apparently, other, more important aims besides. It seems that through their altruism they hoped to help themselves to preserve what they valued, to defend what was theirs. They had vested interests which they were not going to give up without a struggle. The observation that 'the middle classes know that the safety of their lives and property depends on having around them a peaceful, happy and moral population' was made not by a dangerous late nineteenth-century socialist but by that highly respectable social reformer, Lord Shaftesbury.

The ruling sections of the population, which included in Victorian Britain not only the middle classes but the traditional upper classes too, felt themselves throughout the period to be under greater threat than almost any of their predecessors had done. Their fear, especially of the combined strength of those they ruled and of its future effect on their position, inevitably and understandably increased as industrialism made it possible and likely that a shift of power within society would take place.

Many, in particular early in the century, welcomed industrialization as an unprecedented opportunity and were proud of the achievements it had made possible. For those who could identify themselves with its predominant values – and share in its profits – it seemed to be the embodiment of Progress. As the members of this advancing group established themselves, however, and succeeded in gaining some recognition from the old ruling elite, they too began to show more caution. Many of them joined those who, from the start, had greeted the 'new' society as at best a mixed blessing or at worst a disaster. In particular they feared that the social forces which it had released might be uncontrollable. The massed inhabitants of the new towns clearly represented a serious menace to them. The London mob had always been a danger which had only been increased, following the French Revolution, by events in both Britain and France. All over Britain urban populations grew to an apparently staggering size, living in even greater proximity to one another. The 'dark recesses of the city', 'the crowded hives' became objects of mystery – and deepening suspicion. Many, of course, were concerned in a purely philanthropic way with the urban slums, but from the start there were critics of the mass industrial towns who concentrated on voicing their anxieties and pointing to the dangers. Theirs was a theme which was continuous, and as late as 1907 the journalist-historian C. F. G. Masterman was clearly echoing it: 'They dread the fermenting, in the populous cities, of some new, all-powerful explosive, destined one day to shatter into ruins all their desirable social order.'

In part this dread was of the political repercussions of the growth of large towns. For, in the first place, they created a labouring population sufficiently concentrated and numerous to become conscious of an identity of interests, of common grievances and hopes. There was born in fact a working 'class'. Moreover, at the time that this occurred, those who were 'hands' were being separated from those who were 'bosses'. (The impersonality of the actual terms is in itself significant.) As the 'desirable' and the 'slum' areas of the towns grew up, economic and social differences – 'class' divisions – acquired a geographical definition which made them even more clear-cut. There were fewer opportunities for the rulers to control the ruled, since in the towns personal influence in politics grew steadily weaker and mass opinion came to be moulded increasingly by more powerful impersonal forces.

Divisions between the classes and the destruction of the ruling groups' traditional techniques of control were partially offset by the improved means of communication which came in the wake of technical advance, and by the fact that so many more subjects could be reached quickly and simultaneously. But even these changes were two-edged and gave those with the authority and privileges little comfort, in view of the opportunity they created for the 'masses' to exercise power themselves. It became increasingly easy not only for the majority to be influenced, but for them to have influence themselves. Perhaps for the first time since the large nation-state came into being, democracy had become a practical possibility and the whole position of the dominant elite – in fact their raison d'être – was fundamentally threatened. (That the French 'mob' had apparently carried out the threat before the end of the eighteenth century made the ruling groups even more anxious.) From the start of the nineteenth century, therefore, there was a more pressing need than ever before to protect and bolster the existing social and political structure, and to ensure by all the means available that the lower orders were 'loyal', 'obedient', 'respectful of law and order' and 'disciplined'. Good citizenship became an end of education, including social education, very early.

These qualities were valuable too for economic reasons. The original industrial masters required workers who were disciplined and responsible no less than the political rulers required subjects like this. In the eyes of the new employers many of the habits brought from an agrarian and rural background by the early industrial labour force needed to be eradicated. Irregular hours and absenteeism, drunkenness and a liking for distracting amusements fitted ill with the requirements of the factory bell, complex machinery, heavy capital outlay and the threat of bankruptcy which frequently haunted the original industrialists.

Hence there began a continuous stream of criticism about the habits of the poor, about their devotion to the taverns and the fair-grounds and about 'Morning in Bed' and 'Saint Monday'. Hence therefore the attack on the ancient holidays and festivals and the traditional amusements. Hence too the insistence here, as in the political sphere, on discipline, obedience and respect.

Both rulers and masters, who when they were not actually the same people shared similar or identical interests, were helped in fostering these qualities among the working class by the resurgence at this time of older religious ideals. Powerful religious movements, and in particular Methodism, gave valuable support by uncompromisingly advocating sobriety and order and effort. They did not always produce the results intended and many of the less pretty attitudes and values of agrarian society survived into the nineteenth century. Moreover, despite its authoritarian elements, Methodism did much to encourage the independence of the poor and, like many other educational efforts made by the ruling group, came to be used for their own ends by working-class leaders struggling for social and political reform. What is more, where earnestness did take hold, it did so not necessarily because the advocated Christian ideals had been accepted, but almost in defiance of them, by sceptics determined to prove their worth to their 'betters'.

Nonetheless, the restatements of the Protestant ethic gave support to the new habits of work then required and to a much safer range of political attitudes. They placed their emphasis unmistakably on hard work, on discipline and on sobriety by teaching that these were virtues and that they would be rewarded, not only with material success, but also with divine approval. The 'pursuit of individual salvation by hard work, thrift and competitive struggle'[3] is the way one modern writer has summed up this complex of attitudes. The ruling groups were able to emphasize again the qualities which they needed in the lower orders.

Nothing which happened during the remainder of the century made this emphasis any less important to the rulers: in fact, if anything the political and economic pressure on them increased, so that it became even more important to nurture the desired qualities. By the time the first youth workers acted, the 1867 and 1884 Parliamentary Reform Acts had made it even more important for working men – the new 'masters' – to be educated. The working class were beginning to organize themselves not only in industry but in politics too, and were finding in socialism a philosophy which seemed to imply nothing less than the complete over-throw of the existing political and economic structure. Nor were the only threats domestic. In Europe from 1871 a unified Germany formed an immense power which within thirty years seemed to challenge Britain's world leadership. Indeed, despite continued economic develop-ment, by the turn of the century it was becoming clear that economically Britain was falling behind the U.S.A. and Germany and that politically, as the Boer War was to show, there was less reason to take her sway for granted. Uncertainty and pessimism were far more common and explicit in the late nineteenth century society than they had been even earlier on, so that earnestness, determination and discipline were at least as important as previous unspoken uncertainty had made them.

The statements of the pioneer youth workers reveal these anxieties repeatedly. They were as concerned as any of their class had been during the earlier part of the century that their young members should grow into workers and subjects who were 'loyal' and 'responsible'. They were as likely, too, to use their personal Christian conviction to justify their concern. 'A scout is loyal and a scout obeys' said Baden-Powell baldly. Moreover, added William Smith, the purpose must be, in part, 'the promotion of habits of obedience, reverence, discipline, self-respect and all that tends towards true Christian manliness' (words which were repeated almost verbatim by the founders of Southport Lads' Club). The aim was 'discipline and religion', in that order but in harness.

The more immediate dangers of the age are also reflected in some of these pioneers' statements. According to Baden-Powell scouting 'appeals with equal force . . . to the boys of Eton College as much as to the boys in an East End slum. It is therefore no exaggeration to hope for valuable results from scouting in the direction of ultimately solving class differences . . .'. National pride, the vow to 'king and country' also receive repeated emphasis, and even Baden-Powell's awareness that 'the girls' branch is more important since it affects those who will be the mothers of the future generation of boys' bears witness to a current uneasiness about Britain's future which contrasted sharply with the predominant feeling in Britain earlier in the century that the country's progress was inevitable.

Here too support could be had from the Churches, and many youth workers must have shared the pessimism of the Archbishop of York when he said in 1878: 'The Church of England must either come into contact with the working classes of the country, or else her national position will suffer and her leading position be ultimately lost'. As one of his contemporaries put it: 'If we in the Church of England do not deal with the masses, the masses will deal with us. We depend, as far as our organization goes at present, upon the popular vote of the country'.

Yet, though religion was advocated partly as a means of providing a prop for the existing society, it was given emphasis also because the faithful themselves felt Christianity to be under severe pressure. For the growth of a new type of social organization had done much to weaken the traditional adherence of the lower classes. Many of the newcomers to the industrial towns had attended church as long as they lived in villages and worked on the land, since in that setting such behaviour was customary and normal. In their new setting, however, they found the habit of worship less usual and compelling, so that many of them abandoned it very quickly. Those who were born into an environment in which adherence was out of place neither committed themselves nor attended.

Here again the pressure on the ruling minority, with whom religious adherence came to be identified, increased as the century continued. Indifference or sheer ignorance remained a major problem and the heathenism of the urban masses was noted many times. Increasingly, however, and just at a time when the religious fervour of the early part of the century grew cooler and internal differences became acute, the external threat became much more positive. Christianity was challenged directly and intellectually, most sensationally by the work of scientists, Darwin and Huxley, and by the activities of Bradlaugh, the first atheist M.P. The danger had become so great that for those who believed that it was essential 'to teach them [the young] . . . that the service of God is the highest service', there was no honest alternative to their going to meet the unconverted and spreading the faith.

Thus, under pressure, the motives of those who first sought to fill adolescent leisure were mixed and at least unconsciously self-interested. Ensuring that the young grew into 'full Christian manliness', together with training them to be 'good citizens' and for 'responsible roles in society' all involved preparing the young to accept an economic, political and religious structure because it was there and because any radical disturbance of it would have endangered the power of those who controlled it. These are intentions which have been given persistent repetition since. Drawing out latent but respectable forms of such qualities as leadership and initiative has rarely, even since the nineteenth century, taken account of the fact that they can often be well expressed and experienced when their goal is criticism of established order. Instead, youthful rebellion, however expressed, has continued to be taken as evidence either of an understandable but naive and passing idealism or of a deep-seated maladjustment to existing society. The providers cannot usually be accused of evil intent: they have nearly always been in positions of social responsibility and blinkered by their own experience. It has been almost inevitable that they would unconsciously pass on to their clients the assumption that 'worthwhile' pursuits are only those sanctioned within the areas of society in which the providers themselves habitually move. Youth work has often become far less a means of developing young people than of unintentionally restraining and repressing them.

The Emergence of a Purpose

Restraint was rarely the aim, of course, and genuine efforts were made to 'develop' the young, to make them something more than they already were. But here too motives were mixed. Altruism was stressed and still is, but anxiety and defensiveness also played a crucial part. For not only were the ruling groups afraid of the masses: they were also repelled by many of the latter's values and habits of life, especially as these were shaped by the spread of industrialism and the large towns. Successful Englishmen, never fond of the 'bawdy plebeian culture', had for decades demonstrated their rise in the world by leaving the towns where their money had been made, disguising their humble origins and setting themselves up as country gentry. When urbanism made the plebeian culture more obvious and apparently even more bawdy, when industrialism brought grime, new dangers to health and ever-present and unmistakable evidence of how money was made, upper and middle-class distaste for working-class and city life became still stronger, until urbanism came to be closely identified with corruption and depravity. Indeed, many turned completely against industrialism as such and rejected all that was associated with it. What such critics saw first was ruthlessness, materialism and self-centred individualism. For them these were far more significant than any economic dynamism or achievement, and constituted self-evident vice. Urban and industrial life could offer no hope or scope for any educational movement. The new society was so inevitably debasing that not even radical adaptation and reform of it were considered. Only total rejection of almost all its major features, only escape to a purer and more detached code and range of activities would enable young people to develop socially.

Hence the ruling group's resort to standards, interests and activities which were isolated from and unmarred by the brutish and vulgar mass society around it; and hence too its insistence on the superiority of all that was part of its own way of life. In particular, such abstracted concepts as 'culture' and 'character' came to decide what was provided for the young in their leisure: value in social education was determined more and more by what was regarded as 'highbrow' or 'respectable' or 'character-building'. In this way, the dominant members of society set out to mould the unenlightened mass into a more amenable and familiar shape, which meant, in practice 'to make over the whole of society in their own image'.[4]

Youth work was much affected by this movement and by the flight from industrial life which did so much to determine its form. One of its most obvious signs was the actual physical rejection of urbanism and an especially strong conviction that the countryside and the out-of-doors contained all that was most desirable. It was not only that the fields, the hills, the rivers offered relief from dirt and drabness. They were also invested with self-evident virtues and therefore needed to be sought with an almost spiritual intensity. 'Towns were places where men made a livelihood: country houses were places where people lived. Man made the town: God made the country.'[5]

The yen for the outdoor life persisted and deeply influenced the early youth workers. For they too not only condemned the effect of the mean back streets and courtyards on the young who lived in them; they also recoiled from the city as such and turned to rural habits and rural pursuits as an essential antidote. The myth was spread and accepted that Nature contained the greatest purity and could be used to save every young person.

Scouting is, of course, the most obvious product of the mood. Baden-Powell, writing nearly thirty years after his first camp at Brownsea in 1907, recalled his early intentions and claimed that 'through camp-life, boat-work, pioneering and nature study one could find all the attractions for a boy which could at the same time be a medium of his instruction in manly qualities . . . Through sips of nature lore, imbibed in woodland 'hikes', the puny soul grows up and looks around.' He had from the very beginning seen 'observation, tracking and alertness' as self-evidently associated with 'discipline, self-reliance, self-sacrifice and patriotism' and as helping 'to turn the rising generation on the right road for good citizenship'.

These were views shared also by other youth workers in many different organizations and separate units. Camping, at least as an annual activity, gained a firm foothold in many other forms of youth work, as did rambling and fell-walking. All of these were encouraged in part for the very sound reason that they brought the young into the fresh air, gave them exercise which might increase their physical health, relieved the tedium of city life and enabled them to display characteristics and abilities which were otherwise unrevealed. Eventually these excursions came to be seen as the cause of, and not merely the setting for, the developments which took place in personality and personal relationships. Thus they were invested with the more mystical powers of character building, leadership training and initiative testing. Pleasure became almost an irrelevant by-product and outdoor activities came to be regarded as perhaps the most effective social educational method. It was assumed without question that profound personal lessons would inevitably be learned by conquering a peak or negotiating some rapids, and, further, that these lessons would automatically be carried back to the towns and applied there.

The countryside offered one, physical, means of escape from the much despised life of the industrial cities. A second such means, which was emotional much more than physical, was the insistence on standards of behaviour, of respect, of courtesy, which were taken straight from the conceptions of 'elevation' which the ruling groups were expounding more uncompromisingly, even, than in most previous ages. The 'manners' which they advocated were of course their own, which had been 'refined' by abstraction from the crude manners of the masses around them. As is so often the case, the very words may indicate something of the processes of thought and feeling which produced the behaviour.

Youth workers were unembarrassed by these assumptions and had need of few euphemisms, as the sponsors of St Christopher's Working Boys' Club, London, showed quite clearly:

> It is our aim to ourselves mix with them freely, and give them, as far as in us lies, the advantage of better education and tone that a happier fortune has bestowed upon us from our circumstances. We believe strongly that the lads can appreciate and will learn for themselves that subtle something which is called 'good form', which is such an important factor among the higher classes.

In the writings of Charles Russell, and elsewhere, words like 'tone', 'esprit de corps', 'decency in manners and speech' and 'social instincts' recur and are often supplemented, when the discussion moves on to actual club programmes, by 'team-spirit' and 'playing the game'. The assumption that youth workers themselves offer perfect models of good social development has remained undisturbed in much youth work. 'Youth leaders', urged one writer in 1948, 'need to be shop-windows through which young people can see and admire all that is good and worthwhile'.

In the eyes of the early youth workers, the place where the model was most successfully moulded was the public school, and repeatedly the hope is expressed that the young people who use youth organizations will learn from and come to resemble its products. 'Training of character', claimed an early edition of The Boy, 'strongly coloured by Arnoldian public school ideas, was more important than the acquisition of textbook knowledge'. And William Smith, often feeling at first that he needed to defend the Boys' Brigade against accusations of Prussianism and militarism, also turned to this indisputably British institution for a precedent: 'There would be engendered', he wrote, 'that esprit de corps which public school boys acquire as a matter of course but which was almost entirely lacking in elementary schoolboys'. Of course, such writers and their supporters were bound to discuss their purpose in such terms, since they had available to them no models of young people's behaviour other than those which were in their own minds and experience. Nor did they have any way of analysing what they desired to achieve without resort to such models. They were obliged to measure their practice against what they and others like them knew and believed, and many of their descendants still speak as though models and comparisons with their own attitudes and habits are the only available language of communication.

A third sign in youth work of the abstracted culture of the ruling groups was the suspicion, resulting from a rejection of the 'materialism' of the society around them, of almost any commercial provision for the entertainment of the young. Because it was automatically assumed from the start that commercialism must bring debasement and exploitation, youth organizations were designed 'as a counter-attraction to the music-hall, the street corner and the public house'. It was a suspicion which again has persisted and which has led to some extreme attitudes being expressed. Thus in 1929, Baden-Powell juxtaposed 'cinema stars, Test matches, Cup finals and murders' and condemned all of them as 'interest in false values', while in the next year the National Association of Boys' Clubs recorded its 'vigorous opposition to commercialized sport' and classed the cinema with the street corner.

Because of commercial interest in young people's leisure time, the view of the Wesley Guild in 1894 that 'recreation unorganized is a danger' was widely accepted. The fact was, however, that it was recreation and not amusement or simple entertainment which mainly concerned these early youth workers. Thus Russell took 'as the first object, Recreation, for this is the compelling force which brings members to the clubs and to the vast majority of them it appears first also in importance'. Moreover, inseparable from this conception of recreation were the 'cultural' standards which youth workers themselves were evolving to defend themselves against the philistinism of the age. No doubt they had good reason to dislike much that was enjoyed and found entertaining in the world which was the adolescent's 'own'. But, as with the commercial provision, little if any attempt was made to select from within it: often it was simply rejected in its entirety as totally empty and worthless. If the *existing* interests of the urban young were served it was frequently not by deliberate examination and provision, but accidentally, while other superior ends were being pursued. The value or appropriateness of an activity was not judged in the first place by what it was seen to do to or for the individual member (though clearly most of the youth workers thought in all sincerity that this *was* the criterion), nor by what expansion of experience in and concern for human relationships and human beings it made possible. The criterion above all others was whether it had inherent 'cultural' worth. Hence, of course, the assumptions made so easily about the value of outdoor pursuits. Hence, too, the belief, which again has persisted, that 'drama', 'art', 'classical music' and other 'cultural' activities must be 'laid on', because of the value they have as *subjects*, regardless of how *people* may use them or of what people may require. Art and Culture were firmly separated from what the 'mass' resorted to when it wished merely to be entertained: they could be identified instead with a small dominant social class, which could thus define their content, make them part of their own heritage and dispense them gratuitously to the deserving and worthy.

In part too, however, the Protestant ethic which so influenced youth workers' political and social ideals also affected their judgment of what constituted worthwhile recreation. An early result of the spread of urban and industrial conditions was, as we have seen, the disappearance of many of the traditional forms of entertainment. Religious conviction at an opportune moment was reasserted and strengthened in order to support practical need. The distracting interests of the poor were discouraged or repressed, and increased emphasis given to the serious use of leisure time. Much contemporary religion, despite the emotionalism of its ceremony, was in its impact on men's social lives anti-emotional and repressive.

Thus leisure came to be an extra period for seeking self-improvement: as material success was a sign of divine approval, effort and striving needed to characterize all one's activity, and idleness and ease had to be denied even during non-compulsory work periods. Joy was associated with sin, play and pleasure could have no value for their own sakes, all that was done which was not purposeful was laden with guilt.

Youth workers, even a century after Methodism had given the Protestant ethic a new emphasis, did not escape entirely from its effects, and formed their views on what they ought to offer young people partly under its influence. Only those activities which might help self-improvement and self-advancement were recognized as justifiable and worthwhile. This is why just making boys happy seemed to Russell an inadequate aim and why he was willing to accept recreation – that is 're-creation' for work – as the first objective. And this is why, too, the word 'pursuits', with all its overtones of striving and effort has been so much used in social education. Though in some ways the puritan tradition contributed significantly to the growth of the responses and values of that industrial society which youth workers so anxiously wished to avoid, it nonetheless played its part in helping to formulate their purpose and fashion their methods. The Protestant ethic and the reaction against industrialism, although at times they pulled in opposite directions, together were vital contributors to the models to which modern youth work has been firmly tied.

Adaptation and Continuity: the Inappropriate Legacy

Youth work today is not, of course, exactly what it was in the 1910s. A number of new organizations and approaches have been added to the original ones; in particular, a genuine rural form of youth work, the Young Farmers' club, which is very deeply embedded in the everyday realities of most of its members; and the Youth Hostels' Association, which sets out to do no more than help young people enjoy the country-side, but which, perhaps as a consequence, is somehow not usually considered to be a 'normal' part of the Youth Service. There has also been a certain amount of amalgamation – the Boys' Brigade and the Boys' Life Brigade, for example – and a good deal more federation: the establishment of the National Association of Boys' Clubs, of what is now the National Association of Youth Clubs and of the National Federation of Young Farmers' Clubs. Also, the Standing Conference of National Voluntary Youth Organizations has been formed and, perhaps most significant of all, there has been an acceptance of some direct statutory responsibility.

Even apart from all this, however, there have been substantial changes in the voluntary organizations which emerged in the early days of youth work and which have carried a major part of the task of catering for adolescents' leisure needs. None of them has simply stood still; all have to some degree recognized the changes in the social environment in which they work and have altered accordingly. Thus their purposes have under-gone, and in some ways are still undergoing, modification, reinterpreta-tion and shifts of emphasis. In consequence of these and other changes youth workers today are far less anxious to stress and to state openly the superiority of their own refinement, and are perhaps a little less likely to see themselves as shop windows. Actual religious conversion and direct influence for political ends are claimed by far fewer to be the most immediate and important considerations. Rescuing the young from the depths of poverty and basic depravity are less pressing concerns.

The changes of language and of organization are inevitable and necessary. It would be strange indeed if youth workers talked and acted today just as they did almost one hundred years ago. It would also be a devastating indictment, for the society in which they now function has altered so quickly and so markedly. Out of the unrelieved poverty of the nineteenth century has grown affluence for many more young people than ever shared it before: even the crippling depressions of the twentieth century have no living meaning for them. International events and, in particular, two major wars and the dictatorial views of 'the State' held by Nazis, Fascists and Bolsheviks have left deep scars on the philosophy and practice of 'voluntaryism'. Perhaps, most significant of all, however, has been the technological advance: it has immeasurably improved the quality of communication between one human being and another, it has made each one more conscious of what sort of life is attainable, and it has given many more the desire for this life and a better chance of achieving it. Technology cannot be viewed as a remote, rather inhuman 'thing'. It has a profound human and individually personal meaning, for it alters ambitions, relationships and philosophies. In particular, it has continually extended the opportunities in society for those decision-making forces which start, not at the centre to work outwards, centrifugally, but at the edges of a human society to work inwards, centripetally, *towards* the executors of power. For example, the extension of the franchise and the intensification of other, less formal, methods for public opinion to register itself, help to make the politician more sensitive to the wishes of the people whom he serves. But these centripetal forces do not only affect 'political' authority in its conventional sense. They also affect both those who for so long have held the power to make much broader cultural decisions and those who influence the content of education. The spread of literacy, increasing access to knowledge and greater prosperity all ensure that what is right and proper in social activity, in the etiquette of relationships between people, in the way they spend their leisure and so on, will no longer be decided by authoritarian imposition from the centre.

If Britain of the 1860s was very different from that of 1760, the Britain of 1960 is unrecognizable, a foreign land in vital non-material ways, in comparison with that of 1860. Many may regret this and act and talk as if they would turn back the clock. Youth workers have not all been quite as resistant as this and certainly many have modified their vocabulary, tone of voice and some of the externals of their organizations. But it is not clear that they have yet expressed purposes, discovered approaches or adopted attitudes which are as fundamentally different from their originals as is today's society from the one which existed one hundred years ago. Amalgamations and federations have taken place among certain movements, but as much in a defensive response to the growing influence on their work of statutory powers as in positive response to perceived changes in society's needs. Society in general *has* increasingly taken corporate action: but it has done so primarily out of sorrow because no private groups had acted, or out of anger at the real or supposed crimes of the young, or out of fear and economic or political prudence. Only secondarily has it acted out of any deeply felt belief that the community must mobilize itself in order to help millions of individual people to grow and develop their experience and abilities.

Indeed it is clear that, though thousands of youth workers have very personally been influenced by the adaptations which youth work as a whole has made, with many of them it is *only* the vocabulary, the tone of voice and the externals of organization which have changed. Has the mood altered, or the relative position, as far as the youth worker himself is concerned, of 'leader' and 'led'? Though the intentions are more humbly and tactfully expressed, are they as fundamentally different as they now often need to be? Though conversion and influence are mentioned less often, have they been removed from the youth worker's programme or just disguised? Is the pill to be administered to the young a new one – or is it just that its sugar-coating is more lavish and sweeter than it used to be? Have youth workers in fact fully understood and made a conscious part of their mental make-up the revolution – technological, social, political, economic but above all *personal* – which has been wrought in the period since youth organizations were first conceived?

It is clear that deeply embedded in this original conception was a powerful educational aim – a belief that the young were capable of becoming fuller personalities than they would if just left to themselves and of deriving greater fulfilment from life. None even now would want to deny the right of the original providers to have such an intention: indeed, if anything, greater lip-service is now paid to it than a century ago, and the whole practice of social education is meaningless without this belief. But their precise interpretation of this intention was very much their own, very much influenced, even dictated perhaps, by their own education, their place in society, the attitudes and values which their times had given them.

The result was therefore that a great deal of youth work was started from an unqualified and unselective condemnation of large areas of the society around them. This led the providers to reject it, to assume that little if any of it gave a helpful basis for the social-educational development of the young who must live deeply within it, and to search for solutions which would offer self-protection, a defence against encroachment. Having cast aside the culture of the old rural Britain as of no account, they went on to treat the new urban culture in exactly the same way.

Their judgment of this new culture was understandable enough. Much of it offered little if any basis for educational advance. But many of the consequences were unfortunate – and avoidable. For subsequent events in working-class history were to show that not all of the urban culture was worthless – some of it, given more chance and positive welcome might have grown much further. In any case, the responses which were made by the providers often had very little to do with real personal social-educational development but were primarily intended rather as a defence of their own established interests. Finally, the educational content which was added consisted very largely of a collection of negatives or of disguised forms of escapism. The myth of the supreme virtue of the countryside, the code of 'refined' standards, the suspicion of mere commercialism, the abstracted and uncommitted concept of 'culture', the guilt-ridden pursuits of the Protestant ethic, all these meant that the educational programmes of youth work removed the young person from the environment – physical, emotional and intellectual – which was and would fundamentally remain his familiar world.

All education may well mean some separation of the young person from his origins, but the values implicit in early youth work were in direct opposition to the background of young people whom it sought to serve. It was assumed from the start that the ultimate ideal could be attained only if young people were taken almost completely out of the values and habits of the world of their parents and launched into a world which the providers had defined as more desirable. 'They offered a powerful and sustained propagation of the ideology of the middle classes'.[6]

The purpose of this chapter has been neither to approve of nor to condemn the beliefs, ideals and motives of those who a century ago acted according to the assumptions and pressures of their day. The sincerity and altruism of many of them is beyond question, while even the fear and self-interest of others were human and understandable enough. In any case it is not for one generation to sit in judgment on another, only to seek to learn from it. Moreover, it seems worth repeating that much that has been presented above is intended as one interpretation and one perspective which must often be treated as a hypothesis to be tested by more detailed research. What cannot be taken as self-evidently desirable, however, in any historical appraisal is an uncritical admiration for an existing structure simply because it exists and has existed for many decades. The aims and methods, the principles and disciplines required today by adults who work with young people in various social-educational settings must be relevant to the situation in which those young people and those adults find themselves. This relevance can be achieved more certainly and more fully only if the past, the origins of what now exists, is examined with open mind.

1. R. FLETCHER, *The Family and Marriage*, Penguin, 1962, p. 69.
2. J. F. C. HARRISON, *Learning and Living, 1790–1960*, Routledge, 1961, p. 40.
3. W. H. WHYTE, *The Organisation Man*, Pelican, 1960, p. 9.
4. J. F. C. HARRISON, op. cit., p. 39.
5. A. BRIGGS, *Victorian Cities*, Odhams, 1963, p. 69.
6. J. F. C. HARRISON, op. cit., p. 89.

Chapter 3

Adults and Young People in Society

Adults' Attitudes to Adolescents

Many discussions of 'adolescence' naturally concentrate upon the state of mind and body of the adolescent him/herself, and particularly upon the uncertainty of the individual on the threshold of independence, and the 'crisis of identity'[1] which this brings. Such an approach is of course quite valid: the adolescent is uncertain, he does need sympathetic help and understanding from adults, and clearly a book dealing with further social education implies such an approach throughout. More specifically however this chapter will consider the social situation of the adolescent, and the attitudes of adults towards 'adolescence' as a phenomenon. For there are elements in the adult mind which do something to exacerbate the uncertainties of the young person, and crises of adult identity which are to some extent eased by the attention given to adolescent unsureness.

First then we need to consider the way adults employ the word 'adolescence', since their misuse of it has helped to confuse their attitudes towards young people. Adults have gradually come to assume that all those to whom the word 'adolescent' may be applied are different and distinct from the rest of adult society in almost every respect, whereas in fact the word refers precisely and specifically to one particular respect only in which they are different. 'Adolescent' is a word which refers to biological and physiological factors for which evidence can be adduced. Those factors operate in everyone, but they start at different times and last for differing lengths of time. They have a variety of psychological effects whose expressions are unpredictable for any individual but to some extent patterned in any one culture. At its simplest, the psychological uncertainty of adolescence may be said to have two important focal points of enquiry: one, in early adolescence, is the urge to find out 'who or what sort of a person am I?', and the other, coming later, the urge to find out 'what sort of a person am I going to be?'.

However, though there are differences from one individual to another in the period over which each may be said to be technically (that is, physically) adolescent, adults have grown to expect that adolescent behaviour will occupy more or less standard years of life. This expectation alone, being widespread, would probably be enough to induce in young people a pattern of behaviour which would answer the cues given by adults and so match the 'standard' adolescent period. But adults have gone further and have taken certain measures which institutionalize their expectation and enshrine it in administrative schemes. The age range covered by the Youth Service, now reckoned as being from 14 to 21, is one, though only one, example, since it has had the effect of reinforcing adults' readiness to assume that adolescence begins about (compulsory) school-leaving age and continues until legal majority is attained.

There have, however, been some notable moves away from this in recent years. Dr Mark Abrams, in particular, in reporting on the teenage consumer market, has pointed out that, in terms of purchasing wants and spending possibilities, it is young people over 15 but under 25 years of age, or until marriage if it comes earlier, who constitute a fairly homogeneous group.[2] In view of the effect which patterns of spending can have on the range of ways in which young people use their leisure time, many educators and especially social educators have begun to think in terms of this wider bracket. More recently, Dr Musgrove has argued for the removal altogether of what he sees as the humiliating status of 'adolescent', so that young people can assume as soon as possible their rightful role as full members of our society.[3] Far more important, however, are indications that administrative and legal changes may be made which would engender radical changes of attitude on the part of adults: the Lord Chancellor has set up a committee to consider the Age of Majority, and the suggestions aired at the last three General Elections for the extension of the vote to all those over 18 are taking the form of firm proposals within the Labour Party.

This book does not wish to propose yet another set of limits. On the contrary, it wishes to dispose wherever possible of the need to think at all in physical-age compartments, since these in practice are so often meaningless. For the developmental age of the individual may at any time be ahead of or behind his chronological age: it is quite 'normal' for a child of 8 to have developed to the point which the average child only reaches at $9\frac{1}{2}$, or to have reached only that point which the majority reach at 7. He will 'catch' up, or be 'caught' up, later. Emotionally, some adolescents are 'late developers' and some are 'early'. What is important is that, in the case of each individual, educators should be perceptive of the stage he has reached in his development, and not constantly expect and encourage uniform behaviour from all those who can conveniently be labelled 'adolescent'.

To see as largely the same everyone whose age happens to be in the teens is unmistakably to over-simplify. Experienced teachers and youth workers are rarely impressed by such generalizations, since they are repeatedly frustrated by rigid age-groupings and made aware of discrepancies between developmental age (the only significant age for social education) and the chronological age of their adolescent clients. For it is undoubtedly true that there are differences of interests, needs, abilities and so on *within* the age-group. The needs and responses of the immediately post-pubertal young man or woman, for example, are often very unlike those of a man or woman of 19 or 20 calendar years who is at a much later stage of development. Notoriously, too, the 'average' girl develops faster than the 'average' boy until about 19 years of age, at least in our society, so that with different sexes of the same calendar age developing on average to different points, even greater care in our use of the concept 'adolescent' is demanded. Again, the 18 year-old will probably enjoy the company of the 22 year-old more than of the 15 year-old, and the 22 year-old will be more likely to tolerate younger company than would the 18 year-old. And companionship between the sexes certainly straddles the normal boundary of adolescence, if the average age at marriage in Britain is any evidence. Men marry on average at 25 and women on average at $22\frac{1}{2}$. This age differential, assuming a period of courtship preceding marriage, indicates choices of companionship in later 'adolescence' which makes nonsense of our easy assumptions about convenient calendar-age brackets.

There are many reasons, then, why the category of 'adolescent' needs to be reviewed whenever it is used. It is clearly a mistake for adults to approach the near-adult older adolescent in the same frame of mind which they adopt in working with the immediately post-pubertal boy or girl. The features which they have in common should not mislead the adult into the easy assumption that they will respond and view the world in identical ways. If the concern of an earlier generation of educators was to avoid 'mannikinizing the boy'[4] it must be the concern of social

educators today to avoid 'childifying the man or woman' unnecessarily
or inappropriately. Certainly we need to remember that a sound maturity
is built upon many expressions of immaturity, but this is no ground for
adult society allowing a frame of mind to develop which *expects* immature behaviour and therefore provides and structures situations so that it
can be contained.

Particularly those adults engaged in social education, whether as
teachers or youth workers, cannot adopt any such undifferentiated
expectation of adolescent behaviour. For they can neither take up the
position that all adolescents are really children grown bigger, thus
producing or encouraging the immature behaviour which confirms them
in their view; nor can they approach young people as though they were
adults, and then 'mark them down' or feel outraged if they do not behave
as adults in all particulars. It seems quite inappropriate for the social
educator above all to think of adolescence as a frustrating and intrinsically
pointless preliminary to adulthood, or as a suitably chastening extension
of childhood, or as an unrepeatable opportunity to indoctrinate the young
with behaviour patterns familiar and comfortable to the adult. Rather,
adolescence is to be seen as a chance for young people to try out a
multitude of different roles in preparation for mature adulthood. It is the
variety and changeability of the adolescent which need to be in the social
educator's mind; it is the variations between individuals and the constant
changes in each individual which need to be perceived.

For the adolescent retains the potentiality to become a whole range of
different persons from the one he looks like becoming today. Given the
situation in which to explore new experiences, to experiment, he will
'try on' this role, that guise, this attitude. The Youth Service and many
secondary schools are creating opportunities for this to happen, and need
to create for many more young people the kind of situations in which
their potentiality can be developed. If this does not happen individuals
will, in Lady Albemarle's words, 'accept a style of life less varied, less
committed and less meaningful than the times allow', and this 'will be
our loss as well as theirs'.[5] It is no service to adolescents or to society to
recruit them to adult ranks merely for what they are at present. Indeed,
though keeping them at bay, thinking of them as 'adolescent', as 'less
than adult', may seem to be the greatest humiliation, in fact it is not.
A much greater one is contained in any adult requirement that, to qualify
for adult status, they must not express their abilities and personalities
fully. Premature integration is thus much more degrading than emphas-

izing their separateness, since it underestimates what young people are capable of becoming. It acts as a more certain protective measure for adults than any denial or delaying of adolescents' attainment of adult status, since it conveniently dilutes the powers of the new recruits to society by absorbing them neatly but without vision into whichever niche in the status quo they happen to fit. It smacks of a philosophy of 'if you cannot beat them, invite them to join you; win them over but under no circumstances let them get together and develop ideas which might challenge you'.

Adults by contrast need to free themselves from the assumption that adolescents are enemies. If adults can avoid such a defensive approach, those of them who accept social-educational roles need to be prepared for some unexpected repercussions. For, once adolescence is seen as a period in which potentialities can develop, the adults' own personal values and ideas will be far more 'at risk' than if they constantly emphasize to themselves the distance and difference between themselves and adolescents. There is no point in their training equipping them for roles of protected authority-figures, since as we argue in more detail elsewhere, they will be required to be holders of the ring in which young people will disport themselves tentatively and experimentally, and touchstones on which young people will try out whatever latest attitude, guise or role they want to test.

Yet, though their roles will be different, their responsibilities for helping the young to develop socially will be no less. Adolescents will continue to need special consideration from the adult members of society. It is important, however, not to think of this consideration as different in character from that given to other special classes of adult – newly-weds, expectant mothers, immigrants or old people – to whom we give special attention in some respects but by no means in all. If we acted in a totally different way towards any of these groups simply because they can be described by terms which refer to one element in their lives, our treatment of them would be unnecessarily restricted and rigid.

To respond thus to adolescents would seem to be particularly unfair since what is regarded as special to them may, to some degree or other, be revealed by many outside their ranks. For, *any* individual will carry for many years many of the features of his adolescent life. Many so-called and recognized adults behave, frequently or infrequently, in large or in small areas, in ways more characteristic of the adolescent 'phase'. The Crowther Report refers to adolescence as 'that April weather of the soul'.[6] The noticeable thing about April weather is that it contains no elements unique to April. All that constitutes April weather can be found elsewhere in the calendar (not surprisingly). The distinguishing characteristic of April is that no element holds sway for very long since it is quickly succeeded by another, and may or may not be repeated soon afterwards. Adolescent behaviour has the same affinity to adult behaviour. It cannot simply be categorized as standing apart and so assumed to demand responses completely at variance with those made to all other members of society.

The affinity between adult and adolescent is not in fact difficult to discern. On a sociological plane, it can be observed in the much-discussed 'teenage culture' of the late 1950s. What was remarkable about this was that it contained few if any elements entirely distinctive to young people. Individual young people gave heavier emphases to certain elements than would most adults, and new possibilities were fastened upon more readily by young people than by adults. As might be expected, the ingredients were the same, even though the quantities and mixtures differed sufficiently to give the impression to those looking for it that a special teenage culture was abroad.

Adolescents then will best be served if adults working with them in social-educational settings give them special consideration, certainly, but nonetheless accept them as versions of the same things as themselves. Once adults think of themselves as standard or normal, and of adolescents as deviant or abnormal, they do the latter a disservice and make their own approach an arrogant one. Even to view adolescents as 'delayed' adults, people approaching the normality of adulthood, is to fall prey to a complacency about the perfection of the adult generation and to ignore adolescents' potential ability to go beyond the 'type'which society places before them.

That adolescents will, at some later date, celebrate more birthdays than they have already is in fact almost irrelevant in determining the nature of the adult's approach to relationships with them. The philosophy which underlies all work with special groups in society is one which emphasizes the common ground in humanity between two people. 'Please regard us as normal but different' say the blind, the handicapped, the sick, the old, the delinquent, the sexually deviant, the oppressed minorities. With an effort, many people who are 'normal', who differ, that is, in less obvious ways, have overcome the tendency to think in categories about such groups, and, fortified by the thought of 'There but for the grace of God go I', have adjusted until they can truly approach minorities as members of the same unity, different versions of the same humanity as themselves. Is it too much to ask adults who work with young people to treat them also as normal but different?

The Socialization of the Adolescent

What, then, is special about the place occupied by young people in any society? In examining this question, it is necessary to note first a point which will be developed at length later, that their place is fundamentally one of extended socialization – that is, of education or introduction to the ways of life of that society. The adults in a society will, deliberately or not, equip their young to contribute to, to participate in and to benefit from the society in which they are growing up. Many factors will determine the nature of this education – for example, what kind of skills are needed for economic or recreative purposes – and also its length and distribution – whether all young people are given the same training for the same period, or some chosen for special, longer or shorter, treatment. Almost certainly one feature will be early training in some kind of small family unit, and, again in most cases, a longer residence with a family or group of relatives. Through these, some of the close-range or intimate skills are learned while further training in keeping with the demands of the society is carried on outside the family, usually by the agency of some adults designated by the society to undertake this responsibility.

In our own society it is clearly customary during most of the years before marriage for people to be resident within the family home and so to receive much of their education there. It has recently been fashionable to raise an alarm about a decline in this influence and in a family's ability to prepare its young for adult roles. It is true that 'the family' today is a smaller circle than in many periods of history and that it no longer therefore confers upon children and young people the benefits of the extended family. Such a wide range of relationships with relatives prepared young people for, and indeed shaped, many of the roles which they were to play in the society of that period. But in our own society the nuclear family prepares young people for different and no less important roles by alternative and not weaker influences. It is a false alarm to bewail a weakening in family influence, for the educative qualities of richness and variety in inter-relationships have merely been replaced by those of intensity, closeness and intimacy. The rise in material standards and security, the use of the

family as the fundamental administrative unit for so many public amenities and services, the tendency for more and more families to live in units
containing only parents-plus-children, and the advent of both television
and the family motor-car have all contributed to the power and influence
of the family over its children. In addition to the realities, the image has
certainly been strengthened by those advertisers of consumer goods who
see it as advantageous to portray the use of these goods in family situations,
because, they believe, it is with such scenes that a majority of potential
purchasers can or would wish to identify.

As experience of family life has generally become more powerful and
formative, we have been made more aware of the strength of its actual
influence upon the young person's future ability to participate fully in
society. Much research testifies to the profound effect on the child of the
home in which the conversation is stimulating and wide-ranging, in which
there is ready access to a wide variety of concepts, whether through books
or any other medium, and in which experiences are rich and varied. By
contrast, the child unfamiliar with the existence of certain words or
concepts cannot develop his mind to use or identify them. If children are
brought up in a stimulating environment where the multitude of ideas
which make up our world are differentiated and put into words, they
will have an immeasurably better chance of a full rich life themselves.
Their imaginative and intellectual potential will be developed to the full,
and life will be experienced in what is for them the maximum number of
aspects.

In other words, it has been no accident in past centuries that men were
seen 'fit to govern' if they had been brought up in homes where the
paraphernalia of government were common talk, or that sons of landed
gentry who alone had heard the relevant ideas were more admirably
equipped to fit the requirements of a landed gentry than any others of
their generation. In the same way, today, middle-class families appear to
obtain a share of grammar-school and university places which is disproportionate to their share of our society's intelligent children and
young people. By the intellectually and socially educational experience
which it generates of itself, the educative family – 'la famille éducogène',
in the French phrase – plays an incomparable role in equipping young
people for the fullest life in society.

But it will be a long time yet before even a substantial proportion of
the young people in our society have available to them, within the close
range of their families, the fullest possible educative experience. Though

it is doubtful whether exertions on the part of public educative services can ever adequately make up for what will thus be left undone, clearly efforts are still required to provide some form of substitute. And it seems that it will be by informal approaches either before or after the school-leaving age, through social-educational rather than academic or practical educational experience, that the educators, the designated adults of our society, will come closest to achieving this substitute.

For, in any society, outside the educative potential of even the most resourceful family there must lie a whole area of introduction and initiation to society which some form of communally organized education must provide. We have an immensely complex society, and accordingly an immense variety of agencies providing introductions to society's innumerable facets. Apart from the vast array of public and private 'educational' institutions, there are countless courses of induction and training in the working world, there are the mass-media of communication, an infinite variety of private organizations concerned to promote their own activity either among young people or adults, the churches and religious organizations, and the great organs of commerce purveying information about their wares and services.

All of these have their place in the preparation of our young people for understanding, contributing to and benefiting from society. However, though the process goes on throughout life, especially in a changing society, the pace is set increasingly in adult life by the organs of commerce and the courses run to help people in their work. By contrast, those agencies which rely on public funds are, relatively speaking, starved and their capacity and objectives badly understood, so that the balance is weighted heavily against them once compulsory school is over.

The 'Graded Acceptance' of the Young into Adult Society

It seems important to look now at the whole process of the introduction of young people into society with the insights which the social anthropologists have given us. One major lesson which derives from their work is that adolescence is not necessarily a time of revolt and rebellion. Some of the causes of any outlaw-like or violently critical behaviour by young people must be sought in the fabric and pressures of the society in which they live. Moreover, there is ample evidence that an urbanized, industrialized society with plenty of exchange of ideas both by personal contact and the mass media, does produce a situation in which many adolescents experience a period of rebellion. And since most of the countries of the world are developing both towns and industry as rapidly as they are able, there is little point in indulging any nostalgia for simple societies.

However, simple societies do offer us an illustration which helps in the interpretation of the more complex structure of our own. The pattern emerges of young people being 'initiated' into the adult society either at a certain age or between certain age-limits, after passing some tests of performance or achievement relevant to the way of life they will follow. This clearly presupposes a stable society, where the means of economic support and the rest of the culture are undergoing little change and where the moral values are handed down and accepted unquestionably by succeeding generations. We may use the term 'deontological' to denote such a society since questions of right or wrong are answered by reference to an authoritative prescriptive code.

One of the purposes of such 'rites du passage' is that it ensures that the society's future will be secured. It has taught its young how to hunt, weave, navigate or whatever they must do to support themselves, and it has passed on also the lore and values which maintain its coherence. Such tests of a young person's fitness for admission to the full society have another effect, apart from guaranteeing the maintenance of the society in the future. They also, by providing a signal for both the adult and the young person that a certain status has been attained, profoundly influence the attitudes of both. The young person newly accepted into adult society, having previously watched the behaviour of elders in a situation identical with his own, has been given a clear indication of what is now expected of him and what attitudes he should adopt to those younger than himself who have yet to pass the test. The attitudes of the longer-established adult members of society are also helped by the ritual of initiation. They have no need to doubt how they should behave towards someone whom, until last week, they had been accustomed for 14 or 17 years to treat as a child growing up. Now their culture has provided them with a clear signal, and the erstwhile child is accepted as a full member of society

Little embroidery is needed on this over-simple sketch, since its purpose is only to help us understand our own society. One point which may be made, however, is that the tests used need to be not only relevant to the conditions of a society, but also agreed and accepted by the whole community. If the signal is to be valuable and meaningful to everyone, all must appreciate its significance and accept its validity.

Our own society is very complex and so obviously lacks any such clear signal of universal significance. Certain sections or facets of our life do, it is true, still retain rites of passage which have significance within the limits of the group of people involved. Some of the rituals surrounding apprenticeships and other forms of training, graduation, passing-out parades and confirmation or other forms of admission to churches are all examples of sectional rites. But when we look for an indication by society as a whole of its acceptance of its young people, we are disappointed. For, various shades or graduations of acceptance are offered to them at all ages between 14 and 21, so that their entry into full responsibility as, for example, a workman, driver of a motor vehicle, soldier and voter all occur at different times. The law considers a person adult for the purposes of paying fares on public transport at 14 and allows him or her to accept full-time working roles at 15 (soon to be 16). At 16, he or she is seen as sufficiently well developed and responsible to see 'X' films unaccompanied and ride a motor cycle. It is conceded that at 17 he may be able to drive a car with safety and consideration, and that he is capable of being at 18 entrusted with knowledge and experience of the techniques and secrets of modern warfare. Not until 21 may such young people vote, marry without parental or court consent, or make mortgage and certain other contracts, although current discussions may lead in due course to the revision of some of these laws. It is unnecessary to argue for the gathering together of all these legal provisions at one point, so that at a certain year all these rights and duties are granted in a bundle. A case might well be made for a comprehensive re-examination of all of them and of how they relate to one another, and certainly we might look to the morality of a situation in which individuals have no right to participate in a political decision which might commit them to military conscription and risk of death. But in a society such as ours, no single point of entry is likely to be discovered.

Legal gradations therefore supply one source of examples of adolescents' graded acceptance into society: marriage, work and morals offer other spheres of acceptance which are worth examining in some detail, even though the gradations are less clear-cut. Marriage, for example, appears to bring acceptance by adult society. Perhaps this acceptance is partly a matter of support to people facing a new experience, but it seems, in part also, to be a matter of self-protection for those who are established; for if marriage did not merit acceptance as an adult, some 'adults' might be uncomfortably aware that their own entitlement to this status was in jeopardy. In modern society, however, we know that a gradually increasing number of young people marry at an age which surprises many adults because it is a good deal earlier than the average age for marriage within living memory. The precise figures for Britain for 1962 show that $6\frac{1}{2}$ per cent of bridegrooms were 16 to 19 years of age, compared with the much smaller figure of $2\frac{1}{3}$ per cent in 1952. The proportion of teenage brides did not increase to the same extent over this period, but they substantially outnumbered grooms of their own age: in 1962, $26\frac{3}{4}$ per cent of brides were 16 to 19 years old, compared with $15\frac{1}{4}$ per cent in 1952. Yet teenage marriage is not a new phenomenon, since it was a common experience in pre-industrial society. Then, however, it occurred at a period of life which was almost middle-age, whereas today, with the life expectation much longer, there are far more adults alive to whom adolescence appears a relatively early stage of development. There is an understandable tendency therefore for the majority of adults to look upon teenage marriage as somewhat premature.

Our society may itself contain the causes of relatively early marriage. There may be pressures and tensions which urge young people to seek the early security of a close and intimate relationship, or it may be that the nuclear family experience itself prepares young people well for a similar intensity of association with one other person. If pressures in society are a cause, however, they are not of course exclusively felt by adolescents, and there is probably always a proportion of people of whatever age for whom marriage is not intrinsically attractive but, negatively, a flight from lonely strain. Thus, we may be prepared to accept that some 'early' marriages should be the outcome of such motives. On the other hand, some pressures and tensions may be unnecessary and may be adding in unfortunate ways to such 'flights from loneliness'.

Whatever the underlying causes, however, it seems certain that marriage as an indicator of entry into adulthood is undergoing change. If wages continue high and credit easy, we can presumably expect a higher number of early marriages, and we should assume that they will not be confined to those who have left full-time education. And if this happens, it will presumably be followed by two successive changes in adult attitude: first, 'early' marriage will lose its significance and rarity value, and will cease to be a signal of arrival at adulthood; then later, as the practice becomes even more widespread, society will come to conceive of adolescence as ending earlier.

The working area of life might be expected to be one in which society would demand that young people prove themselves and pass a test which shows unmistakably that they are fit to help support the society in the future. Our complex society does, of course, make such demands. Yet it earns its living in ways which, for many, require a high level of preliminary training, and for many others, a low level of personal involvement or responsibility. The consequence is that for the many young people who undergo training, acceptance for one's value to society as a workman comes either at yet another graded stage in the progress from school to full acceptance as an adult, or even in some cases at a stage beyond 21. For other young people who undergo little or no training (and who constitute by far the majority), the chances are slim that they will find a job in which the physical strength and zest which is their potential can be expressed. Most will do work which demands little involvement or responsibility, and so they are unlikely to merit, or to feel that they merit, adult acceptance on this ground. In fact, many of those who receive little or no training are those who experienced successive rejections in the 'selective' processes of our education system, and left school already convinced that society would be reluctant to accept them. Streaming in the primary school, selection at 11 or 13 plus, streaming in the secondary school, aptitude tests for technical training – all are frequently defended as necessary for practical reasons and as inevitable in some form. We can of course help to erase irrelevant social differences and give every schoolchild the opportunity to shine by widening further the range of the curricula. But two facts will remain. One is that those young people with skills believed to be of economic value will find early acceptance for trainee status, but not until they are trained will they be accepted as full members of society. The second is that the others will lack even the security of traineeships while they await acceptance, and later, when they are finally acknowledged by society as adult, it will rarely be on the basis of the economic contribution of their work.

Again, there is no argument here for wholesale social engineering to overcome these disadvantages. The complexity of our society must surely mean that there are few occupations in which a young person can, spontaneously, do all that is necessary to make him a valued and respected member of society. The exceptions are perhaps in sport and entertainment, where high prestige may be accorded comparatively early in life, although even here there is frequently resentment at young people's earning-power. And while it is excellent that in our society so many of our population complete and live well beyond a working span of life, the effect on young people even in those jobs where little training is required is to defer promotion or advancement. Once again, therefore, most young people feel little involvement or identification with what they see of adult society in the working world and, as with marriage, they are provided through work with no clear point of accession to adulthood.

The third special 'area' requiring examination is that of moral codes, values, standards and customs. In truth, this is even less separable from the fabric of a society than either work or marriage, but needs to be disentangled in order that it can be discussed and evidence provided of how our current society, in this respect, makes initiation and acceptance difficult for young people. Ours is, clearly, a markedly different society from the simple one sketched earlier. While that society settled questions of right or wrong by reference to what has been laid down by *previous* generations, we concern ourselves much more with the *consequences* of doing or not doing what is proposed. Relatively few people are prepared to settle a question by simple reference back to an authoritative moral dictum. In fact, we may fairly be described as a 'teleological' rather than a 'deontological' society, since we habitually answer moral questions by reference to what end-result would be produced. We do, of course, refer back to certain moral values whose fundamental concept is not being challenged, since Western thought has developed a number of abstract 'goods' which most people continue to accept. But rapidly changing social conditions mean that we are constantly faced with dilemmas about how the abstracts apply in new kinds of practical situations. Sometimes circumstances alter cases, but more often the difficulty is to see which of two conflicting cases is the proper precedent for a new circumstance or to discern precisely what the relationship is between some acknowledged moral principles and particular day-to-day situations. Moreover, as part of an attempt perhaps to reassure ourselves that our current scepticism is well grounded in the precepts of the past, increasing attention is paid to those parts of the established codes which imply that it is right and good for individuals to question and judge independently, *not* to accept authority or tradition uncritically.

There is nothing surprising about our situation. Naturally a society which comes as much into contact with contrasting cultures as ours does, and whose members are as well-informed as ours are about the different values prevalent in these cultures, will have to undergo some rethinking about its own values. Any society subject, as we have recently been, to relatively large shifts in economic power and changes in the distribution of individual wealth and income is bound to have an injection of new practices into its code of behaviour, based upon the experience and habits of people who were previously hampered by poverty and whose views were therefore submerged below the level of action. Any society which has only relatively recently enfranchised the majority of its members and which has ever since experienced widespread social and occupational mobility must expect the patterned attitudes and assumptions to be disarranged in the process. The liberated centripetal forces to which we referred in the previous chapter have inevitably had their effect here too.

As a teleological society, the spectrum of moral values which we present to young people growing up is thus a thoroughly confusing one. Almost any kind of behaviour will be championed as right, or at least not wrong, by some group or faction in society, and so intensive is our intercommunication system that young people are almost certain to know this. On the morality of hardly any issue is there widespread agreement. Within the last two decades even the law, usually slow to reflect changes in moral attitudes, has been changed on capital punishment, corporal punishment, obscenity, betting and prostitution, and very nearly changed on homosexuality. All these are areas of intensely emotional and moral commitment: in other fields, churches, perhaps the most noticeable organizations concerning themselves with values, have set up commissions on euthanasia, sterilization, smoking, drinking, abortion, contraception and artificial insemination. And intensive public debate has raged on such, perhaps peripherally moral, matters as the use of Sunday, hire purchase and the persuasiveness of advertising. In sum, even if a majority of people avow a certain attitude, any young person *knows* that many of those who say 'X is right' in fact practise Y, the opposite, or at least fail to practise X. He knows, too, that a vocal minority will be recommending a divergent value or standard. We argue elsewhere that this disputation is a healthy sign in a free-speaking democracy, and it is both inevitable and good for young people to be aware of its existence. We need, however, to understand and appreciate the effect upon young people when such a babel, such a discord, such a free market in values constitutes so prominent a part of their environment.

A child who passes puberty achieves a potential independence. Soon he wishes to make that potential actual, and he wishes to find out for himself whether what he has been led to believe as a child really 'works'. So far in life he has heard many precepts: he now wishes to see what the evidence is in adult practice. Now, though he does not of course think this all out consciously, he wants to see and feel with his own senses what fits and what does not. If he were to find that practice corresponded broadly with the precepts he had heard, then he would indeed be fortunate, undisturbed and, dare one say, he would have no need to 'rebel'. Perhaps stable, simple societies are especially fortunate in the degree of correspondence between precept and practice which a young person is likely to find. In our society, if such a young person were to find only that adult practice *uniformly* conflicted with what he had been led to believe were the right and good ways of living, then he would no doubt be mildly confused, but might well conclude that things had moved on a little since his parents and teachers and other mentors first perceived them. But in our society he will find more than that: his confusion will be the worse confounded, because he will discover that there is no uniformity of adult practice. He will find conflict with the precepts he has previously heard, but the conflicting practices themselves will contain many crosscurrents, many fine distinctions of shade, many different contradictions of what is preached, an assortment of rationalizations and hypocrisies.

No plea for a simple life is being made here, nor is any persecutor's cause being established to subject our society's moral behaviour to a 'clean-up', whatever that may mean. Nor is it being implied that any child who has reached puberty is still pure and unsullied. But it is important to throw into relief the unnerving moral turmoil which young people in our society experience as soon as they seek to distinguish for themselves an allegedly 'good' act from an allegedly 'bad' one. The variety of moral practice means that the young person can gain no sense of acceptance into our society as a whole simply because of the moral values he adopts for himself. Whatever his own practices, he will constantly meet people who withhold acceptance from him because they see him as not yet having 'grown up' enough to adopt their standards.

The Need for 'Adolescence'

Why is our society able to accept its young only gradually and reluctantly? What need do its adults have for this period of adolescence and what function do they expect it to perform for them? One possible answer would seem to be that adults wish to defend themselves against the young, and that they have therefore artificially created adolescence for their own ends. In a simple society, whose immediate future mode of life will contain very few, if any, new features, there will be little scope for alterations in the social structure or in social relationships and arrange-

E

ments generally, and therefore comparatively few opportunities for the young to innovate. Our own society, by contrast, anticipates that its immediate future will contain many new elements. Indeed, our commercial viability in a competitive world depends on our readiness to adapt and to take advantage of new technological possibilities. If prosperity allows it, human taste for novelty will ensure that we exploit new opportunities in the use of leisure, just as increased expectations of convenience, comfort and ease will insist that we advance our provision of welfare and social amenities. In this atmosphere, quite radical change apparently becomes inevitable, and adults, who almost always feel a greater identity with and attachment to what already exists, can be expected to be at least suspicious of the adolescents. For it will be the young, as persons, who will usher in and be the agents of so many of the 'new ways' and who will live with novelty much more easily than will their elders.

Nor is this the only factor which is likely to cause adults to be perturbed at the emergence of each succeeding generation. For to it must be added the hypothesis that the longer a society withholds status from the young, the greater will be their frustration and the more determined will be their search for the reforms which will give them that status. Ours, as we saw above, can be regarded as such a society since it is giving young people very little clear indication of how and when they have achieved such status. The clear implication of all these arguments is that adults are likely to have increasing cause for concern about their own roles and security and to feel themselves under mounting pressure from the young.

This, however, seems to be only one function allotted to the period of adolescence by the adults in our society. A second arises from the fact that adults habitually expect some form of respect in return for the advice or education which they give. Clearly, in any society, young people depend immensely upon other adults than their parents for education, information and advice over small as well as large matters. In consequence, it is more widespread for adults to assume that an ability to dispense needed information, interpretation or advice automatically merits respect. And yet, it is not clear that all adults have that ability to the degree which they believe they have. Moreover, it can be argued that having been born chronologically earlier constitutes more of an *obligation* to make available the fruits of experience than a right to choose to do so only in return for respect. In our society also there are increasingly practical reasons why adults may find, not only that their information or advice sometimes fails to earn them respect when they offer it, but also that they either have no relevant advice to offer or are offering it on a topic which has been 'covered' in a school or technical course. So rapidly, in fact, do new factors affect situations which young people are meeting or skills which they are learning, that individual adults are now often seen to have little experience which is relevant. Inevitably, in a rapidly changing culture, the experience of one generation has *relatively* few lessons to teach the next, and, even where it has, the habit of learning from older experience is not ingrained enough in young people to ensure that they recognize a part of the collective wisdom they need in the potentially helpful adults they meet. The young tend to acquire a scepticism about what their seniors have to say and offer.

In view of the potential threat to adults which adolescents now apparently constitute, and the decreasing willingness of the young to respect the old simply for their extra years, it is perhaps to be expected that most of the separate groupings which make up society still need to insist on the concept of the 'novice'. Two particular functions for this can thus be discerned. The first is to ensure that the newcomer will acquire the considerable body of knowledge which most situations still do demand. The other is to confirm the established members of the group, to give them confidence and enable them to measure their expertise by directing their attention to the inexpertness of the newcomer. Thus, any organization is more or less encouraged by the uncertainties of existing members to establish 'done' and 'not done' practices, if none already exist, and to insist on their observation. Those who are established members thus often perpetrate much more in the name of morale, cohesiveness, organization and identity than is strictly necessary for the group's continued existence as a human enterprise (which would, if left to itself, almost certainly generate its own intrinsically necessary customs and mores anyway!).

Consequently, whether deference is due or not, and whether there is need for any form of novitiate or not, adults are well able to make it appear so – and indeed young people may often welcome the stability and ordered progression which such a convention implies. Thus the period of adolescence appears to serve a valuable function, both for adults who are suspicious of young people as agents of social change and for adults who, for the sake of their own self-confidence, need to feel the superiority of the person already initiated, to whom deference is therefore due from the novice.

The 'Protection' of the Adolescent

However, although adults may need to believe in 'adolescence' as a phase of life through which the younger generation must pass, do young people themselves gain anything – or, more properly, does society as a whole gain anything from the deferral of young people's entry into it as full members? For it could be argued – indeed, it has sometimes been argued – that, because adults must impose this special status on the young, the young are bound to be degraded. Yet there is nothing *intrinsically* humiliating about making special provision for sections of society having special needs, or with special contributions to make. If society gives special status to the adolescent, even though adults' motives may be to preserve their own position, then the effect on young people need not inevitably be to lower their standing. Schools, youth clubs, students' unions are in this respect no different from old people's centres and mother-and-baby rooms: all display thought and care in provision, and their administration and staff can convey all manner of attitudes. But there is no *need* for any of these attitudes to imply some kind of superiority, nor for the adults who contact young people in the places specially provided for them to be disdainful of their clients.

It will be the contention of this book, therefore, that we should retain – improve and extend, certainly, but at least retain – the special provisions we make for young people, both in the interests of the development of the individual to live in our kind of society, and in the interests of the vitality of our society itself. This contention rests on two characteristics which young people can be enabled to develop and to make available to society. One is freshness of approach and the other, youthfulness, a characteristic which in the future should not be confined to the chronologically young.

To take freshness of approach first, many people are by now familiar with the kind of induction course to an organization which asks the newcomer to do two things simultaneously: to familiarize himself with the structure and methods of the unit, and to make an appraisal of the suitability of that structure to serve the unit's purpose. This technique, used easily in small and defined units like firms or businesses or schools (by the staff only, usually), is valuable because the fresh mind of the newcomer is uncontaminated by the habits and conditioned responses of his new environment.

In society at large, an organized use of this technique is unthinkable.

For the 'purpose' is not so clearly definable and the structure – if any – is so ramified as to be mysterious. But the mental approach, the critical and discriminating appraisal, needs to be developed for the sake of individual and society alike. Special effort needs to be made therefore to give the young person at least some refuge, so that he is in contact with others taking similar 'time out' *and* has a chance of *not* being smothered by the existing mores of society. For we cannot afford to encourage young people to be accepted prematurely by society and to accept in return society's existing methods, structure, solutions, assumptions, schemata, categories, and so on. We need rather to enable them to take an objective look at them and so to ensure that young people have some part of their daily or weekly lives where *they* predominate, in a 'place' set apart, in provision specially made. They are, as adolescents, not yet wholly contaminated, predisposed, committed, and they deserve the opportunity to be in the wilderness, free of the yoke of established habits and practices.

To offer special provision of this kind is not so much to protect young people from reality but to protect them from preceding generations' response to reality, from adult society's interpretation of reality. Those responses and interpretations are not sacred, they are only set historically and perhaps accidentally. They will thus bear examination by uncontaminated newcomers who in no way identify themselves with past developments and expressions of traditional views of reality. It *may* not be practicable for young people to put alternative responses into effect or even in some cases to conceive of any until they attain adulthood themselves, but they need to cultivate in adolescence, when they have the best chance, that habit of mind which does not assume that a solution or an arrangement is the most appropriate one merely because it is the existing one.

By contrast, to dispense with special provision for young people, to seek to absorb them into society with as little time for reflection as possible, seems like a thinly disguised measure for maintaining the status quo. To admit young people to full status in adult society at all the points where they touch it is to offer them status in the existing system in return for their endorsement of it, and such a device is of course likely to succeed. Indeed to some extent it can already be seen at work. A feature of the attitudes displayed by many modern secondary school children is their concordance with 'reality'. They make realistic appraisals of their future lives and careers (though in their fantasies they picture these quite differently), and they appear to feel less strain, tension and conflict with the values of the society into which they are 'absorbed' at an earlier age than others in their generation. Such a readiness to conform observed in these young people and commented upon frequently by other adults ought to be disturbing to the social educator. 'Education', according to one important dictum, 'must communicate the type and provide for growth beyond the type'.[7] To instil the ability to discriminate and make independent judgments might be thought part of most educationists' aims. Certainly it is important to help young people to admire before they are taught to criticize, but it can hardly be wise for a society such as ours to encourage the teaching of the first without making provision to ensure that young people have the opportunity to develop and strengthen the second.

Such criticism, born out of tension and conflict in the individual, may perhaps be readily seen to be of advantage to society. But there is advantage for the individual, too. For, as we shall repeat in a variety of contexts, a certain degree of strain is inherent in most kinds of educational experience that are not mere parrot-learning, since no individual advances very far if he is not stimulated to grapple with discordance. Progress comes from the resolution of conflict between disharmonious concepts, not from avoiding them; it emerges from synthesizing apparently discordant ideas rather than by merely accepting their separateness. Conflict can be constructive and provide a platform for development, and it is no service to young people to protect them from it.

Clearly young people need to have some adult support available when needed, both to provide a setting and to personalize from time to time the established responses and interpretations of an earlier generation. But this does not mean that teachers and youth workers should merely transmit the accepted versions of reality and not ask young people to look and interpret for themselves. In a later chapter, we argue at length that more and more adults working with young people need to envisage their work as being to stimulate and support an emerging independent judgment. The didactic function of teaching must clearly remain, but in social education, whether by teachers or youth workers, a very high proportion of the work must inevitably be much less authority-based, far more permissive. What we need to ensure is that adults responsible for the educational process are helped through training to become aware of, and to apply, the principles and understanding which can guide them in the relationships which are required, and that more adults than at present are allowed and encouraged to make these relationships, whether in school or through the Youth Service. As a society we need to retain and improve provision for young people so that they can continue to develop their independence and their discriminatory powers by regular refreshment away from the stifling pressures of established society.

For as society benefits by reappraising its arrangements, and as the individual develops his ability to work out solutions unawed by those that exist already, it will be possible for more and more people to retain for a much longer portion of their lives that flexibility and openness to new ideas now associated only with youth. The developing adolescent has a much wider potential than his immediate or current environment calls upon. Inevitably as he is admitted to adult society, as he does 'settle down' and absorb its values, he at present often loses a great deal of the adaptability or ability to develop in quite new directions. And yet, full social maturity, as we suggest elsewhere, requires the retention of as much of this flexibility as possible. If we 'absorb' the adolescent into society at the earliest chance, as whatever kind of person he happens to be, as whatever figure he is cutting at the time, in whatever roles he is then experimentally adopting, we fix his own image of himself by our responses to him as he then is. Society's special provision for the adolescent is justified therefore: it is not merely protection for its adults from the threat of young people, but also protection for its young from premature stabilization in images whose contours disturb the adults least.

It is difficult to describe the quality of youthfulness without lapsing into the lyrical, but we need to conceptualize it in some way because it is something which young people need room to exercise, and adults need to preserve. In a society which will receive a rapid succession of adaptations as new inventions and possibilities arise, the unpredisposed approach which is most spontaneously made by the young will be at a premium in all age-groups. Established links and contacts, habitual responses, existing structures and provisions may simply not be appropriate to each year's or month's crop of unprecedented situations or to the new tasks which follow from them. Open-mindedness, suggestibility, approachability are the ways in which a person shows 'youthfulness' in personal relationships. In his approach to a problem, he will be flexible, adaptable, prepared to be radical, pragmatic rather than dogmatic, objective, comparatively unprejudiced and analytical. Of course, the adolescent lacks some of the characteristics which enable the adult to make best use of youthfulness or flexibility in approach. He will grow less mercurial as he grows older, changing his allegiances to different reference groups less readily and less frequently. He will temper the keenness and extremism of his emotions with greater discernment and depth. But the opportunity to let this radical approach flower at adolescence must not be missed: this period is crucial both for the individual and for the society in which he must later exercise his judgment. For the person who has not tasted 'open-mindedness' at adolescence is likely to find that it is almost impossible to produce it on demand later in life. Unless we approach further social education with a determination to give young people the opportunity to experience 'youthfulness' sometimes unpressed by established patterns, we shall do them a disservice individually and weaken our society's future adaptability.

The Effects of Society's Graded Acceptance of Young People

It is clear that the graded acceptance of young people into society has an effect both on the adults and on the young people themselves. For the adults, it means that they are left without any clear guidance about how to 'take' young people. A boy or girl who has left school and yet is neither 21 nor married is an enigma. His place in 'the system' is not clear, for he is neither totally a child nor totally accepted as an adult. The adult finds himself in a state of ambiguity, receiving conflicting signals about what attitude he should take up. The individual confronting him has some of the characteristics of an adult, some of those of a child, and some almost alien to both. The adult is like a baby or a dog faced by strange and disturbing sense-impressions, and he reacts accordingly.

He may do one of a number of things. He may, as it were, put his tail between his legs, or turn his face to the pram-pillow and so avoid the issue. Or he may try to propitiate the mystery by tokens of homage, by conceding the young person's every indicated wish and by endorsing his every act and attitude. Alternatively, he may try to make the disturbing image fit a familiar one which he does know how to deal with – by perceiving the young person as a child, as an awkward customer or as an adult. Or again he may, as a variant, be prepared to offer full acceptance as an adult but only to those who satisfy some criterion arbitrarily selected by himself: certain educational qualifications, ex-membership of a certain school, membership of a certain family or club, or even participation in some course or movement. But more often the adult resolves his uncertainty in the way we frequently react to ambiguous situations, by adopting aggressive attitudes.

The adult has repelled the threat of young people to some extent by exploiting the concept of adolescence, but he still has to meet with and treat with certain young people, and they are still personal embodiments of a passage of time which implies the eventual decline of the adult's own powers. Time and again the response is to pour defensive scorn upon any observable behaviour which differentiates some section of young people from the adults concerned: almost equally often the scorn is followed by speculative fascinated horror about what might be going on unobserved. The young are selected for special treatment, their foibles and weaknesses made reasons for special comment, as if every young person broke society's ideal standards and their elders were blameless. The verbal pyrotechnics of our threatened 'civilized' adults must surely outstrip the most frenzied incantations of simpler societies, which we are wont to describe as 'primitive', when they are frightened by the weather or an eclipse. Yet adults' morale clearly needs a boost. If such aggressive responses against the young provide one, and if, however insubstantial, they offer some comfort, no doubt they will persist.

The effect of 'graded acceptance' upon young people themselves is more noticed in our society, perhaps because it is a more congenial topic for adults. It is usually described as some kind of 'teenage culture' or 'adolescent revolt'. Young people fundamentally are somewhat puzzled and hurt by their evident estrangement, their statelessness. Much of what we may see as 'teenage culture' is an elaborate disguise of this hurt, which they no more wish to advertise to others, especially adults, than to themselves. But individual adult-adolescent contacts frequently suggest a state of affairs in which young people feel estrangement from their parents and other adults, rather than any actual rebellion or revolt. Whenever a young person seeks to make an independent judgment it *appears* to adults to be rebellion. This is partly because, in order to demonstrate both to himself and others that he *has* made a judgment independently, a young person often *has* to reach a conclusion different from that of the adults concerned: if he reached the same, there would be no evidence that he had not simply toed the adult line. But adolescents themselves appear to feel far less hostility to adults than is projected onto them by adults, though, inevitably perhaps, once cued by adults that a state of hostility exists, young people have little room to manoeuvre. They must either capitulate or rebel.

Graded acceptance into society has the effect on young people as a whole which studenthood formerly had upon university students. Society has long accepted the variant, alien and cloistered subculture which life in a university produced. Poses could be adopted, enthusiasms worked out, follies perpetrated, all manner of individual tastes indulged. The ways of students were a law unto themselves, their goals were their own, their morale dependent on internal and, to the outsider, secret affairs. Society at large might take over to its own use some of the features that excited, amused and entertained the student, but not very often. Until recently students have been the only identifiable group of adolescents with time and money to express their different choices. The increase in unsupervised leisure and the additional 'discretionary' spending which became the adolescent's in the 1950s paved the way for the true nature of 'studentry' to show.

For student culture had only accidentally been confined to students. It was essentially an adolescent culture closely connected with the deferral of status which a modern complex society imposes on all its young people. The economic emancipation of postwar years gave all young people the opportunity to 'join'. Certain activities and interests, which we can readily recite as being predominantly adolescent, gave outward expression to that independence of view of which we have spoken. Young people needed settings and vehicles and business to be about, so that they could 'live' their indigenous approaches to life.

They were not only in need of settings and vehicles, but they could pay to hire or have them. Commercial interests were readier – by almost a decade – than public services to help the emergence of a subculture probably always latent since people congregated in towns. Coffee bars, bowling alleys, microgroove 'single' records, 'pop' stars and disc jockeys, the friendliness of the 'local', succeeding styles of dancing and clothes, transistor radios, amplified guitars, motor-cycles, cinemas, TV shows, were all pressed into the service of the emergent adolescent subculture. Its ingredients, as observed before, were the same as or versions of the culture of the surrounding society, but young people placed different emphases and often took a much quicker initiative in exploiting a new medium. The 'teenage consumer' industry boomed, though not so much as has sometimes been believed. Dr Mark Abrams's oft-quoted figures of 1961, for unmarried young people between 15 and 25, showed that this 13 per cent of the population spends 5 per cent of the money, noticeably on entertainment items. But undoubtedly the volume, concentrated on a relatively narrow range of expenditure, caught the attention of the sociologist as much as the entrepreneur.

Much has been written and said about 'teenage culture', though 'sub-culture' would be more accurate. Its impact has not always been uniform in all geographical and social areas of the country, but often its form has been surprising or melodramatic or bizarre. Yet its existence should cause no surprise. Young people, given no clear role to play in society yet serviced by eager commercial enterprise, have developed for themselves a cultural medium and a social role. A group whose full acceptance into adult culture has been variously deferred has partially found a substitute and temporary culture. Adult society meanwhile has been slow to adapt the aims of its educational services and has thus failed to make the best use, both for the individual and society, of this period of protection, estrangement, flexibility and potentiality.

1. W. D. WALL, *Guidance in Adolescence*, The Twelfth Charles Russell Memorial Lecture, November 1964, p. 3.
2. M. ABRAMS, *Teenage Consumer Spending in 1959* (Part II), The London Press Exchange Ltd, 1961.
3. F. MUSGROVE, *Youth and the Social Order*, Routledge, 1964.
4. WARDEN SEWELL of Radley College, 1858, quoted in *Radley College* by A. K. BOYD, who is in turn quoted by F. MUSGROVE, op. cit., p. 55.
5. LADY ALBEMARLE, writing in *Youth Review* Vol. 1, No. 1, October 1964, p. 9.
6. 'Crowther Report', 1959, – *15 to 18* (A Report of the Central Advisory Council for Education (England)) – para. 166.
7. W. E. HOCKING, quoted by SIR FRED CLARKE, *Freedom in the Educative Society*, University of London Press Ltd, 1948.

Chapter 4

Aims in Social Education

Mistaken, Mis-stated and Misanthropic Aims

In speaking of aims in social education this book will not attempt to collect and restate all the aims of all the organizations which are concerned with it. Nor does it necessarily presume that any common aim is definable since, certainly at a practical level, the diverse and even divergent operations which actually take place in the name of 'youth work' alone make it difficult to believe that there is a unifying purpose behind it all. Indeed, any statement of common aims may do little more than betray its author's particular anxieties and wishful thinking. However, this is a risk which must be taken since the social education provided both by the Youth Service and by the schools is now more than an aggregate of organizational aims and personal motives. Social education, in fact, is being incorporated with social policy and into the thinking which shapes our broader educational and social environment. In consequence, it seems worth trying to state an overall, justifying aim, and to establish a unifying language with which social educators can identify and in which they believe it is meaningful to speak of their work.

A number of methods have been adopted in the past to define aims in the Youth Service which have often been taken over by social educators generally. One which is sometimes proposed is rooted in the assumption that preventing delinquency and anti-social behaviour is the most pressing demand on those who work with young people. Those who advocate this view see young people – to some extent – as dissatisfied with themselves, but mainly as threats to society in general which need to be contained. The primary justification for the provision of social-educational facilities for adolescents thus becomes the negative one of keeping them from crime.

Such a justification is inadequate partly because in our present circumstances it ignores inescapable and severe practical limitations on the Youth Service and even the schools, but chiefly because it is based on a false diagnosis of the needs and situation of young people in our society. The limitations it ignores are those of social pressure and of the shortage of time and skill among social educators for dealing with the individual emotional disturbance which causes the worst forms of anti-social behaviour. For, firstly, workers who wish to meet and offer help to 'problem' youngsters, or who operate in areas where the latter constitute a major section of the adolescent population, are sometimes discouraged and even prohibited from doing so by sponsoring or governing committees, or by officials, by the police, by parents of 'good' young people, or by these young people themselves. Though these sections of our society are usually as shocked as any at the exploits of the delinquent and near-delinquent fringe and are anxious to see them converted to more acceptable habits, in their capacity as sponsors of or as workers or participants in social-educational institutions they are frequently antagonistic to young people who do not readily toe the line. In an effort to maintain a respectable image and to avoid the discomfort and material damage which may result from accepting 'rowdy' and 'disruptive' elements, adults subject adolescent out-groups, including delinquents, to discrimination and exclusion. They are regarded as too hot to handle.

And there are senses in which such adults, whether workers or sponsors, are right. For much of the time of social educators is fully committed. Youth leaders and even teachers at times are required to work with large numbers of 'normal' young people, to manage units of work, to service committees, even to raise funds and perhaps to be trained themselves or to help train others. Little time, emotional energy or effort can be left for catering for difficult groups. Moreover, such groups, though no doubt too easily labelled and stereotyped, often require special understanding and approaches which can be given all too little consideration in a comprehensive course of training for youth work or teaching. Thus most adults in social education are not only not encouraged or given time to rehabilitate the delinquent or near-delinquent: they are not provided with the skills which are essential if such a task is to have any chance of success.

The practical limitations are, however, only the more obvious reasons why it is difficult to make delinquency prevention a major justification for social ecucation. More fundamental and significant is the fact that any effort to do so must start from the false assumption either that the vast majority of young people are social 'problems', or that only those who *are* problems are worthy of educational attention after they leave school. But it is clear that most post-15 or 16 year-olds do *not* exhibit serious anti-social tendencies. Most do not have problems which are liable to lead them into serious and illegal conflict with their society. Most of them are personally stable and adequately adjusted.

Because most young people are 'normal' does not however mean that they are not worthy of continued educational consideration. As we hope to show – later in this chapter – their social and emotional needs are as yet far from completely satisfied, so that some deliberately provided opportunities for seeking and attaining further development are necessary. This development will certainly demand that adults allocate much of what time and skill they have avilable to catering for the 'special needs' of individual young people. But meeting these special needs will include not only providing help in avoiding brushes with the law and other forms of anti-social behaviour. It will require, too, that adults stand prepared to be involved in the whole range of human problems and decisions which young people must face. In consequence, they must be ready to play roles in relation to the young which are far more individually oriented and far less critical and judgmental than any approach which starts by assuming that all young people need saving from a criminal way of life.

To work as a social educator, in fact, entails a much more wide-ranging and demanding concern than the prevention of delinquency. There are, for example, many other signs and kinds of malaise and disturbance, and the social educator needs to be ready to concern himself with any of these. But, even more important, most of his work cannot be seen as corrective of some deviation or deprivation. He must begin by trying to understand the broad spectrum of human interaction, all the many kinds of normality. The majority of what he does will be positive, developmental of actual social skills rather than healing social inadequacies or incompetences. And this will require a deepened and extended understanding of young people, an enriched variety of ways of relating to them, because it implies a less single-minded purpose lying behind the approach. The aims of social education must be much more individually relevant to the needs of young people than the straitjacket concept of delinquency prevention allows. This latter may well be achieved but much less because it has been sought as an end in itself than because it has been a consequence of the attainment of other, much more sensitively humane and personally meaningful ends.

A second means of defining aims in the Youth Service has been to call upon some of the highest aspirations of Western man. It is difficult to disagree with this kind of definition and it receives much attention from those who savour literary expression at its best. For both these reasons, the definition used by Sir John Maud, the then Permanent Secretary to the Ministry of Education, deserves the repetition it has so widely received since he used it at the Ashridge Conference called in 1951 by King George's Jubilee Trust:

> To offer individual young people in their leisure time opportunities of various kinds, complementary to those of home, formal education and work, to discover and develop their personal resources of body, mind and spirit, and thus the better equip themselves to live the life of mature, creative and responsible members of a free society.[1]

To some people, words like these are warming and inspiring and encrusted with associations which give them special values and meanings. Others however call attention, on hearing them, to the impediment to understanding and cooperation in our society which can be caused by the communication barrier, and demand that such words be translated, examined and given a closer definition. These others include many men and women who will work most closely with young people, and indeed they include the young people themselves. Certainly if the ideals represented by Maud's words are ever to be seen by young people to be relevant to their own condition, some reinterpretation is urgently called for. In 1960 the Albemarle Report referred to the need for restatement:

> Much in the foregoing raises the involved question of communication in a society which has been to a large extent hierarchically divided in its speech and is now becoming, especially through the activities of 'mass communication', almost demotically 'classless' . . . We have been struck by the great number of occasions, in the evidence presented to us, on which words such as the following have been used *as though they were a commonly accepted and valid currency*: 'service', 'dedication', 'leadership', 'character building'. Again, we wish not to be misunderstood. We in no way challenge the value of the concepts behind these words, or their meaningfulness to those who use them. Nor do we think that young people are without these qualities, or that they cannot be strengthened. But we are sure that these particular words now connect little with the realities of life as most young people see them; they do

not seem to 'speak to their condition'. They recall the hierarchies, the less interesting moments of school speechdays and other occasions of moral exhortation. Yet though many young people may be inclined to turn away if they are asked for 'service', in the relationships of their neighbourhoods and at the work-bench they often show 'service' in action. We believe that they are grateful for help in seeing, defining and acting according to moral standards, but that they wish to see these relevantly embodied, and that this relevance must be shown in language. They are often today in a peculiar wasteland; by instinct they reject many of the false values offered by elements in their society; but they are unable to accept the terms used by more disinterested and sincerely devoted people. Their failure to attend youth clubs may be less often a sign of apathy than of the failure of their seniors properly to adjust their forms of language.[2]

The implication of the Albemarle Report here is that it is by young people that such statements of aims go uncomprehended, while adults en masse can identify with such language. The same implication is contained in a comment on this passage by Mr Jack Longland, Director of Education for Derbyshire, speaking in Oxford in 1960:

The gap of mutual intolerance and incomprehension between old and young is always necessarily a wide one, and may be this is a condition of human progress. But it is wider now than it has been for generations, and in moral education it means that much of our talk, most of our precepts, slide traceless off the backs of the young. . . . what has happened is largely a breakdown in *communication* – the words that mean much to us are empty noises to the young – and, as all education depends fundamentally on communication, the breakdown is serious.[3]

The extraordinary thing about the clear recognition in such statements of the difficulty of communication is the concentration on adult-adolescent misunderstanding, as if the only language barrier were one that is surmounted by getting older. What must surely be apparent on reflection, however, is that it is not merely young people who do not acknowledge or comprehend the language in which 'moral' education is commonly discussed: large sections of our adult community, the services of many of whom are used and needed in youth work, do not find meaning or significance in such language either. It is not good enough to blame such incomprehension on the absence of common religious assumptions among

the adults in our society. It is certainly true, and probably healthy, that
fewer of us are ready to use the pious terminology of moral exhortation.
More adults in society have had a good basic education at school and are
aware of more of the aspects of life in society through mass media of
communication. Words are too commonplace, especially persuasive
words, to exercise much influence on action unless they call close upon
the individual's real motives. Moreover, since the majority of men and
women in our society lack acquaintance with the classical-liberal tradition
of Western culture and do not hold religious assumptions and language
in common with the religious minority, we must seek another language
in which to understand what we are about. The gap in communication
between adults and young people is in practice much less significant than
the subcultural divisions within our society generally.

Another completely different approach to the definition of aims is that
of the sociologist and the psychologist. Their expertise is certainly
relevant to social education and when they speak of the emotional, social,
physical and psychological 'development' of the individual, and of the
'social acceptability' of his behaviour, their language can go far to describe
aims for it. However, such concepts are not always acceptable to educationists, who argue that the 'development' spoken of must be in some
direction and that it is no help to be told that your purpose is simply
'the development' of young people unless the experts also advise on
direction. They argue, too, that to speak of the 'social acceptability' of
the behaviour of particular groups is to be mainly concerned for the
maintenance of the 'status quo' in society and is to neglect young people's
potential contribution to social change and development. In fact, the
discipline of the sociologist makes him aware of the shifts, from time to
time and place to place, of what is 'acceptable' in behaviour, and aware
too of the forces or groups, including young people which induce such
shifts, while the discipline of the psychologist offers built-in criteria for
measuring 'development', although these criteria often lack the type of
moral content demanded by some educationists.

In view of this, it might be expected that the educationist himself could
produce a definition of social-educational aims, and indeed it is from this
source that much help and attention has come. Unfortunately, in current
debates, too many educationists are handicapped not only by relatively
imprecise analyses of society, but also by their aloofness and timid withdrawal from the society into which their charges must go. One would
sometimes think that schools or youth organizations were monasteries

F

from which pupils escape to the outside world unexpectedly, rather than places of preparation to meet its demands. One would think too that the values of such educational institutions were as uniformly wholesome as those of the 'world' were abhorrent. Educationists at the moment start too often from a belief that it is their task to protect the young from 'society', fearing that otherwise the young 'as individuals' will lose their identity. The argument is that 'mass forces' are submerging the young man or woman and that the unique facets of their personalities are becoming less noticeable and less valued, lost in what is externally imposed by uniform impersonality. Sometimes 'the welfare state' is the evil cause. By the overprotection it offers 'from the cradle to the grave', by removing from people the need to overcome by their own resources the severest crises of poverty or sickness or family breakdown, it is sometimes said to be undermining individuality and inner strengths and self-exertion. At other times, blame is placed on 'the mass media', especially television and advertising, since they impose patterns of leisure and of buying which apparently are most significant for their uniformity and the automatic nature of the responses they invoke. Individual decision and differentiated choice, it seems, are increasingly less likely and less possible. Sheeplike, uniform, massive responses are more and more the rule.

An example of this modern pessimism even occurs in as sensitive an appraisal of the individual's need for further emancipation as that of M. V. C. Jeffreys in his book *Personal Values in the Modern World*:

> Political enfranchisement, education, and a raised standard of living have given the average individual power and responsibility which even half a century ago were enjoyed only by a few. It is one of the great ironies of history that, in the same period of time, large-scale economic and social organization, the extension of State control, and the development of mass media of communication have largely neutralized the individual's capacity to use those opportunities.
>
> We live in an age of mass culture which is not only increasingly standardized but also manufactured and synthetic. More and more we look at the same things, listen to the same things, think the same things, and passively receive the same services as they come off the conveyor-belt of the Welfare State.[4]

It is undeniable that many of the modern technological and social developments have brought problems and created attitudes which traditional moralists can only deplore. Moreover, it can be shown by objective, carefully documented enquiry that the effects of some of these changes have been unfortunate and depressing for many individual people, young and old, who are living through them. Nonetheless, one is entitled to ask how accurate is the historical perspective of some of the critics, and whether the mass of labourers and shepherds, out at the break of dawn, seven days a week perhaps, long months of the year, tilling soil or delivering lambs, lived lives so much more differentiated and varied than do today's car assembly-line workers or televiewers.

The interpretation of these changes in our society as 'massive uniformity' betrays a remoteness and non-involvement which no educationist should allow. A greater sympathy and understanding for the multiplicity of individuals leads to an interpretation of the same social phenomena which is quite contrary and which might almost be summarized as 'infinite individuality'. For it is possible to argue that never before has the individual in our society been under such persistent and exposing pressure, that he or she is now responsible for a disconcertingly and almost unbearably large number of personal decisions, taken with less reference to socially-determined or authoritatively-imposed limits and criteria than at any time in the past. We have already discussed that babel of voices which suggest conflicting moral standards and beliefs and which advocate different, often contradictory, solutions to human problems. It places each young person by whom it is heard – and that means the vast majority – at risk more often than has been possible before. Each adolescent is constantly expected to distinguish his own preferences, feelings, opinions, attitudes, desires, expectations and needs, for himself, in a very great number of areas of life. Of course, his choice on any one issue will be the same as the choice of thousands, perhaps millions, of other people presented with the same alternatives. But as many, perhaps more, thousands will take another course on this issue, and, moreover, those who take the same course on this issue will take other courses on other issues. Because we know 1,000,000 people do 'X', and 1,000,000 do 'Y', and 1,000,000 do 'Z', and because we know there is *some* overlap, we tend to think of *all* those who choose 'X' as choosing 'Y' and 'Z' as well. Of course, we find it easier this way to organize the world in our minds, and we may be forgiven in idle moments for composing stereotypes or 'mass man' images in this way. But, on reflection, we must see that even if any man makes a whole year's choices in the same way as any other (and the chances against this seem to be astronomical) he is still unlikely to be doing so always for the same reasons and motives.

The individual, in fact, not only has more choices to make because he has more money, more free time, greater mobility and improved capacities for mental differentiation of concepts: he has more choices to make, also, because the choices are less and less made for him by established custom and tradition. The situations are new or have new components, and custom has not built up. It is the individual himself who is expected to decide how he is to behave in his relationships, not just with his sister and the girl in the next cottage, but with the many girls in his social life, the works, the holiday camp and the bus, and to decide what is good and right behaviour for him. He is expected to choose a wife according to his own judgment of what he wants and needs and not according to any considerations of market value or even parental demands; complementarily, the individual herself is expected to participate on an equal basis in this mutual choice. They are expected to raise children, not according to any definite regulations of family or community or state, but according to what he and his wife themselves interpret to be the best practices in a whole selection available to them. And so on. Much of the responsibility which tradition, custom and convention in a *less* differentiated society would have removed from him is now his alone or almost alone. The individual, in fact, far from losing significance and the opportunity for self-assertion in a 'mass' society, now has almost more of these than he can cope with. He is very much more at risk.

Even if there is any truth in the 'mass uniformity' interpretation, it is clear that the educationist will not be helped if he places too great an emphasis on it, since it succeeds only in alienating him from the experience of the individuals he is concerned to help. It is clearly his responsibility to 'start where the individual is', to 'speak to his condition'. The dimension of social change which must be the basis of educational theory is that which focuses upon the infinitely increased choices confronting the individual. The relevant educational response will, equally clearly, be a different one from that which starts from the assumption that it is uniformity which needs to be tackled. That is, the need will not be to present people with more comprehensive and uplifting philosophies and ideals than the standardized, manufactured, synthetic ones imputed to the mass society in general and the mass media of communication in particular. It will not be to assume that the critics of these mass media are really the repositories of 'true' culture or values and to ensure that these penetrate down to the masses. Recognizing that the individual is already greatly at risk, under severe pressure to find personal solutions to a whole array of problems, the educator must offer the conditions, facilitate the means by which the individual will be enabled better to make for himself the decisions which will come his way.

But the desire to present people with ideals and philosophies is rooted in other soil than merely the fear of mass uniformity. The leadership of the young has long meant prescribing for them the ways in which they should respond to certain situations, the choices they should make, the values they should observe. The Youth Service is particularly likely to be saddled with this kind of aim since it is the focus of many an adult's last chance to make good by proxy some of the shortcomings of his own life. If he can urgently impress upon young people between 14 and 21 the standards which he has learned by experience to honour – if not to observe – then he feels his duty by posterity the better done. Whether he clears his conscience by donating money, serving on committees or actually making contact with young people, he can exercise himself to see *his* standards accepted.

Time and again, in fact, speeches and statements are made which suggest that the education system, and not least the Youth Service, should be inculcating values which *it* knows and understands, and which differ from those of the real lives of its clients. The habits are well set, since for centuries the passage of accepted, acceptable values and ideals, customs and activities, has been from small dominant groups to the majority. Certainly it has been customary in this country for those in economic and political power to assume that they should dominate culturally and socially as well, to pass on their values of proper behaviour, right standards and worthwhile interests, and thus to inculcate the acceptance of their views over whole areas of life. In practice, they have probably had less effect than appearances suggest: but at least the appearance of their moral and cultural leadership has been upheld as a complement to their rule in other spheres. Gradually, however, other non-central – literally ec-centric – groups are ceasing to defer and are grasping the opportunity to register the fact that they formulate and express philosophies and values which conflict with those of the central opinion-formers. As education in depth releases their ability to communicate what has long given real meaning and purpose to their lives, these non-dominant sub-cultures are slowly coming to articulate the standards and norms which are their own and are impressing these on the awareness of society as a whole.

But it is not easy for us to forget habitual assumptions. Values have previously come from those in positions of political and economic leadership and have spread centrifugally; recent actual changes in society – including the release of centripetal forces in the wake of technological, economic and educational advance – have not been matched by changes in attitude. The cultural elite is still widely assumed to be 'right', to have the 'proper' values.

And yet the social changes which lead some to believe in 'mass uniformity', have also created the possibility of the multitude of individuals exercising their choice, of being consulted, of influencing and formulating the opinions of others, in their own interests and according to their own ideals. One can argue that these opportunities are being abused or missed, but one cannot argue that they are not there. They are eroding the custom and the possibility of an elite making decisions on behalf of the 'mass' without consideration or means of knowing what 'the mass' wants. Every additional use of the gallup poll, of market research, of the follow-up or preparatory questionnaire adds to the power of the non-elite to shape their environment and their lives. The much-vaunted power of the advertiser is only exercised within the band set by the needs or wants of those who consume the goods or service he offers, so that his constant concern is to find the needs most common in the community and then to vie with his rivals to persuade the consumers that *his* product satisfies them best. Moreover, as we saw in Chapter 2, what is true in the economic and material fields of life is no less true in the fields of culture and morality. For in the widest sense and probably in unprecedented ways in such a large and heavily populated society, democratic forces have been at work at least since the nineteenth century, cannot now be resisted and are exerting their influence on the broadest range of that society's values and assumptions. Traditional forms of leadership are no longer appropriate. The majority of people are no longer certain, if the majority at any time ever were, what is absolutely good and right, and what is more they say so. Doubts are quickly raised when any group or individual claims special insight into what is best and correct for others, or special knowledge of of what young people ought to become. It is against this social background that any definition of the proper aims of social education will rest.

Maturity for Their Own Society

Chiefly, we take the maturity of the next generation for *their* society as the most useful way of conceptualizing the aim of the social education of the adolescent generally and of the Youth Service in particular. 'Maturity' appears often in the statements of aims of youth workers and of many teachers, either as the overriding aim or as one in a list of qualities which it is hoped to develop in members. It is made one of those words which describe characteristics or qualities in vogue at a particular time or among a group of sponsors of work with young people. Certain qualities, it is implied or even explicitly asserted, such as maturity, initiative, leadership, etc., can have an existence somehow unconnected to particular situations. They are seen as continuing entities, ready and waiting to reveal themselves when opportunity presents. As 'entities', they can be developed or inculcated. Even those who speak of the inculcation of such qualities, however, admit to the inherent weakness of their view, since they frequently agree that the qualities concerned are 'neutral' and capable of being turned to individually and socially undesirable ends.

We would go further, however, and take the opposite view that these 'qualities' are not continuing, enduring phenomena at all, that they are not even 'neutral' entities because they are not entities at all. Certainly the words themselves are meaningful, but they are applicable only to certain people's behaviour in particular situations or classes of situation. No one, for example, 'has' initiative. He or she may take the initiative in particular situations or in a series of situations, and may even be expected to do so in later ones because of a reputation gained and because of a belief by others in the possessibility of 'qualities'. Such behaviour how- ever is *relative* to situations, not inherent and inalienable in the individual. He who takes the initiative in one kind of situation, say on a mountain, may not take it in another, on the shop-floor or in a play. Moreover it is good that he does not: he would be a predictable and boorish demi-god if he did, he would display a pitiful inflexibility, he would often behave inappropriately due to his rigidity, and he would himself lose the poten- tially rich experiences which playing a wide variety of roles could bring.

Maturity is often assumed to be one of these 'qualities' and is included among the special ones to be inculcated in young people or aimed at in education, especially social education. What is really meant? Is it suggested that life is an upward progress during which the schools and the Youth Service can help the individual, until at some point around 18 or 20 overall maturity may be attained? Thereafter is there only a plateau left to cross until some future point of decline is reached? Presumably not, or, if this is what is meant, the adults who use the term are engaging in the purest self-delusion. For it is quite clear that many 'adults' are themselves still far from 'maturity' in almost any sense of the word, and that many adolescents have in some respects already reached it.

When 'maturity' is put forward as one quality to be inculcated, is it assumed that it is something a person attains over the whole area of life at once? This seems patently untrue. Words like 'freshman', 'greenhorn', 'rookie', 'sprog', etc., remind us that an individual entering a new field or way of life is generally not expected to make immediately what more experienced hands would call a mature approach to it. It is almost inconceivable that full adjustment to a new situation should be made at once. The individual human condition is one of interdependence and interaction with many other people and features of the environment. If new people and new features come into view, a period of adjustment is inevitable. If this be so, the adolescent who is judged absolutely mature is hard to find, for, even if one leaves aside other unexplored fields, relatively few of their age have yet experienced marriage or parenthood. The boy or girl regarded as a mature secretary to a members' committee or as an experienced dance organizer or school captain, may flounder as much as the next when the experience of marriage or a change of job confronts him or her.

Among adults, the man who has to change careers in mid-life presents a clear example here. He may be manifestly mature while in the job to which he has grown accustomed for 20 years, and yet may look and feel an absolute beginner when, say, he is compulsorily retired from the Services and seeks to 'settle in' to a civilian post. No one, of course, will think any the less of him for being 'adolescent' again in this respect, for needing a period of adjustment, for needing to grow to maturity again in the 'work' aspect of life.

Similarly, no one need criticize the adolescent who needs periods of adjustment in different areas of *his* life. The 'mature' club member may well be a 'fish out of water' in a work situation, as well as being completely unnerved by a new experience like a foreign holiday or a sudden call to help with a sick neighbour. Within the Youth Service, of course, this fact that maturity is a piecemeal attainment is widely acknowledged. It is recognized by implication firstly in the *statement* by many workers that they do not wish to have their members too dependent on the club. They accept that young people will want to spend much of their available leisure elsewhere – at home, at the 'Tech.', at the bowling alley. They know that members' best interests will not be served if they spend all their free time in the environment and social groups of the club. It can be seen, too, in the admission that some of the recruits to work with young people who find it most difficult to adjust their roles are those who have 'come up through the ranks', as senior-member helpers and the like. The adult who never grows out of adolescent behaviour in some areas of life is a well-known caricature in the Youth Service. He has learned the responses and behaviour patterns of his leisure-time while he was still himself adolescent in the club, and often he carries these with him largely unchanged through later years if he stays in the same environment. It would be difficult for him to alter his responses appreciably, since familiar environments and people provoke familiar responses and behaviour. Because other people's expectations do not easily change, the trained youth worker or the time-served apprentice are often advised not to continue in their new capacities in the old environment.

Maturity, then, is not a plateau attained, nor is it a blanket to cover all circumstances. Some people have attained it over large areas of life, many are never 'settled in' to some situations. It appears too that maturity as an undergraduate, say, or as a salesman, depends on some length of experience in this role, and presumably on having learned by that experience what behaviour this role calls for.

In talking of this process by which we cease to be a greenhorn or a beginner in each succeeding field of experience, are we confusing maturity with that staidness, that lack of youthfulness which, in the last chapter, we argued was one of the prices we pay for our attempts to induce young people into adult habits of thought and behaviour too quickly? Are we equating maturity with the stability which, some may hope, will be reached anyway in each of these fields eventually, but which may not in fact be a worthy aim for social education? Surely we cannot be falling into the trap of wishing to make young people old before their time. This is indeed the implication of much earnest endeavour in the Youth Service and in schools. Adults so strongly desire that the young people with whom they have contact should behave in an adult way and join the adult ranks, they so clearly indicate their expectations and approval of conventional manifestations of adulthood, that quite a number of young people are 'forced' to maturity in this or that field. There is little value in this superficial adultness. In fact it can do positive harm to individuals by cutting them off from their peers' acceptance. It often means little more than that they have learned tricks of behaviour accepted as indices of maturity a decade or more ago depending on the age of the adults concerned, and it can encourage attitudes and habits which are out of phase with much else in their developing personalities and which will stifle that quality of youthfulness already too rare in our society.

Are we, then, if we talk of aiming at maturity in young people, perhaps presuming to interfere, in some cases unnecessarily, in a process which in any case will go on unaided? It is certainly true that, teacher or no teacher, youth worker or no youth worker, young people will start work as apprentices or greenhorns, will join some sort of club as new members and perhaps get 'initiated', will have their first date and their first heart-breaking romance, will have their first experience of responsibility for the welfare of others, and make their first submission as an independent-minded adolescent to the will of the majority. Most of them will begin married life, will change jobs several times, including for the girls a change from 'work' to 'housework' and probably back again, and will become parents.

Successive experiences in life will be met and coped with, fortunately, whether social-educational opportunities are deliberately provided or not. The youth worker has a limited field of operation – directly he can communicate most about leisure-experiences, less about work-experiences and less still about family-experiences. The teacher as social educator works in slightly different areas, but they are no broader and may be narrower. The distinctive part for each to play, however, is not to attempt to pile experience upon experience for young people, not to bring them to full growth as quickly as possible, as if its premature achievement carried a special prize. To give each young person a variety of leisure-experiences and experiences of responsibility is certainly part of his *method*, but the justifying aim of social education could surely not be to enable young people to accumulate a multitude of such experiences, however many varieties the schools and the Youth Service might add to a process which we have admitted will go on anyway. The boarding-school house-master or mistress is not concerned to put boys or girls through a variety of experiences merely to add notches to their stick: the experiences of the student in his or her union have taught little if they have left only an accumulation of learned responses to different kinds of situation: nor is it for the social educator simply to parade young people through as many different realistic situations as possible.

For we have oversimplified. In speaking of attaining maturity in certain 'roles', we have implied that the role of 'husband' or 'employee' is a single one. In fact it is not: the description 'workman' covers a multitude of situations lasting a lifetime and calling on an almost infinite variety of responses. The same man, as workman, will play an immense number of roles in one week – to his employer, to his foreman, to his mates, to the apprentice or 'lad', to the customer or the visitor. This same individual in his home will in one week appear as the breadwinner, the chastiser of his children, their gift-bringer, their protector, and so on. Outside his family he will be one night the customer or 'regular', another the member joining in his club's programme, and another a godsend to his neighbour. Maturity for this man could not, then, consist of the accumulation of responses learned and brought into play like a pack of cards. His 'learning experiences' could never be varied enough to cover every eventuality.

Where schools or youth clubs or universities have succeeded in educating mature pupils or members, they have done so not because they have turned out men and women with an accumulation of responses learned in widely varied experiences and held in readiness for use later. Their success has been by contrast, because men and women have been enabled to engage in an intensive social intercourse and to extract from it certain social skills. These skills have helped them to respond appropriately to the variety of situations with which they have later been confronted.

The method in schools or clubs or universities may often have seemed to be to subject the pupil to a range of 'stretching' experiences, or to see that these are available. But the element which has made the lasting contribution to the development of maturity has been not so much the most easily observable content – the football or the netball or the dramatics – but the making of many different kinds of relationship, the experiencing of many different kinds of role. It is not sufficient simply to try to train young people to be experts in certain practical tasks as if it were the school or the youth club's purpose to attain standards of 'activity' skills as high as those of say, the colts' team of the local club or of the local dramatic society. If such standards, and even higher ones, are achieved alongside the central purpose of social education, well and good. But social education must above all be about relationships, and although these elements in every human situation cannot be easily conceived of separately from the tasks involved, they must nonetheless become the area of young people's experience on which adults in social education need to concentrate and which they must deliberately develop.

The Youth Service, and in part of their work the schools, can and should offer opportunities for the individual to increase the social skills through which he will be enabled to take his part in each new experience. This surely is the central aim in social education: to help young people acquire the social skills of cooperation, of membership of and contribution to a common effort, of sociability, of colleagueship? In doing so, however, it is inadequate to assume that some will always be leaders and others always followers since there are not just two kinds of roles to play in any group, whether at work or play. Moreover, the most difficult thing is often not to play the role, but to determine which role it is appropriate to play. Making such modifications to one's role according to circumstances and particular relationships is not to be unswervingly conformist to what others expect. The man who knows when to do the unexpected is valued at work and play alike. Nonconformity of expression is often the appropriate, indeed even the essential, response. But to rebel indiscriminately, to overthrow convention as a matter of principle, is no more a sign of maturity than to observe convention in all particulars. To rebel at the opportune moment and in an acceptable way is both more difficult and more effective. The unthinking bore who assumes in every situation that he is expected to take the lead, to give orders, or, slightly different, to act as chairman, is every bit as immature as the shy person who has ideas which he never knows when to reveal. Again, the impetuous rebel who cannot consult is as immature as the over-dependent man or woman who always needs the support of authority or group decision before acting. It is not the leadership, the followership, the chairmanship or the consultation which are immature, but the monotony, the inflexibility, the inability to adapt to a situation.

All this implies a view of society which now needs to be made explicit. The urbanized, industrialized, leisured society which we now take for granted in this country demands of its members both an incessant capacity for the choice-making of which we spoke earlier and a very great deal of flexibility of performance in networks of relationships. We are mobile, geographically: we must adapt in hours or minutes to a city rather than a village, or vice versa. We are mobile, socially too: the man next door may believe he has changed his social status overnight because he has changed his job. We intercommunicate intensely, by private letters and public media: so we are made aware at shorter and shorter intervals of new information which demands of us a new appraisal of our own situation and a slightly changed view of life and of our relationships to others. We have more time at our disposal when the basic bread-earning job is done and an increasing variety of ways of utilizing that time: so that there is an increase in the possible number of groups to be a part of and in the possible variety of functions we may perform within them. We may change our place of work several times more frequently in a lifetime than in previous generations, for a variety of reasons; and, within the work experience of a growing number of people, success depends on the kind of relationships, collaboration and communication achieved with other workers.

Such an analysis of society is not new. But it is important to deduce its relevance to the kind of education our young people should receive. Their work will be productive and their leisure rich if they can learn to mix appropriately with other people. Their exposure to the succession of individual choices will not be so stressful if they learn to be self-confident, whether they make a choice which coincides with their acquaintances' or strike out independently in disagreement. In our society the mature adult is one who, avoiding both self-effacement and self-conscious importance, enters a new group with open mind and sensitively takes its pulse. He does not have a preconceived idea of how he will behave, what he will say, whom he will speak to and in what language and tone. He avoids the temptation to short-circuit the richness of human responses by deciding in advance what behaviour pattern to follow. He has learned to tolerate, even to enjoy, the uncertainty and the excitement of an imminent new experience by *not* drawing up plans, by *not* making assumptions about 'what it will be like'. He is confident enough to be ready to trust himself to respond *when* he is in the situation. Far from being in some way untrue to his 'real' self by sensing out for each occasion how he will behave, he is a man of many parts, a many-sided character. He is ready to display whatever side of him is called for by the situation as he finds it, and he is willing to discover that he may not sincerely be able to meet the demands made upon him. He is ready to lead or not, as the situation and the other people in it require, to be laughed at or not, to play a servicing role or not as the circumstances seem at the time to call. He does not determine his course of action because his status in another, temporarily irrelevant, setting is different from that of others present. He does not inherit from past decades or past experiences, when customs suited other environments, stereotypes of what tasks and behaviour are properly his.

To be so flexible, so sensitive, so versatile, requires a very high degree indeed of social skill. It is valuable to taste a wide range of different social experiences, to gain the feeling of a great variety of roles within them.

This is maturity in the sense of a highly-developed sensitivity to the requirements of others on oneself and a flexibility to express the appropriate aspects of one's individuality to meet the situation. Such maturity does not grow rapidly, and assumes the self-discipline and humility which come from a careful discernment of one's own social situation and personal potentiality. What is required of social educators today is that they help young people to this self-understanding and self-expression. Forcing is useless: the adult can only offer sympathetic support, once he has created in his club an environment which will ensure as many learning experiences as possible. In this way young people will be enabled to define a code of morality and ideals appropriate to their condition and to society as they see it. To make their lives satisfying, coherent and pointed they will need an understanding of what they value, believe, enjoy, love, reject and oppose, and this must emerge from a realistic appraisal of their own situation, opportunities and needs.

This chapter does not claim to have defined maturity for all time or for every kind of society. It has attempted to portray urbane, sophisticated man in a society whose value-system is open. Most of us now live in urban settings, where contacts with many other people are innumerable and of many different kinds and where we must make choices over a very wide area of human experience. Such an approach to the definition of maturity thus emphasizes that its nature is rooted in the society and environment of the people about whom it is used. It is fairly clear that to be classed as a mature Polynesian islander a man or woman needs to display many qualities which the mature Western European does not, and vice versa. Behaviour which is well-adapted to one society or culture is not so to another. Even within our own society there is an infinite variety of subcultures, and what passes as suitably mature in one may appear ill-fitting behaviour in another.

To summarize, then, maturity seems a very proper aim for social education. But maturity is not a quality which is in any sense an entity, to be transported from place to place and brought into play. Nor is it an accumulation of expertnesses at different aspects of life. Instead it relates to a particular culture and indeed subcultures, and consists of behaving in a way well adapted to the environment. In our own society human beings figure prominently in the environment, because we are a closely-packed urban community. Good adaptation to the environment requires a sensitivity to the demands upon one of the situation and particularly of other people, as frequently as these demands change. It assumes too a capacity to modify that environment when modification is appropriate. The mature adult in such a society is one who has the sensitivity to perceive the role he should play and who has the flexibility to play it.

1. SIR JOHN MAUD, reported in *Youth Service Tomorrow:* A Report of a Meeting arranged by King George's Jubilee Trust and held t Ashridge, 27-30 April 1951, p. 13.
2. 'Albemarle Report', 1960 – *The Youth Service in England and Wales* (Report of a Committee appointed by the Minister of Education, November 1958) – para. 145.
3. J. L. LONGLAND, reported in *Youth Leadership and Responsibility.* An account of a residential course at Somerville College, Oxford, September 1960, University of Reading Institute of Education in conjunction with the Duke of Edinburgh's Award Scheme.
4. M. V. C. JEFFREYS, *Personal Values in the Modern World*, Penguin, 1962, p. 51.

Chapter 5

Methods:
The Effect of Language in Practice

Conceiving of the Methods

A great deal of social education is done with this aim of increasing young people's maturity for their own society. Its starting-point is an acknowledgment that human personalities and human situations are infinitely varied and that workers therefore need to be prepared to approach the young flexibly and open-endedly, with as few preconceptions as possible about how they might develop. Some workers who take this view of the purpose of social education, however, are often prevented from seeing its implications because of the very ways in which they are invited and encouraged to conceive of its content, its most appropriate modes of work and its most useful vehicles. For the language in which so much social education is discussed acts as a straitjacket: where the result which is being sought is an individually relevant response to a personal and unique situation, where the approach is open-ended, and the desired consequences infinitely varied, it is not possible to forecast in detail what the component elements of any young person's social education must be. These elements, too, must be variable, relative to people and their condition, adaptable in some of their most vital respects to needs and events as they arise.

Yet much social education is conceived and conducted as if such a prefabrication were possible, as if the adult could be forearmed with a battery of verbal formulae which will have inevitable and universal validity, as if, provided he has a wide enough stock of ready-mades, there is no need for tailoring. Human needs, and especially adolescents' needs for growth, demand greater differentiation than their physical shapes, and ready-made social education is in any case too impersonal to be real education at all. Yet many social educators are encouraged to practise as though they can know *before* they ever meet the particular young people who require their services exactly what facilities and adult responses will be required. A conceptual framework is fashioned out of their own and their associates' enthusiasms and interests, faiths and values as though these can enable them to make confident and unambiguous statements and generalizations about 'the young', their needs and the adult's role in his relations with them. Adult behaviour in social-educational settings is then discussed as if it can be to a large degree factory-produced, precast. It is talked of, for example, in terms of 'planning your winter programme', 'activities for girls', 'the incentive of competition', 'members' committee work', 'applying a group method', and so on.

The function of each of these languages is broadly the same: to give adults a set of mental concepts with which to plan, justify, discuss, make coherent, give meaning to the relationships which they must form with young people in social-educational settings. In anticipation of the unpredictability and untidiness of their encounters with the young, the adults are equipped with certain terms and ideas which will help them to prepare for their experiences. They are supplied with means of giving these experiences direction and so of imposing greater order and logic on them. Because social educators must work amid the pressures and uncertainties which are inherent in almost all social education, they do need some form of encouragement and reassurance. And because the formulae listed above can be applied to some young people in some circumstances, many workers are reinforced in their confidence in them and are thereby helped to deal more positively with some at least of the demands which inevitably are made of them.

Nonetheless, the dominance of these ways of conceiving and describing the content of social education needs to be challenged fundamentally. For, though they do not misrepresent the truth, they do miss out an important element of it. These conceptual frameworks refer only to part, or to one dimension of the essential field: constructed out of activities, competition, girls' needs and the rest, they do help the thinking of some adults for part of the time, but their basis is extremely insecure and their possible scope very limited. For, in the first place, the emphasis of such frameworks is on the superficialities of the experiences which can fulfil the young's social-educational needs. It is comprised mainly of the elements which are obvious, and indeed often includes only those which are capable of a

G

material expression. Such a framework, in fact, concentrates above all on tasks – on the occupation of people in operations which have known ends and concrete results and which assume that only the conscious motives of those involved are significant and worthy of educational attention. It touches too little, if at all, on the less apparent, more subtle reasons for and consequences of people coming into contact with each other and forming *human* enterprises. Moreover, such frameworks are not only superficial: the content which they entail is very largely selected by adults and so collectively represents what *adults* conceive to be essential to young people's development. Thus there is no guarantee that they convey what *adolescents* see to be valuable in a learning experience, nor do they necessarily employ terms or adopt criteria which are meaningful to younger, fresher personalities with fewer responsibilities and vested interests in the existing order.

What such frameworks attempt to do, in fact, is formulate prescriptions for future action out of the 'successes' which some adults believe they have achieved in the past with some young people. They seem to assume that the points of *identity* between one human situation and another do more to decided the outcome of these situations than do their points of *difference*. For although two situations may bear some superficial resemblances, and indeed the young people in them may be persuaded to react similarly by identical approaches, the really significant thing for a social educator ought to be that each one of these young people is an individual, with private motives, personal requirements and characteristics exclusive to him or her. It is with these idiosyncratic factors that a social educator must mainly grapple, and not with the generalizations and labels which can be attached to collections of individuals.

Thus the predetermined patterns of action proffered by adults regardless of immediate circumstances and actual people, the prescriptions which are formulated out of apparent past achievement with some young people, are extremely unreliable guides to what really needs to be done for the great many young people whom any adult may encounter at a later date. Indeed, at best, such prescriptions would seem to provide the worker with rules of thumb, whose relevance to some young people will be precise but accidental, and to others non-existent. The adult can never be sure that any prescription is going to indicate to him responses, procedures and approaches which are appropriate because they are what are required by the actual young people he meets. Because they are only rules of thumb, because they are so dependent on the superficialities and reveal nothing of the individual needs which will determine successful social education, they leave him far too reliant on a trial-and-error, hit-and-miss form of practice.

However, such a way of conceptualizing social education's content is more than inadequate and unreliable: it restricts an adult's view of what is required of him and how he might behave. Because it prevents many adults thinking about their approaches to young people with an open mind, it becomes a barrier to making real human relationships and enabling deeper and fuller human lessons to be learned. Indeed, the confidence which it proffers to practitioners is a false one which unnecessarily limits their achievement by encouraging them to emphasize only the extraneous aspects of their relationships with the young and by preventing them from discerning what is much more meaningful to many young people in any human encounter.

To say, then, that activities or the special needs of girls or particular types of groups have *no place* in social education is not the intention of this book. What is being challenged is in part the claim which is sometimes made that these particular attitudes and formulae *by themselves* constitute an adequate language in which to speak of social education. Even more fundamentally, however, doubt is being thrown on the assumption that it is possible and helpful to construct a framework and conceptualize the content of social education by predetermining what will be good for young people and which vehicles will be especially successful. Consequently, before going on to propose in the remainder of this book concepts and a working discipline which appear more reliable and more revelant to social education, it seems important to examine in detail some of the more conventional generalizations and prescriptions and to assess more precisely what their limitations are.

Activities, Badges and Competitions

Perhaps the most common and all-embracing misconception is that which results from social education being discussed only in terms of 'activities', as if it were only such behaviour as may be categorized under some activity heading that had any significance in social education. The adults who adopt this particular view thus see it as vital that they involve as many young people as possible in well-defined tasks which often have long-term objectives and which are advocated mainly because the adults themselves approve of them. The activities recommended, in fact, are almost invariably those which are believed to be 'cultural', or 'character-building' or in some other way 'worthwhile' by adult standards. Because their content is acknowledged by adults to be valuable, it is assumed uncritically that all young people will be socially educated only if they are brought into contact with some at least of them. They thus provide a frame of reference within which adults feel they can work purposefully. They offer a language which enables certain adolescents to be known and understood, to be described as 'actors', or 'footballers', or 'artists', or 'Christians', and so seen as 'good' members or 'responsive' pupils. Complete and reassuring administrative procedures are made available, and relief from the strain of having to decide what needs to be done is given to hard-pressed practitioners. By starting from an assumption that social education must be conducted through 'activities' and 'activity programmes', a large number of adults are helped to make apparent sense of their relationships with young people.

Undeniably, such an adult attitude and approach suits many young people very well. Perhaps because these young people already know what they want and require, perhaps because a clearly presented and well-established structure gives them the initial confidence to become involved, they respond positively to adult-prepared programmes of this kind. And yet, as a general and final statement of what will ensure sound and desirable social education, the activity concept seems at least naive and indeed often completely out of touch with reality. For there is no way of knowing in advance that any particular activity, however uplifting the adult believes it to be, will be the one which will best serve any young person's social education. What may be necessary for one adolescent's personal and emotional development cannot with any certainty be understood merely by examining and judging the nature of the tasks he might perform and the practical skills he might acquire. What he may need for his social growth does not automatically become clear just because an adult believes or knows certain interests – 'classical music', or 'the theatre', or 'the arts' – to be cultural and others – 'outdoor activities', or 'community service' – to be character-building.

Such a method of establishing the content of young people's social education seems to be *mis*conceived because, even if it is possible to establish that an activity has inherent and absolute quality as a form of human expression, it does not for that reason alone represent a medium through which any individual can achieve what he or she most needs. 'Folk' or 'pop', the 'picture-house' and the 'palais', interests such as pigeon-fancying and rugby-league football which have their roots in a local environment but which are not usually recognized as belonging to a 'high culture' or as being notably 'character-building' – any or all of these might provide a much more appropriate means of bringing some young people what they require. It is not necessary today, as it seems to have been in the nineteenth century, to rely for definitions of what is educationally good and stimulating on the subjective judgments of adults who have only their own past experiences to guide them. It is possible now to discover some standards at least which are more objective than these and so more individually relevant. And it is important to think in terms of what people 'do' with activities and how they perceive them and react to them rather than what activities are believed – on the basis of unrepresentative experience – to do to people.

To conceive of social education as being achieved only or mainly through 'activities' chosen by adults for their inherent worth thus seems to start at the wrong point. Instead of beginning with young people and what in reality they require, the point of origin of this language is the adults and the apparent absolute value of what they know they can offer. The result is that it confuses means – the content of social education, in this case activities – with ends. It makes what is provided for young people valuable *in itself* without ever enquiring whether it is the vehicle for what is most socially desirable and meaningful for the recipients. Often, the mere fact that young people have participated in what the adult approves is apparently taken as sufficient achievement in itself. Certainly the extent to which they have personally developed a greater maturity for their own society barely seems capable of discussion because of the limitations of the language. For the concentration is on tasks and interests extracted by adults from society in general and given special weight by them.

Even, however, where further results are sought and defined – where, for example, 'qualities' such as initiative, self-confidence or a sense of responsibility are made the objects of involving young people in activities – there are serious weaknesses in the approach. For adults cannot assume, as many of them seem to do, that the desired ends will be automatically achieved because the approved activities are being pursued, and indeed, the possibility exists that the outcome will be precisely opposite to the one which was sought. Thus, a young person who performs in a play or who is a regular member of a climbing party may acquire a great many practical skills and may also, in the process, learn something of the value of cooperation, team-work and acceptance of other people's commands.

But he may also learn blind obedience and succumb unjustifiably to group pressures. He could, of course, discover new talents in himself and with good reason increase his self-esteem: on the other hand, his successes might unduly and even dangerously inflate his assurance about his own abilities and importance to others, and make less likely any balanced appreciation of his own worth. Nothing in cultural, character-building or any other form of activity is *especially* suitable for developing any of the personal and social qualities which so many social educators make the purpose of their work.

What is more, the qualities themselves, the very characteristics which adults see as laudable and which bulk so large in their conceptions of social education are ambiguous and can be seriously misapplied by young people. For example, perseverance and persistence, which appear so regularly in the vocabulary of the activity-minded, might be displayed in some situations by some participants as stubbornness or foolhardiness, just as an especial concern for long-term objectives might be turned by some into rigidity and an unwavering loyalty, and steadfastness of purpose might produce in others a narrowness of view and even fanaticism. The 'qualities' which gain immediate and uncritical approval from a large number of adults, and which are so often seen to be the product of keen participation in an activity, are not themselves entirely evil of course. But, although some young people may gain much from joining an activity, others will almost certainly gain little or nothing by doing so and some may even be harmed.

The adult cannot therefore conceive of his task as if he were carrying on crusades for certain interests or pursuits or faiths, and indeed there may be occasions when he has a responsibility to help young people to avoid, for example, acting in a play, learning an instrument or joining a church. The adult who recruits twenty-three out of twenty-four members or pupils to an enthusiasm or interest which he happens to believe to be good cannot take this as unquestionable proof that he has succeeded in a social-educational sense, since it is possible that only one of the twenty-three will be genuinely and personally helped by the new commitment. The mere involvement of young people in 'activities' is no automatic guarantee that their social education has been furthered.

Despite this, however, there often exists among youth workers and teachers a hierarchy of activities and pursuits to which they refer when they wish to ascertain what is good for the young people in their charge. This structure has of late become rather more flexible and has admitted certain 'interests' which at one time would never have been considered as educative agents. Thus, dance-drama productions at times incorporate the latest forms of teenage dancing, an interest in motor-bikes is often fostered and groups playing music in the modern style may be encouraged. Indeed, some adults become so anxious to be seen as accepting and utilizing contemporary (and sometimes commercial) trends that the activities they sponsor deliberately and self-consciously emphasize aspects of what they assume to be 'pop' culture.

Even this, however, does not mean that the activity-conception has altered fundamentally, since to 'lay on' activities just because they are 'modern' is to adopt precisely the same attitude of mind as do those who insist on certain activities because they are cultural or character-building. It is still to prejudge what will touch the personal needs of the young people whom an adult meets, without first attempting to assess what these needs are and whether what is being offered is relevant to them. What is more, a great many youth workers and teachers are uninfluenced even by these marginal shifts of emphasis, and continue to take their lead on what should be provided from the more traditional activity hierarchies. Indeed, their approach has as recently as 1956 been embodied in an important new structure, the Duke of Edinburgh Award Scheme, whose scope is as broad and whose statement of what is desirable is as detailed and confident as any that has appeared in the past. It is undeniable that the Scheme has done much to bring more adults in the community into contact with young people by encouraging them to share their interests and skills. It has also created a framework through which it is possible for young people to develop 'all-round' and so restates the intentions of older organizations – like the Young Men's Christian Association, for example – which have attempted to help young people grow on many fronts and to avoid an education which is lop-sided. Clearly and unambiguously the Scheme demonstrates the assumption that young people's social education depends upon their occupation in certain adult-approved activities.

In particular, the prestige and widespread adoption of this Scheme have harnessed and given impetus to two families of activity which have in any case been growing in popularity among social educators in recent years – outdoor activities and community service – and have enshrined in an appealing and impressive way the scientific, bureaucratic impulse to *measure* young people. No one would wish to deny that these fields of activity can be for some young people important and valuable media for social education. However, both of them engage the emotions of all who try to think about them without necessarily being seen in their exact place in the lives of individual young people. In consequence, on both outdoor activities and community service in the abstract, are piled unreasonable and unreasoning hopes that they will act as panaceas. As with the activity concept in general, however, both of these particular aspects of it seem to have little if any special merit as social-educational vehicles, and indeed appear often to set up unnecessary obstacles to the achievement of the ends of social education in our society.

For, in the first place, it is clear that all adolescents are no more fitted to undertake a service to others than are all adults. For some in their teens any such commitment is inappropriate because it is viewed too lightly or carried out for dangerously selfish reasons, or even because the young are providing palliatives for serious social problems, and so enabling society as a whole to avoid reacting as vigorously and radically as it ought. What is more, to make a 'programme' out of young people's altruistic sentiments may once again never touch their very personal requirements in this field and may even do them some harm. Some young people will undoubtedly respond very positively and helpfully to suggestions that they serve such impersonal groups as 'the needy', or 'the sick', or 'the elderly'. But some may take up the suggestion without ever seeing the relationship of what they are doing to their own grandparents' need for consideration and aid, or to their physically handicapped brother's demands for attention: they may be led to feel that they are doing elsewhere all that is required of them. 'Community service' in its generalized sense may help some young people to achieve greater understanding of more intimate problems, but this connection between the two will not occur automatically.

Community service as a vehicle for young people's social education has another even more fundamental weakness. For it imposes on the adult social educator who uses it an immediate and inescapable responsibility, not only to the young people he meets but also to those whom the young people set out to serve, and this additional responsibility can prevent the adult from working with certain young people in ways which are most appropriate to their need. Thus, even though the latter may have, in the first place, committed themselves voluntarily, the adult may be forced on occasions to insist that they act in certain ways and continue to fulfil certain tasks. For some young people, such insistence may well be an essential element of social education, and certainly for a large number, adult suggestion, clarification and advice will be an important ingredient.

But for many others, the most vital aspect of a social-educational experience may be freedom from adult direction. What they may need more are opportunities to decide for themselves what they will do, to live with the consequences of these decisions and to learn from the mistakes as well as achievements which all this may entail. Too often, where community service is being used as the medium for social education, the adult cannot work as permissively as this. To safeguard those being served, he must act as an authority with some young people whose greatest need may be to free themselves from a dependence on or a suspicion of authority. The principles underlying service to others, in fact, can contradict and even conflict with those on which sound social education must be based. None of this is to say that no young person can or should offer his services to the community, since many young people will do this effectively and conscientiously and will derive from it much that is beneficial to their own development. What such considerations do seem to do, however, is to undermine fundamentally the special claims made by many adults for this particular method of working with young people. To put forward community service as helpful to all adolescents' development, or as having superior social-educational capacity to any other form of activity, once again demonstrates a serious misconception of the way adults need to practice. And to talk of it in activity terms, with merely a gloss of social conscience as many adults do, is actively to *prevent* oneself from considering the motives of young people and their needs.

Much the same can be said of those outdoor activities – of climbing, walking, canoeing, sailing, pot-holing – which are also increasingly being advocated as social-educational vehicles which have special merit. Here, too, it is not necessary or useful to argue that such vehicles have no place at all, since, in a society where town life can still be (as it was in the nineteenth century) limiting and depressing, contact with the varied wildness, with the openness and the colour of the countryside can give pleasure and a form of personal fulfilment which many adolescents cannot achieve amid streets and buildings. Within limited areas of human activity and expression, a self-knowledge can be acquired and a discovery and release of latent abilities made possible, and on these *some* young people can build greater confidence and a deeper awareness of potential skill. Because the countryside offers a different set of experiences from those which most young people meet day by day, in certain respects it can widen horizons and deepen self-realization. Deliberately, however, this definition of appropriate purpose and possible achievement is a narrow one. What is being sought and most often gained is pleasure and self-fulfilment by means of a certain type of experience which would otherwise not be available. The skill that is gained is a skill in rock-climbing or canoeing, the greater self-knowledge is knowledge of one's own responses to a scarcity of footholds or an unexpectedly rapid current. These are the only certain conclusions which can be drawn.

Indeed, it is especially difficult to be confident that outdoor activities have any more profound or long-lasting effects than these since, by their very nature, they exaggerate a problem inherent in all education – that of achieving a transfer of what has apparently been learned from the situation in which the learning originally occurred to other situations in which the lessons must be utilized but whose conditions may be considerably less favourable. For outdoor activities deliberately remove young people, both physically and socially, from the milieu in which they must continue to work and play, and then give them no clear guide as to how they can transfer what they have acquired and discovered to their everyday lives. What is too rarely acknowledged, in fact, is that resilience and persistence may be acquired or discovered when, for example, the task is to walk twenty miles in a day of rain and wind, but that these same qualities will not necessarily be revealed when a long and painstaking preparation for an examination is called for. Nor will the ability to take a group of like-minded peers from point 'A' to point 'B' by use only of map and compass develop in itself the qualities of leadership that will impress a group of fellow-apprentices or a foreman, when the subject matter may be morals or productivity. The transferability of understanding and skills from one situation to another is not so simple a process and may not be improved at all by exposure to physical hardship in the out-of-doors.

Indeed, the social education which strenuous outdoor activity makes possible for young people is likely to become less and less relevant to their everyday life in the 1970s and the 1980s. For whatever relief is to be had by escape to the countryside, the fact remains that urban living and industrial forms of work are with us and are extending. The challenges these create – challenges to choosing a mate, deciding one's own moral code, forming satisfying relationships with other people and developing the social skills which make these relationships possible and mutually acceptable, raising children, formulating one's ideals and discerning which political party best expresses them, deciding which brand of food to buy and why, understanding why prices rise and why wage policies are negotiated, and so on, and so on – these are challenges for which the young can only be prepared *within* an urban-industrial setting. Moreover, by themselves, they would seem to offer challenges enough. One may wish that some of them at least did not exist and one may even try to eradicate these. But it is impossible to pretend that they do not exist or that they will not make considerable demands on young people who are searching for a maturity in the society which surrounds them. To invent more challenges would thus seem to be irrelevant, and even perhaps presumptuous.

There is one final reason why social education which is too dependent on outdoor activity is likely to be inappropriate to many young people's needs. This follows from the fact that, though adolescents are at the peak of their physical *strength*, they are not at the peak of *judgment* in physical matters. Calmness, precision and many of the qualities required for real expertise in outdoor pursuits will only come to them later, in the twenties at the earliest. What is more, young people, in addition to their above-average strength and energy, have also a keener emotional perception, fuller feelings, a greater sensuousness and aesthetic vigour. In these fields too, therefore, though time will again temper judgment and refine discrimination, there are immense opportunities for development. Adolescence, in fact, is a time in which young people should be able to feel justified in having a taste of as wide a range of activities as possible. It is then that their potential for taking up new experiences in the emotional as well as the physical realm is highest and, in so far as advancing years will later rob them of a chance to play any but a spectator's role in physical pursuits, the latter offer a comparatively shortlived sphere of activity and interest. If there is good reason for taking the chance and exercising physical prowess while one is at one's strongest, there is even more justification, perhaps, for fostering early a liking for experiences which will be available for one's increasingly sophisticated pleasure over a much longer period. It is a palpable disservice to young people to give lop-sided prestige to the physical.

Yet, in the physical pursuits school there is at least an implication and often a categoric statement that the view from 3,000 feet is infinitely superior to viewing a Van Gogh; that driving oneself hour after hour up 600 feet of rock is much more important in the expression of personality than is training one's breathing to master the subtleties of a French horn solo, or that the ability to choose a camp site well and pitch the tents securely is a considerably clearer sign of human capacity than is the ability to coax one's fellows to express pain, surprise, joy or frustration on a stage. Because of the overweening devotion to the physical, in fact, a premium seems to be placed on a very limited range of human behaviour and abilities, and a conception of social education is accepted which has too many disturbing overtones of the 'blood and soil' ideals of a much less worthy philosophy. The highest virtue comes to be identified with strength, with intense physical striving, with the ability and desire to exert one's body for long periods. Other human attributes – bodily poise, grace and freshness, restraint and gentleness of response, softness and sympathy, tenderness and sensitivity to immediate human need – come to be devalued and certainly are subordinated to loyalty, to abstract causes, the pursuit of impersonal objectives like mountain-tops, and respect for others as climbers and canoeists rather than primarily as fellow human beings. Many of the arguments for the great outdoors suggest a suspicion or a rejection of intellectual and aesthetic responses which can hardly be regarded as creditable in those purporting to be educators for an urban-ized society. In addition, the outdoor pursuits movement will con-tinuously be in danger of achieving the very opposite of its intention. For the pastoral romantics will almost certainly convince many a young person that the countryside is all hell and high water, and not for them – and even that all social-education opportunities deliberately provided by our society are unworthy of their attention.

The main conclusion that one must draw from all this, however, is not simply that outdoor pursuits or community service are credited with exaggerated educative powers, but that no activity, whatever its content, deserves to be offered as an automatically relevant and successful medium of social education. For, far from any single form of leisure occupation providing the ultimate and perfect vehicle, the wider the variety of situations and experiences to which young people are introduced, the greater the range of responses they may be able to make. No single kind of experience is better designed for, or can be guaranteed to produce, development in all and sundry, or even in the majority. Some will display different aspects of personality in one kind of situation, some in another. Take a young person, remove him from the young people with whom he has established his role, and place him with other young people similarly selected. Then, no matter what experience he is offered, there are roughly even chances that he will or will not 'discover more about himself', 'develop traits unknown', and reach other 'worthwhile' ends. Or even, take a group of young people who are well known to each other, offer them an experience quite new, and, whatever the nature of this experience, they will reshuffle roles within the group, and individuals may reveal unsuspected 'characteristics'. The pattern of young people's behaviour in such a situation, however, is not an inevitable one. They are simply becoming more aware of their needs and giving evidence of how the adult might practise with them in the future.

For it is not being suggested that activities as such have no place in social education: on the contrary, activity by and interaction between young people when they meet will provide the essential medium for the social educator to attain his ends. But the adult must have sufficient insight to be able to identify what activity-medium might be appealing and available to any particular young person or group of young people. He must also be able to utilize skills, within a circumscribing set of principles, which will enable young people to formulate and develop this activity in ways more appropriate to what they want and need.

There is a further drawback, however, to a language which describes social education only in terms of the activities or tasks which are measurable, or in terms of the concrete achievements which such activities and tasks make possible: it draws attention almost irresistibly to those aspects of young people's leisure experiences which are measurable. Merely to put a name to any particular passage in the experience of a young person during his leisure, merely to label it, is in one sense to measure it: for any part of our experience which can be described in words is liable to be discussed objectively by others, and often without reference to the person for whom alone it had the unique meaning which his life and perception gave it. But beyond this, a large number of adults are apparently fascinated by the feeling of having tangible proof about the way in which young people spend their leisure time. They take pleasure in accumulating evidence about the nature and quality of their activities, and indeed help to create structures and patterns which channel young people into measurable performance.

The most obvious manifestation of this tendency is the competition. The supreme advantage of *competitive* activity for the adults responsible for young people's education seems to be that by its results they can make even greater sense of what young people are doing, and 'judge their worth' even more certainly. It is a means of conceptualizing and describing the groups of young people which have 'what it takes' and which have progressed in the directions sought and approved by the adults. A whole pyramid of leagues and festivals, cups and shields, a pecking order of divisions and tables and grades, a mathematical play-exercise of points are thus introduced and institutions intended to aid young people's social development come to be pervaded by an obsession with results rather than with the enjoyment and experience of an activity, or with the appreciation of the human contacts which this activity makes possible.

In international and even inter-city or inter-area competitions, such assistance to the individual in bringing order into a chaotic universe may be helpful. If we are to retain our balance in society, we must believe that some things are tokens of significance, that something, easily comprehensible, gives us a meaningful indication of the greater value or importance of one thing over another. It may even be that competitive activity, and in particular sport, sublimates our aggressiveness and acts as a channel for attitudes and emotions which otherwise would need outlet and release in far more damaging and dangerous ways. It is no doubt right, therefore, to pay our gladiators to fight those of the next town, or country, or, even if we do not pay them, to let our fellow-adults or star young people perform unpaid as representative of our combative thoughts and feelings if they choose to do so. But it seems vital to examine much more carefully the effects of talking about social education and of publishing tables about it *only* or primarily in terms of the competitions entered, fought out and won.

But even where outright competition is inapplicable, or loses favour, other forms of measurement seem to be resorted to and gain ground very quickly. For example, as soon as outdoor pursuits grow popular and distract some young people from adherence to competitive and team sports, as soon as young people's interests through better education and greater opportunity extend to pottery-making or modern ballet, then adults begin to grow uncomfortable. What are young people doing, with the clay, on the lake, on the stage? Is it a profitable use of time? The only known means of answering such questions apparently is to turn young people's experiences into some describable, definable, rewardable shape, to lay down 'standards' by which they can be measured. Thus, regardless of its personal meaning to the human beings involved, there follows the introduction of score-sheets on to the stage, log-books on to the lake, and a points scale into the pottery-room. Every self-respecting youth organization lays down its own scale of attainments and hurdles, and many schools, too, insist that their pupils are tested even where academic examinations are known to be inappropriate. 'Schemes' and 'courses' thus become a means for measuring the extent to which the young have placed their leisure time under the scrutiny of adults for the largesse of merit ratings, and the young person who enjoys the same experiences without giving the adult the bonus of measuring it is clearly at a discount. The question to ask about an individual becomes not 'what kind of a person is he?' but 'what badges has he got?'; not 'what have been his experiences, pleasures and pains?' but 'what tokens of approval (defined and offered by others) has he fought for and won?'; less 'who is he?' than 'what has he?' This is not to deny, of course, that incentives are highly reputable teaching aids when used with discrimination by a teacher who understands that they are subordinate devices. But to the layman, to the administrator, to those teachers who are more concerned with form than content, the incentive becomes all. Instead of a gimmick to extract the best performance, the attainment or non-attainment of the goal becomes the key issue.

There is no doubt that in the 'working' part of life certificates, degrees and diplomas are going to be used for some time and, indeed, as the need for technical, measurable competence or demonstrable intellectual skill grows, so too will the demand for 'paper' qualifications. Moreover, even in their leisure, some young people will find the award systems, the league tables, adjudication and all the other paraphernalia of measurement to their liking, will express themselves in them, and will develop to ultimate maturity through them. Having been given the confidence of having done 'well' in such adult-constructed measurement systems, they may be helped to move on to independence themselves.

For many young people, of course, this would be sufficient, and many adults would emphasize that for other young people what should be valued is not the medal or the victory but the experience and the human contact. However, many adults involved in face-to-face contact with young people are not easily distracted from the award of tokens. Perhaps because they feel that the only signals of their own success are the badges, cups and medals which 'their' young people acquire, perhaps even because they do not conceive of what they are doing as being concerned with human relationships and personal experiences, such adults fail completely to make the social education which they offer meaningful to many of the young people they encounter. More likely, however, the adults are imprisoned in the language of measurement, unable to conceive of or talk about the dimension of the work which is its prime social and educational justification. Moreover, many young people too will perceive the measurement systems in a quite different way from what was intended, since such systems can quite easily encourage the socially insecure to seek the artificial props and crutches to self-confidence which tidy structures and demonstrable successes can bring.

It must be realized also that to tie young people's social education too closely to measurement schemes is to cast their use of leisure time into a rigid shape, and so actually to inhibit them from developing the forms of expression most helpful to them in adolescence and most permanently useful to them later in life. For two fundamental reasons, in fact, such an approach can be seriously disabling to young people. The first is that it will often prevent a young person from experiencing an activity simply as a form of enjoyment, with no end-reward. Indeed, the chances are against him doing so unless he is fortunate enough to meet an adult and some fellow-participants who ignore the form to some extent for the sake of the content. The consequence of such so-called social education in the past is to be seen in the many adults who are 'lost' in their expanding leisure today, not because they never had interests in their adolescence but because they never learned to enjoy those interests outside a structure which gave rewards and made measurements. The other fundamental reason which makes the measurement approach a possible disservice to young people is that it may never encourage them to meet the other people involved as people: each young person participating may always view the surrounding adults and young people as coaches or measurers, as fellow-competitors or as hostile rivals.

The whole system is thus an elaborate and indeed effective device for doing many of the subsidiary things in social education, but it totally misses the central purpose. It also loads the dice against the achievement of maturity and obscures the fact that many who submit themselves to measurement by adults are not 'success' stories if judged by the wider objectives of social education to which many of the adults concerned subscribe. Even though they may have produced the 'results', they have often learned 'wrong' reasons for action and had some irrelevant attitudes to the use of leisure reinforced or imposed on them. Forcing growth by means of incentives can nurture ability without discrimination and can leave the individual's motives for displaying that ability completely unexamined.

Competitive and measurement schemes, in fact, absorb a dispropor-tionate amount of effort, skill and time, and they hinder at least as many young people in their progress to maturity as they help. For the language of such schemes does not help the adult to cater for certain characteristics and certain young people. All are put out of court: they must appear as 'unknowable' qualities, or as young people who did not join or who failed to stay the course. Yet such young people are clearly worthy of attention, and ways of conceiving of a form of education more appropriate to them are needed. It may be *easier* to measure human beings than to get to know or understand them, but measurement and the competition which so often accompanies it provide no firm platform for any social educator's practice.

Undeniably, for some young people, the level of skill developed in an activity will be important: high standards and tools of measuring them are what *some* clients will want and need if their social development is to occur and are therefore something of which they ought not to be deprived. And as activities also help to broaden young people's ability to deal with their environment, competence and especially measured competence in them can give confidence based on this power to cope with surroundings – 'everyone needs to do well at something'. Activities help, too, in young people's use of increased leisure, giving relief from the tensions of working life – 'everybody should have a hobby'.

But the restrictive language of activities, and the allied confining concept of measurement, conspire to prevent the adult who uses them from seeing the *social* in social education. For activities also attach young people to a concensus of and a commerce in ideas, an intercourse with other people: they introduce the young to company and give them reference groups in the community with whom to identify. Even when the young people concerned attain a level of skill lower than that which, potentially, they seem able to reach, the activities are worthwhile because they constitute an arena in which human interaction takes place around a theme chosen by common consent. Activities in their proper perspective may be seen as providing a medium through which young people can increase their involvement in and appreciation of human behaviour, and so experience much that is essential to 'man as a social animal'.

'Boys' Work' and 'Girls' Work'

The language and concepts of social education are limiting also when they imply that practice with boys is bound to be inherently different from that with girls. Perhaps because social education began in the days of male dominance in our society, approaches have first been devised for work with boys and have then been transferred to work with girls and mixed groups. Often, however, in these new settings these approaches have seemed to be much less successful and, in searching for a reason for this,

H

workers have come to assume that there is something 'special' about 'the needs of girls'. The tendency until recently has therefore been to deal with the 'problem' of what to do with the girls by dismissing the latter as 'different' rather than by attempting to rethink the original approaches afresh. 'Boys' work' has become the standard from which 'girls' work' is seen as a variant.

Clearly, differences in sexual characteristics do affect the needs of boys and of girls. But the conceptual framework which many social educators have been offered makes it appear that the most important needs of girls are those which they have *because* they are girls (and likewise with boys). In consequence, because the vast majority of the adults in social education have so far been men, they have been made to feel personally excluded from a mystery and hence seriously inadequate in their contacts with half their clientele. In fact, the needs of any individual young person will be determined far more often by other factors than his or her gender. For, the variations in need between the individuals in a group which happens to be composed only of girls will probably be much wider than will the difference in the needs between each of these girls and an individual boy of similar temperament, maturity, intelligence, home background, etc.

Two interrelated assumptions apparently produce this conceptual muddle. One of these we have already dealt with in some detail: that activities – that is, certain types of adult-approved tasks – are an essential ingredient of any social-educational provision and that participation in them can be used as the major criterion of young people's success or failure in social education. The other is that boys are more interested in activities than are girls but less interested than them in relationships. When these two attitudes come together it leads some adults in social education to see a problem in working with girls in general. For the girls, on the whole, seem to want most of all what is least valued for its own sake in much social education – contact with people, especially boys and men, but also girls and women. Conversely, girls refuse to be distracted by the activity sideshows which many social educators judge to be of most worth and so supply most often. The consequence is that they become 'difficult to cater for'.

Jalna Hanmer in her authoritative study, *Girls at Leisure*, admirably traces this line of reasoning:

There seems to be a tendency to think in mutually exclusive categories. This is reflected in the terminology used to describe young people and their leisure activities and in the concepts used to discuss girls. Terms such as active and passive use of leisure, being with or without interests, being clubbable and unclubbable are dichotomies. Each has its opposite, or opposing concept. A system of values is implied by the approval and non-approval given to these categories. One is considered good and the other is considered bad. In addition, one is often identified with girls and the other with boys. It is considered good to be placed in the categories 'with interests', 'active' and 'clubbable'. Girls sometimes achieve this but more commonly are classified, 'without interests', 'passive' and therefore 'unclubbable'. Boys are more often equated with the 'good' categories and girls with the 'bad'.[1]

And so, Jalna Hanmer goes on to point out,

What constitutes an interest, an active or passive pursuit, or clubbability is defined by society, in relation to its values, thus producing a hierarchy of judgments of leisure uses. It seems, for example, within the youth service to be frequently assumed that a boy who spends a large proportion of his leisure playing football has a better use of leisure than a girl who spends a similar portion of her leisure dancing. A visit to the theatre is judged to be a better use of leisure than a visit to the cinema. The judgment is not related to what is being shown or performed and, in both examples, it is not related to the quality of the experience to the individual.[2]

Many adults, as Jalna Hanmer says, attempt to solve the 'problem' by conceiving of relationships as an activity. They notice what it is that girls are most interested in, assume that they can extract the essentials of this and then attempt to build it into a formal or semi-formal programme of structured exercises. Satisfying girls' 'special' needs thus comes to equal providing more tasks which can be recognized as specifically feminine because they are *about* relationships. And so, for example, the moment some workers recognize that many girls are more interested in their future roles as mothers and wives than in playing games, they establish a 'home-making' activity group, or something similar. Certainly, this will be the way to help some girls. But for many other girls (and many boys too, as we shall see later) it starts at completely the wrong point, since these young people would have been satisfied (less spectacularly, it is true, and in less easily measurable ways) by meeting in the club married men and women and by these adults making their personal qualities and their reflections on marital experience genuinely but humbly available. The girls concerned will not necessarily be *told* about married life but will rather use the chance, by testing themselves against those who are married, to discover, informally, in their own time, by methods which appeal to them, what they think, feel and fear about courtship and marriage. Mature adults – men and women – can, simply by their presence and relationships among young people, ensure that actual human needs are being met and that experience of human relationships is being made available without ever ostentatiously pursuing task ends.

The relationships-as-an-activity approach at least has the advantage of making possible a greater variety of response and a more sensitive appreciation of one general area of human differentiation. Nonetheless, it appears to be fundamentally misconceived, since to provide activities which are *about* relationships is not necessarily to offer the *experience* in human relationships which young people want in the setting in which they want it. As Jalna Hanmer says, 'to view relationships as "programme" is to depersonalize'[3] and is thus a certain way of removing the very element in them which made them appealing in the first place.

This approach, however, is not the most serious consequence of thinking of social education in terms of 'boys' work' and 'girls' work'. Much more fundamental is the assumption that it is only girls for whom relationships are important. It is undeniable of course that some people are in general likely to be more interested in other people than in things, in relationships than in subjects, in human attributes and human feelings than in skills and activities. Such people will probably ponder first how a person will treat them, what that person thinks of them, what they feel about him or her, and only afterwards enquire what that person does or how well that person does it. And it is undoubtedly true that it is more acceptable in our present society for the girls and women among such person-oriented people to show these interests overtly than for the boys to do so.

However, such attitudes cannot be explained merely in terms of the gender of those holding them. They are not dependent on any inherent difference between the sexes which always makes boys want only to pursue task ends and girls simply content to experience relationships. Regardless of their sex, such person-oriented young people are clearly hoping at least on some occasions and from some of their activity experiences for a deepened appreciation of human relationships. While many of those who have this outlook are girls, an increasingly large number of boys also can be seen to disdain the characteristic task-oriented programmes offered to them.

Girls and boys must be offered media for their development in which activity tasks continue to have their proper value but in which human relationship processes are valued at least equally with, and at times more than, these tasks. More and more young people will want the unmeasured freedom and opportunity to learn more about themselves and their contacts with others and to understand how and why they and others feel and react. These gains will have to be encouraged by adults certainly no less diligently than are victories in netball (or football) matches or the making of pretty dresses (or canoes). Only then will the young people most concerned respond to the adults and make use of the facilities at their disposal. As Jalna Hanmer says,

> Young people . . . need help with their heterosexual development – not just by an occasional talk, even less through a course on home-making, but through making and sustaining contacts with their own age-group and with mature adults of both sexes – adults who are able to take young people seriously and who can furnish an example within the club of relationships of friendly respect.[4]

Such work with young people is of course commonplace in some youth organizations and schools, but there remain many adults in social education who are bewildered by the young people who do not respond to the activity-bait offered. Some boys are then dubbed effeminate simply because they also refuse to be fobbed off by activities in which human interaction is at a discount, and the girls who do have an interest in activities for the sake of competence and mastery of the skills involved come to be regarded as more or less conveniently masculine. But masculine and feminine traits are in reality far more subtly mixed than the boy-girl distinction implies.

Moreover the signs accepted by society of male-ness and female-ness change perceptibly over a long period, even if the change is imperceptible in any particular decade. In recent years the differences in the social roles of men and women have consistently tended to disappear. There is still a long way to go before women have equality of opportunity in careers, but in leisure, social and home life, there are few activities now reserved exclusively to the male, or to the female. Men and women share shopping, housework, baby-care, gardening, home maintenance and many other spheres previously assumed to be the preserve of one sex or the other.

The adolescent generation, which has grown up in a society where equality between the sexes has reached such a high degree, has itself indicated, in much of its dress and personal decoration, that it recognizes the erosion of distinctions based on sex difference. Less and less does it seem appropriate to define the responses which work satisfactorily with many boys as the standard ones and those which have to be adopted for the majority of girls as the variant. It may not even be very helpful any more to use the differences between the sexes as an especially significant indication of how the social education of any young person should be conducted.

Indeed, the fundamental error that adults make may well be to think of young people as girls (or boys) first and only afterwards as individual human beings, and therefore to allow their hypersensitivity to any client's sex to determine their approach. For the other generalizations which can be made about human beings and young people in particular will probably be much more helpful to them: even more important, social educators need to be much more intent on responding to the essential and unique nature of a personality and to recognize that the sex is only one of a number of contributing factors. In fact, if they look first at the individuality of a young person, they may become conscious that they are liable to be blinded rather than helped by their generalizations about gender. Thus in this case they may discover that they have been so busy trying to decide how this or that girl fits into their faceless, generalized image of what 'girls' are that they have missed the personal points of contact which they might have established, the personal interests and the personal needs.

All this leads once again to the conclusion that to a large extent social education is unnecessarily restricted in its scope by the way adults, and perhaps in this context male adults especially, conceptualize their roles and responses. The reasons for this in the work done with girls seem complex. They may well be closely related to those which impel some adults in social education to lay such stress on physical exertion and achievement, since the devotion to the outdoor myth and the feeling that girls are a problem seem to be very closely related, and both apparently stem from the underestimation among the adults concerned of those gentler and more sensitive qualities which in our society are normally associated with women. Certainly it is worth considering how sure of themselves in the presence of girls and women are some of the men (and some of the women, too, for that matter) who act as social educators, and how varied are the roles which such people can play when associating with girls. If they are uneasy at not always possessing the necessary skills to have a non-courtship relationship with women or girls on a genuinely equal footing, and if this uneasiness transmits itself to the girls, it may give the adults involved an excuse for blaming on others what is really their own disability.

The substitution of a meaningful language for the misconception about 'boys' work' and 'girls' work' has very important practical implications for the place of women in social education. Frequently, even traditionally, their place and the value set upon their work are unmistakably indicated by the way they are designated. In the Youth Service, for example, many are dubbed automatically as 'girls' leaders', and this is often taken to imply that their job is with the girls because girls need separate treatment which a fellow-woman will understand, and that the appointed person can have no contribution to make to the boys' development. Or, the women in a club, are seen simply as appendages to activities – 'girls' P.E.', or 'canteen lady' – with apparently no human relations functions at all.

But in practice it seems certain that for some girls a *man* will make a more suitable worker because, for the particular personalities being served, regardless of their sex, he is a more suitable adult. It could also be that the functions which the women in an organization fulfil – as instructor or canteen lady or girls' leader – are incidental to other services they bring to members, boys and girls. What is important here is *not* primarily that this worker is a woman who therefore will do this range of jobs best for the girls, but that she is an adult with certain traits and skills which seem most appropriate to the needs of this and that young person. The part that a woman has to play in social education may be not firstly as girls' leader or as instructor in activities best suited to girls, but as a sensitive, skilful and mature person capable of discerning and responding appropriately to some of the demands of a growing young person, whether boy or girl, either privately or in the company of his or her peers. Indeed, one might go further. Far from women in the Youth Service being thought of as just 'girls' leaders', for example, they might be recognized simply as youth workers and, with certain boys or groups of boys, it might follow logically that they have a special part to play. It may well be, in fact, that more women capable of doing this are not available to the Youth Service and even to teaching exactly because they suspect they will not be considered for such roles, but will be confined to working with girls.

Thus society would seem to have ample reason not only to introduce girls to men and manly qualities – there is already a host of youth organizations trying to do this – but also to increase boys' contacts with adult women and their appreciation of more 'typically' feminine qualities. Even this, however, cannot be turned into a dogma. What is crucial here is that the adults concerned cease to see themselves as providers of distinctively masculine or feminine types of activity, since such an approach ignores the individuality of an adolescent and seriously inhibits the range of adult work. If, instead, adults regard themselves as working with individual young people, they will be much more likely to discern the most appropriate responses to both girls and boys who at present are not attracted to social education at all, or who are rarely helped by the provision which adults assume their sex requires.

Members' Committees

The language and concepts most commonly used in social education may be said to limit adult thinking about its practice on another, quite different, front. For although social educators agree that they should afford young people the opportunity to gain a first-hand experience of self-government, their interpretation of this, their effort to put it into practice, is usually singularly narrow.

In schools, the actual exercise of responsibility by pupils is dependent on the bestowal of some authority on prefects by adults who retain its ultimate sanctions in their own hands. Also, efforts are made through classes on 'citizenship', 'civics', and 'social studies' to acquaint young people with the more general aspects of the community's elaborate governmental machinery. Youth workers and many teachers, however, have long recognized that no one learns the *sense* of participation in a communal responsibility by a *knowledge* of the machinery, however great this knowledge may be, and that only by experiencing a process of deciding in a group does an individual have the chance of understanding, by extension of feeling, his involvement in the body politic or in any vast corporate entity. And so in the past youth work provision has very frequently aimed to create opportunities for young people to manage their own affairs and to exercise genuine responsibility independent to some degree of adult authority.

And yet the fact that by far the most common youth work expression of this aim is the members' committee suggests misconceptions about what needs to be attempted and what forms need to be established. It is true here again, of course, that this particular method of implementing a general adult intention can and often does offer some young people an experience of self-government which suits them. But adults' great faith in it and their disproportionate dependence on it once again demonstrate that they have allowed preconceptions and a somewhat inflexible language to limit the effectiveness of their work. First-hand experience of and participation in democracy can be gained through many forms of provision, and the members' committee is one such form which is available to the social educator. However, except among mature adolescents or in an organization where it is very well established indeed, this particular form almost demands adult involvement and detailed advice. In practice, therefore, it is often adopted less because it is helpful to young people as a means of controlling their own affairs and more because it is convenient for the adult who wishes on the one hand to give the impression – to his members, to other adults and to himself – that self-government is a feature of his club and with the other to retain a reassuring control of events.

Young people's development towards maturity for their own society is in fact restricted in many cases by the members' committee, since it is a form of self-government which bears no resemblance at all to the media of democracy which young people already know best and are most likely to use outside the youth organization. For it is patently obvious that most of the public policy-making groups which young people know about do not operate on the committee basis. The members' committee is encouraged to function as a forum in which individuals, sometimes elected by fellow-members, consider matters disinterestedly and for the welfare of the club. Cliques and coteries are discouraged; the committee is regarded as a failure if it is dominated by a strong, disciplined group. If its processes are compared with the functioning of local government or with Parliament, it is possible to see at once why many club members regard their committee as a form of democracy entirely unrelated to real life, and possibly designed to occupy their energies harmlessly. It is true that, as adults, they may experience committees which do operate by individuals exercising a concern for the whole as they see it, and voting or speaking accordingly. More often, however, they will see committees consisting of representatives of other interest-groups, who are, if not mandated, at least delegated to safeguard certain concerns, and some *club* committees are indeed composed of representatives of such subgroups in the club.

Adults in social education need to consider both the kinds of democratic government which young people already know about and the other kinds to which they might be introduced. It is likely that, in school, they will know only the government of prefects appointed by authority, although some young people will come through schools experimenting with or using other patterns entirely. Apart from this, the young person's only direct experience of social organization may be in the family and at work. Obviously the structure of the family means that parents can neither be appointed by a process involving the child nor expected to exercise their role in a completely non-authoritarian way. At work, the chain of command in the organization is also established by the time a young person arrives, while in any case his place within any enterprise is hardly likely to permit him to participate in any major decisions affecting its affairs.

The only participatory social organizations young people are likely to know about, then, are local and national government, and, when they leave school, union-management organizations in their place of work. From the local council they are likely to 'learn' very little in the true sense of 'learn', since most of them cannot be involved. All that one can hope is that, because of their rather academic knowledge of the existence of the two-party system, or government-opposition dichotomy, they will be perhaps more prepared for an opportunity to participate in such a system than in any other.

The union-management system, however, they will be participating in, or at least they will be aware of its method of operation after a short time at work. The bargaining system as a test of brute force may be disappearing, and we may be passing as a society into a more advanced, cooperative, relationship between those who manage, in many cases employees themselves, and those who do not. Nonetheless, whatever progress we may make in industrial relations, employees' associations and employers' associations, shop stewards' committees and management committees will continue to exist and will guarantee for some years to come that it will be that form of social organization which will create the strongest impressions on the minds of many young people.

Thus if the social education of the adolescent is to be based on experiences he knows, and if it is then to introduce those which are similar but new, some at least of the schools and clubs concerned will need to devise a form of member participation in the management of the enterprise which resembles the social organization that is met at work. Much action in fact will need to be through management-member committees, not unlike the employer-employee councils in many factories and businesses. In such joint committees, it could be explicitly demonstrated that the club's management committee has responsibilities and objectives which the members do not share, and that the members have concerns and insights which the management should not ignore. Clearly the relationship is not one of employer-employee, but this is one of the first lessons to be learned, one of the first distinctions in social organization to be drawn. What is important is that this very normal pattern in the lives of young people, should, in some clubs at least, be used as a teaching method. It not only asks for participation of a kind which many members understand, but also reflects the actual balance of power or pattern of relationships and responsibilities between management and members. The point is not that one form of democracy is right and others wrong: what is important is that a variety of forms coexist in our own society, that young people need to be prepared for more than just one, and that therefore adults need to conceive of the social-educational media for doing this as flexibly and realistically as possible.

If adults in social education believe that adolescents in general are capable of programming their own leisure, they might also hope to draw some lessons from the settings in which members of the age-group pursue full-time higher education. In most universities and colleges, for example, a very different type of collective relationship with sponsors is found from that which normally exists in the conventional youth organizations. The contemporary social educator may be able to learn far more from the comparatively untrammelled form of communal responsibility enjoyed by the student union than from the patterns worked out in the past by youth workers catering for juveniles and unemancipated adolescents. Though part of a much larger institution and subject ultimately to the surveillance and even at times the veto of adult sponsors, students find in their unions a freedom to govern and a scope for independent action which is customarily denied most 'youth club' members. They handle thousands of pounds each year and account for this money themselves, they book leading dance bands and star American cabaret artists, they stock a bar and control its use, they negotiate with their sponsors and intercede on behalf of members. In the broadest sense, they will carry economic, social and political responsibilities which will provide some of the most real experiences of self-government.

Together with comparable, self-governing institutions – Young Farmers' Clubs and Young Conservative Clubs, Working Men's Clubs and Country Clubs – the student youth clubs suggest conceptions of adolescent management of their own affairs rarely approached in the remainder of social education. Clearly the analogy can never be complete. Both school clubs and youth clubs cater for younger members than the other social-educational agencies mentioned, so that more active adult involvement with and support for the young people concerned is often appropriate within a pattern of self-government. Youth clubs and organizations, again, will almost always cover fewer aspects of a young person's life than will most student unions. It is certain, however, that even in the present Youth Service more responsibility could be delegated if adults – both management committees and actual workers in the clubs – were less fearful of diminishing their own areas of authority, less in need of seeing their own wishes put into practice.

Such an approach, however, conflicts with many deeply entrenched views about adolescent social education. It calls into question some of the commonest adult attitudes to financing the necessary provision since there exists a sharp contrast, for example, between the way the costs of running a youth club and a student union are met. Indeed, participation in union life is thought to be so important a feature of a student's education that society goes out of its way to encourage it. It does this firstly by including in student grants an amount intended to cover the membership fee, thus often making membership compulsory, and then by providing buildings and equipment whose style and quality could be afforded only by the most exceptional of youth centres. Moreover, because of the manner of financing a student's involvement and because of the extent of his direct and indirect personal contribution to his club's funds, a degree of personal commitment and 'ownership' is implied which very few youth clubs, mainly dependent as they are on impersonal subsidy by a distant 'authority', can hope to purvey. Adult assumptions about the financing of social education in colleges and universities are thus much less likely to cause the 'we-them' attitudes which are so common among members of conventional youth organizations, and, in consequence, make it more usual for students to expect to undertake full and direct responsibility for their own affairs.

If the methods of government of the student unions were adopted for use in other social-educational settings, there would clearly be significant consequences for adult-adolescent relationships. For, although youth workers and teachers would still be deeply involved, especially where younger adolescents were concerned, they would need, even more than they do for other reasons, to think of their roles more in terms of stewardship and counselling than of authoritarian leadership. Their positive dictation of affairs could be considerably less, and there would be the opportunity for many more of the springs of spontaneous adolescent action, for many more of the grass-roots of young adult leadership to be tapped.

Social educators' preoccupation, then, with the language of members' committees unduly restricts their provision of forms of self-government by young people. However, their attention is also distracted from the purpose of self-government in social education by the committee language of agenda, of decision, of proper procedure. This is a constant reminder that a committee is normally established only to make effective administration possible and that, in order to be reliable and consistent over a long period, it must proceed according to agreed conventions. But in social education self-government is designed much more to provide young people with a vehicle for fuller growth to maturity. The criteria of efficiency applicable to an adult committee apply equally to a well-experienced committee of young people. But an adolescent group deserves other criteria when it is learning to manage its own affairs: it is not always composed of experienced and responsible young people (nor are adult committees for that matter), and since it is operating as an educational medium as well as an administrative one it must be judged accordingly. In particular, it is important for the adult to understand that, judged by educational standards, conflict can be valuable whether it occurs between young person and young person or between members and sponsor or manager. For enforced orderliness may be useless, and, although good administration requires committee decisions and so demands that order come out of chaos and compromise out of conflict, the conflict itself can teach many lessons. Thus, in a group which is partly an educational medium, concern for efficiency must at times be neglected in order that what is valuable in temporarily unresolved disagreement can be gained. It takes substantial experience for a group to achieve harmony for the right reasons – that is, not out of deference, or fear, or inarticulateness, but as a consequence of dignified concession and a reasoned standing of one's ground. Whether the group is formally a committee or not, harmony will not come easily if inexpert participants are numerous. For harmony is not the absence of conflict but its resolution, and a committee of individuals all expected to reach decisions for the general good is not always a suitable medium for learning such a difficult lesson.

Too many adults regard situations of conflict as disastrous, especially when they bring members and sponsors face to face. Often they see them as an indication of their own failure to get members to make 'good' decisions, or dismiss the young people concerned as 'bad' on the grounds that they are 'irresponsible'. Once again, however, there is no absolute definition of what is good and responsible in this context. Many actions now judged 'good' were only committed because some citizens were prepared to behave 'irresponsibly' and to be dubbed 'bad' by some of their contemporaries. On the grander scale, the barons who humbled the king at Runnymede, the men who rejected Charles I's 'tyranny' and who later carried through the 'revolution' of 1688, the suffragettes – all these may today be seen as contributors to a democratic tradition. Yet their contemporaries would have been conscious not so much of their loyalty to the established order as of their criticism and ultimate rejection of it. Though methods of expressing 'irresponsibility' will usually differ, the same principle may well apply in the much smaller organization of a youth club. The irritating young people who ask awkward questions about those who manage the club, criticize the programme vehemently, find themselves repeatedly in conflict with the adults, and doubt the wisdom of their policies, may all be judged to be fitting in badly, not seeing their role as members of the community clearly and therefore not learning the lessons of good citizenship. Sometimes their opposition *is* so persistent and unreasonable, and so anti-socially expressed, that it *is* they who are showing the signs of poor adjustment. But it is hardly possible that it is *they* every time. It could be that it is as often the organization which is failing to adjust, and that the accusation of 'bad citizenship' and unsuitability for self-government made against the young person is in fact a defence behind which the discomforted and personally affronted adult retires.

The social educator, in fact, needs to see conflict, not necessarily as a dreadful evil to be eradicated as completely and quickly as possible, but as an inevitable consequence of the concession of any degree of self-government to young people. It is a part, in fact, of the human circumstances in which he will have to work and at times a positive vehicle of the learning which he hopes will occur. Conflict, tension, the clash of personalities and opinions, are not always or only destructive forces. They enable a number of important and valuable opportunities for development to occur. A situation in which two people openly and strongly differ makes it possible for each of them to define, perhaps for the first time in a conscious way, the ideas that each has, and to test their worth by articulation and defence against the rebuttal of the other person. At the end of the discussion or argument, they may know much better what they really believe and even why they believe it. Or again, the clash between people in a group over what the group wishes to do and who is to lead it will enable a number of people to test out the degree of acceptability to other people of their own personal ideas and influence. Once more, the conclusion could be that both of the contenders for status have discovered more that is true about themselves, seen more of their actual impact on other people, had more of their false self-images exposed, than they could had the conflict never occurred.

Harmony and good fellowship are warming and reassuring experiences. On the basis of them, a good deal of learning will always go on. But if they are all that people ever experience, other learning will not occur because the opportunities for it will not be available. In any case, outside an educational organization young people experience much else besides harmony, so that if they are protected or inhibited by such organizations, they are not being given a meaningful and constructive preparation for their own society. Intrigue, power-seeking, the adjustment of personality to personality and policy to policy – in fact, 'politics', in all its senses – are not unfortunate and degrading: they are real and inevitable in the meeting of human beings in groups and so in young people's experience of life.

To short-circuit living experiences for the young in case they find them disturbing is not, in fact, necessarily to do them any service. For, *all* true learning may at some time involve disturbance and pain, since the fitting of some new piece of knowledge or understanding into established schemes of ideas and practices does challenge and create tension and disquiet, both for individuals and groups. Cooperation, compromise, corporate responsibility are not easily or painlessly learned, and young people will not thank the adult for pretending that they are, or for truncating the learning process of human tension and strife in the name of sound administration.

The Abuse of 'Groups'

The language of social education has recently acquired a new set of concepts which, though of considerable value to its practitioners, are nonetheless open to substantial misinterpretation and misapplication. These concepts are rooted in the need, on both practical and educational grounds, for the social educator to use as the main medium of his work the relationships which young people form in groups. However, some adults, in an effort to adopt this approach, embark on their social-educational practice as if they can specify certain forms of group membership, certain kinds of shared goals and common interest as the only ones through which they personally will work. The adult, in this case, attempts to define the type of group which is suitable for his social-educational work by asserting in advance that it must have certain characteristics: or rather he asserts that, if a group he meets is to be accepted by him as a medium for the social education of its members, he must perceive it as having a certain kind of purpose, ethos and network of relationships. He then becomes the judge of whether any group is potentially or actually valuable for the attainment of one or more of the limited number of ends deemed by him to be 'social-educational'.

'Group work' in this sense, therefore, represents something very much less flexible and productive than the interpretation given to the phrase later in this book and indeed by many other practitioners and writers. When misconstrued, in fact, and used to give expression to adult pre-conceptions about what they will do in social-educational situations, group work becomes merely another device with which practitioners arm themselves before they ever come into contact with the individual young people who want their services. In other educational fields – in the grammar school or technical college, for example – it may well be justifiable to predetermine the setting, content and even the membership of a teaching situation in this way, since an adult may be able to foresee in detail that certain facts and ideas will have to be communicated and will definitely be needed by certain pupils or students. In social education, however, because such a forecast cannot be made with any confidence, it is seriously misleading to suggest that only particular definable types of relationship pattern or group goals exhibit the features necessary for particular adults to work through them.

It is largely the way in which the word 'group' is used in social education which leads to misconceptions about how the worker might actually operate. At the root of the misunderstanding seems to be an assumption shared by many adults that only two 'types' of group are worthy of recognition. One is the activity group, formed initially to foster a particular interest or develop a particular skill and put directly under the supervision or instruction of an adult selected primarily for his ability to achieve this end. At times, admittedly, allowance is made for the fact that while the skill is being imparted or the interest stimulated, much else in the way of experience may be derived also. Nonetheless, it seems a regular practice among social educators to ignore this 'bonus', or, if it is acknowledged, to treat it as irrelevant. In fact, because in this context too the conventional attitudes to 'activities' tend to operate, such a group is often taken to be the supreme, and perhaps even the only legitimate, educational group experience.

The other 'type' of adolescent group, which is sometimes also said to have a supreme or exclusive value, is the so-called 'friendship group', the 'natural' groupings which young people form when left to themselves and which they use above all as means of expressing their sociability. These, it is sometimes claimed, the adult must recognize, accept, 'work with' and perhaps occasionally 'stretch'. In these groups, young people will get their most 'real' experience. Because they are principally *social* groups, and because this particular form of education is concerned to develop social skills, they are assumed by some adults to have an inherent perfection which gives them a clear pre-eminence.

These two contrasting images of 'group' are often made to seem mutually exclusive and so tend to produce a great deal of reciprocated antagonism and mistrust. What could be simply aids to adult thinking about the settings in which they will work come to be seen as actual methods of working quite different from and indeed rivalling each other. Yet in practice, the two settings are not exclusive, since 'activity' elements and 'associational' elements always coexist in any group. At times the expression of one of these elements may seem to be so strong that it may appear to an adult that some particular gathering of young people completely lacks the other element. However, the young people concerned will be experiencing a better balance of the two elements, inextricable as they are, than the outsider may perceive, and in any case whichever element predominates, the setting can still provide the social educator with a valuable means of fulfilling his purpose.

For, within what the onlooker may class as a formal or semi-formal activity group, the skilled worker can offer all the opportunities which are necessary for young people to achieve the social maturity which in Chapter 4 we suggested ought to be his aim. In such a group there can be, alongside the acquisition of a skill, experiences of setting a purpose and testing whether it is realistic, of accepting responsibility and exercising

I

authority, of coping with conflicts between individuals and helping to resolve the tensions which are engendered. The depth and degree of 'activity' experience may at times be less if ample opportunities for these other experiences are to be created, but both are closely related, in fact normally completely interwoven, and what is to be gained from both can be had simultaneously.

In the 'friendship group', too, such experiences can be concurrent. Because these groups are 'natural' they are not perfect; because they are 'social' they are not devoid of activity. The sociability may be dependent upon a common activity, but being 'sociable' in itself implies intensive activity of an important kind. It brings into play a large number of skills – verbal skills, skill in projecting one's own personality and in grasping the differences between one's own view of oneself and that of others. It makes possible an exploration of personal ability, a testing of personal potential in an accepting atmosphere among people who are exploring and equally uncertain and yet open to new ideas. It enables participants to discover what is and what is not permissible in their relationships with their own and with the opposite sex, what is appropriate humour and when serious response is needed. It enables them, too, to discover which ways of behaving are normal, which ones break conventional codes acceptably and which break them unacceptably. Much that a poised and capable adult simply takes for granted, many of the social skills which to him are second nature, have to be learned through their own group experiences by young people in their teens.

As membership of an 'associational' group requires participation in activity and the practice of many skills, and as membership of an 'activity' group means involvement in many relationships, it is unrealistic for an adult to conceive of two 'types' of group with fundamental differences from each other. An adult cannot make up his mind in advance about the characteristics which a group ought to exhibit. For as a social educator he has a responsibility to individual young people whatever group goals and relationships are seen by him to exist at any particular moment. Moreover a group primarily concerned at first to carry out an activity together may move, either after conscious decision or without any deliberate plan, towards a widening of its scope and may seek new experiences and wish to test new outlets. Or a group which originally simply enjoyed each other's company may find itself going beyond the initial purpose which brought its members together, and turn its energies to acquiring other than social skills: its purpose may become more specific, its product in a sense more material. Though this does not mean that either element in the original intentions was unjustified, it does not mean that either gathering has been transformed into an essentially different 'type' of group.

The fact is that any adult who attempts to determine the setting of his work simply by defining beforehand a kind of group experience which will enable him to be helpful to young people must very seriously handicap his social-educational practice. Such predetermination fails to allow for the real complexity and changeability of human relationships and for the variety of individual experience derived from them, and thus needlessly blinkers a social educator's attitude towards his work. For he cannot say: 'The groups with which I am concerned must all exhibit certain common characteristics. When young people do not do so, the fact that they are mixing with one another for another purpose is irrelevant to me and I cannot work with them'. For, at one moment, in one set of circumstances, some young people will congregate in one way with one kind of purpose in mind, and will 'do' something through a clear-cut and formally established structure. However, at another moment, in different circumstances, some – perhaps the same people, perhaps some of the same ones with some others, perhaps altogether different ones – will come together with another kind of purpose and form entirely: 'merely' to associate, to 'enjoy each other's company'. In between and even beyond each of these extremes, many other gatherings with many other purposes are possible. The value of these processes cannot be determined simply by referring to the labels arbitrarily attached to them by adults, since one group may have a clearly defined structure, shape and size, and yet lack any regular or constant aim, while another group which does have a precise aim and end-product may display little conscious organization.

Indeed, a 'group' need not even have an existence except in the mind and eye of the onlooker. The actual relevance of the word to a number of individuals who have relationships with each other may depend on nothing more than the highly personal judgment of someone completely detached from the feelings and opinions of those he is judging, and so in no way expressing their own interpretation of their situation. Though an articulated or implied common purpose and a mutually accepted structure do often give to people in association a consciousness that they have a form of unity, frequently their association occurs so spontaneously and is so transient that the individuals involved may in no way be conscious that the network of their contacts constitutes an entity which might be called a group. To others outside their own circle they may appear to be a group, but their behaviour and their self-image may in no way be affected by this.

Moreover the social educator whose conception of any group suitable for his own ends is crystallized in advance is in danger of not discerning what his response to some young people needs to be. If he always thinks of individuals as members of 'X' or 'Y' groups, or only contacts them as members of such groups, he may well be failing to discharge the whole of his responsibility to them. For young people above all, whether in 'class' rooms, youth clubs or in coffee bars, on motor-cycles, on dance-floors, or in the theatre, experience a wide variety of shifting as well as constant, accidental as well as deliberate, unconscious as well as conscious, influences and associations with other young people. Those concerned for their welfare will not automatically assume beforehand that they know which of these experiences always offers the most favourable opportunity for growth and self-realization. Rather, they will be flexible enough to respond as and when the interests of any one of the young people involved in these group situations requires them to do so.

The situations in which young people learn are thus highly complex, subtle, varied and changing, and so can hardly be prepared for simply by the adult imagining particular types of group settings and then acting as if these were perfect representations of the real circumstances he will meet. Young people do congregate in groups and spend a great deal of their leisure in association with contemporaries, and they gain immeasurably from doing so. Their meetings and relationships, therefore, provide any social educator with invaluable media through which to work, and give him reason to think of himself as a 'group worker'. However, the educational opportunities with which these meetings and relationships present him are in important respects both transient and unexpected. Even if there were definable 'types' of group, it would be impossible for the social educator to forecast which kind of goal and networks of relationships would exist among a particular group of young people on any occasion. Any attempt to prefabricate the pattern of his actions and reactions in a group setting would diminish the flexibility of response which is essential. The adult who specifies in advance the characteristics which groups must exhibit is therefore not only misconstruing the meaning of 'group work'. He is also adopting a concept of social-educational practice as restrictive as those others dicussed earlier in this chapter.

1. J. HANMER, *Girls at Leisure*, London Union of Youth Clubs and London Young Women's Christian Association, 1964, p. 17.
2 Ibid., p. 17.
3. Ibid., p. 66.
4. Ibid., pp. 66-7.

Chapter 6

Towards a Client-Centred Practice

A Change of Language

In this book so far we have attempted, against a historical and sociological backcloth, to examine the aims of social education and some of the ways in which its actual content is conceived and discussed. We have seen that social educators' statements and actions often assume that there are certain exact points which must be reached by young people and certain well-mapped paths which cannot fail to take them to these points. Thus the activating concept in the minds of many social educators is a model which not only exemplifies what the young should become, but also to some extent prescribes how they should be helped towards it.

It is the argument of this book, however, that such a model-centred approach to the social education of the adolescent is no longer appropriate. Those who work with young people need no longer employ the language of activities, measurement systems, girls' work, members' committees and 'types' of group simply because it embodies their own personal faiths, interests and enthusiasms. The conceptual framework produced by this language is incapable of conveying the wide variety of paths by which the current aims of social education can be pursued and attained. To speak in terms of this or that model is therefore to take up a rule-of-thumb prescription which is bound to be appropriate only to a small proportion of groups of young people, and is thus more of a limitation than a guide.

More positively, therefore, the suggestion of this book is that the paths of progress for adolescents' social education must be decided primarily by the requirements and expectations of the young people with whom an adult is actually working, according to the circumstances in which these young people actually find themselves. It is true, of course, that neither the personality and philosophy of the worker nor the demands of the society which to some degree he represents can simply be ignored, and we shall argue strongly in the following chapter that their influence needs to be acknowledged and their exact place carefully discerned. However, in any search for guidance and sanction on what ought to be provided for the young and what the end-product ought to be, the potentiality and needs of the young people themselves must now receive the major emphasis. Hence the open-ended definition of purpose in terms of young people's maturity for their own society which was offered in Chapter 4. And hence, too, the criticism of prescribed patterns of practice and abstracted formulae for action which we advanced in the last chapter, and the claim there that realistic adult responses can be determined only after the young people concerned are known and to some degree understood. If those in their teens are to have available to them a service which is meaningful and productive, such an orientation on the clients and their situation is essential. Short-cut, mass-produced solutions are inadequate.

Thus, social-educational practice needs to be carried out within a framework which is *client-centred* rather than *model-centred*. The discrepancy between these two approaches is not of course absolute and clear-cut, but client-centred work involves an attitude to young people, to their potentiality and to the possibilities of releasing this potentiality which is strikingly at variance with the attitude which underlies work done in a model-centred way.

Model-Centred Social Education

Clearly there is nothing sinister about adults working to recruit others, whether young or old, to their own interests and values, and to see others following in their footsteps. To help others gain where one has gained oneself is a common, indeed a normal, phenomenon in our society and as such is open to no criticism. What is more, there is a host of young people very grateful for having met such campaigning adults and having been fired by their enthusiasm. Though the benefit derived from the contact of an enthusiastic adult with a willing young person is in a sense unreliable and haphazard, since it is entirely dependent on the accident of their meeting, it frequently means that the young person has an opportunity to undergo an experience which otherwise he would have missed. The educational advance which this makes possible should not be underestimated.

What does seem dubious, however, is that such adults should comprise the staff of what is intended to be a young person's general social club in a district. For then the young person does not get what he bargained for, which was a chance to be sociable, to spread his own wings, to discover his own needs and express his own choices. Had he gone in the first place to a club which said over the door 'amateur dramatics' or 'judo club', he might reasonably expect the staff to have fairly clear ideas about the way he would wish to spend his time. However, in joining an organization or society for its general social (or perhaps social-*educational*) amenities, he would seem entitled to expect much less pressure and adult organization of that time than in fact he often encounters.

Moreover, model-centred social education often means that young people, because they can afford little other educational or commercial provision in an area, have to put up with quite a slice of what they do not want in order to get out of a youth club or society what they do. Stated like this, their dilemma appears to be a commonplace of daily life. But in fact a large part of what they do not want is *justifiably* not wanted. It is undesirable as a part of social education because it consists of adults suiting their own ends, pushing their own interests, advocating their own ideas and views of the world, in a setting purporting to be for the benefit of young people. As the Bow Group pamphlet, *Responsibility for Youth*, pointed out in 1961, 'This compact is fundamentally unsound'.[1] The results are cynicism in the young who go through pleasing motions in order to get their deserts at the end of the day, and either self-delusion or despair in the adults. It would be more honest, and more beneficial to young people, if the adults who wish to popularize their own hobbies and hobby-horses worked under a banner which proclaimed the nature of the relationship they wish to make. They need to say quite categorically that they act as specialists campaigning for adherents to their enthusiasms, as men and women putting sectional views to all they can attract.

Some adolescents badly need an all-absorbing enthusiasm, of course, and although contact with adults is by no means the only way in which they can 'catch' one, there is every reason why they and the adults who can service them should meet to their mutual benefit outside social-educational settings. For no one would deny their right to be entirely wrapped up in their hobbies. It is when the adults meet such young people (or any others) within a social-educational setting that they have a responsibility to try to communicate their hobbies and interests only when these hobbies and interests would genuinely help the social education of the particular adolescent.

Much of the social education which is available to young people, then, is offered by society through adults who conceive of their work in terms of proliferating the enthusiasms and interests which give meaning and coherence to their own lives. Far more often than not, such social education is carried out at no financial cost to society by part-time youth workers and by teachers taking unpaid extracurricular 'activities' at school. While we may take pride in the willingness of so many adults to give up time to what they see as the needs of young people, it is pertinent to ask if society is unwittingly paying another price. For young people are being served often as part of another process: the reinforcement by certain self-selected adults of their own model concept. Social education of this kind permits young people to be subject to the attentions of adults whose own satisfaction comes when young people take up particular pursuits or beliefs. The range of possible enthusiasms is so great of course that if any young person were exposed to them all he would have a great deal of choice left to him. However, the actual experience of any one young person is far more likely to include a contact with only one or two adults in social education, so that the pressure is to 'progress' only towards their models.

For the fact is that at present social education attracts a disproportionate number of such adults, model-centred and peddling their own enthusiasms because they believe in them. A service which should offer opportunities for specialist enthusiasms among a general, much broader educational provision centred on the client's personal needs and relationships, is in fact offering to many young people an arbitrary – because it depends on what the adults of the district feel like peddling – selection of special or sectional enthusiasms. Provision of this kind is of course a political and financial necessity. Even in schools, and certainly in the Youth Service, funds do not permit the paid provision of general client-centred work whenever volunteers do not come forward, and volunteers naturally include a large number of model-centred adults who wish to spread their enthusiasm, hobby or belief among as many young people as they can attract. Moreover, since so much of the paid staff in social education (especially in the Youth Service) has been recruited from these volunteers, model-centred adults abound among both paid and unpaid workers.

Nonetheless, initially a challenge must be mounted to the fundamental assumption that the social development of young people can be helped in a disinterested way by adults whose motive is to proliferate a model. To service young people's social education is more difficult than this, because desirable forms of 'human nature', desirable expressions of it in behaviour, and desirable means of attaining these expressions are infinitely variable and not reducible to types or models. While there is a place in social education for some such adults, it requires most of its staff to have a subtler conception of their role. Anything calling itself a service to young people must surely reduce, both in proportion and in total, the number of adults within it who are seeking to fashion young people according to models.

A few determinedly model-centred adults will never wish to approach young people otherwise and their attitude will not be changed by denial or even probably by training. Their point of view is certainly sincere and frequently well worked out, since many of them would maintain that their particular approach *is* the one best designed to meet *all* young people's social-educational needs. However, as social education is defined in this book, the extensiveness and benefit of their contribution would seem to be limited to that of a specialist in certain fields with certain precise but confined objectives. No one will deny the place of such adults in a comprehensive social-educational provision for young people, if they establish, or work within, an agency proclaiming itself to be for the pursuit of particular enthusiasms only. Nor indeed will anyone deny their place if, like the special counter run by an exclusive cosmetic or jewellery firm in what is otherwise a comprehensive department store, they set out, within an institution or area which offers good general provision, to proselytize on behalf of their own special enthusiasms. What must be doubted, however, is their predominance within a service which in any case has the resources to cater for only a small proportion of the young people who might have need of it.

Yet not all social educators are irrevocably model-centred, and not all adults who have enthusiasms or hobbies or beliefs bring them into their social-educational work. Many adult enthusiasts who have a clear model of what they want themselves and perhaps their children to be, succeed in serving other young people in an entirely disinterested way, and, presumably, so could many more if they were given an alternative way of approaching their job and an alternative conceptual framework. There are indeed few model-centred adult workers who would not examine and respond to a different conception of their functions, if this were presented in a meaningful language which offered a real alternative to the familiar vocabulary of their subject or enthusiasm. In fact, while still talking of their work in model-centred terms, many adults may be gaining satisfaction and success already from practising in a client-centred way to which they have been led by their own personality, by accident or by force of circumstances. Their adherence to client-centred criteria, however, is likely to be inconsistent and incidental, since they may well abandon them when they become aware that an action dictated by the needs of the clients conflicts with their own desire to have young people approach nearer their model.

Training facilities do exist, of course, but for both youth workers and teachers too many of these, by concentrating on induction into a particular enthusiasm or belief, purvey model-centred approaches and use a model-centred language. What are required much more, however, are courses which would make proselytizing, building according to models and the promotion of particular hobbies all secondary to the prime object of a service to young people as they are, with the expectations and requirements they bring with them. Model-centred workers need to be offered a vocabulary and a set of concepts for thinking in an equally systematic way about their clients, and principles, understanding and a discipline to guide a more disinterested response to them. Since no alternative sovereign concept has been open to them but their own pursuit or belief, their habit has in the past inevitably been to see young people in the terms of their own enthusiasm, rather than to see their own enthusiasm as only one among a whole range of possibilities open to each young person they meet.

There is, then, no hard and fast dividing line between model and client-centred approaches to social education. Some adults can be recognized as extreme representatives of either one or the other, but many embody elements of both with only a difference of emphasis in practice separating them. No absolute dichotomy can or ought to be established, no attempt ought to be made to separate model and client-centred types of relationship completely, as if each actual practitioner were either wholly one sort of worker or wholly another. To do this would be, once again, to ignore the complexities of human personalities. Nonetheless, at present in social education the emphasis seems disproportionately on models and apparently needs redressing a good deal. If this is to happen, however, predominently client-centred practice needs a more appropriate theoretical framework.

A Framework for Client-Centred Practice

What is needed is something to take the place of the misleading language of model-centred work, and its somewhat simple mode of conceptualizing the content of social education. Since the client-centred worker cannot measure his practice against a model for young people's development, he needs another framework for guiding and evaluating what he is doing. This will have two essential elements: one of these must be an understanding of the experiences which social education entails and the other a set of principles appropriate to the work. The understanding called for will be deeper and more conscious than that derived from an intuitive response to everyday events: it will have to be enriched therefore by the accumulated experience of practitioners and by the work of the human scientists. The principles will be deduced from an analysis of the relationship between three interrelated elements of the social educator's situation: the society within which he operates, the wants and needs of the young people he serves, and his own attitudes, abilities and feelings. It will be the fusion of these principles and this understanding in the mind of the social educator which will give him the necessary discipline to guide his ongoing practice.

Much of this framework social educators *as a body* undoubtedly already have. Out of what they have acquired from their sensitive responses to life in general, as well as from what they actually do in their social-educational work, can emerge a body of recorded and recalled empirical knowledge of unchallengeable authenticity. For this to happen, however, each adult still needs to become much more self-conscious about the well-founded judgments which experience and insight make possible. He must make yet more fully available in a more orderly way, first to himself and then to others, what his 'natural' shrewdness, his 'common' sense, his 'native' wit tell him. The 'knack' he has with young people must be worked out, its principles articulated, his understanding brought to the surface of his consciousness and all contributed to the pool of systematized knowledge. What is intuitive and unexplained is certainly not to be scorned or disregarded, but it needs to be more fully verbalized and ordered.

For, in the first place, the understanding of human relationships needs to look beyond the personal experience of any individual worker or group of workers. It will need to take into account, and indeed to be refined by, what the human sciences can teach. Their contribution is not to be exaggerated, since much of the knowledge derived from them is still tentative, and in any case a proportion of it will either have no relevance to the everyday preoccupations of the youth worker or teacher, or will be beyond his training and competence to understand and apply. Nonetheless, a great deal of what the human scientists have established cannot simply be ignored by social educators, however challenging it may be to traditional practices and modes of thought, since it can add significantly to their appreciation of what young people are seeking, doing, lacking.

It is important to be clear about the nature of the help which the social educator can gain from such an understanding of human behaviour. If he is hoping to gain from it a set of certain answers and predetermined responses he will be disappointed. It can however help him to illuminate what is involved in the complex human situations he meets, and it can clarify the range of alternative ways of reacting to these, but it is categorically not a collection of hints and tips passed from one worker to another as if they had a universal and timeless application. For it has regard to the indeterminate number of variables which cause each successive human situation to be distinctively different from the last and which make it impossible for one educator to fit the procedure of work, the habits, programmes and approaches of another educator, in their entirety, into his own unique experience. It is not the type of learning which assumes only one correct reflex action to a particular stimulus or situation – which teaches that to stop a car a brake must be depressed and no other action is appropriate, or that to call an ambulance 999 must be dialled. To claim, for example, that in order to prepare for a members' committee meeting one need only learn the rules of committee procedure is again to ignore the human relations element of any learning situation, and so to overlook the key factor in a client-centred approach. It is rather like saying that, in order to treat a chest complaint, all a doctor needs to know is how to put a stethoscope in his ears and where to tap the patient. For what the doctor eventually prescribes derives only partly from this visible activity, much more from his interpretation of what he hears. Though circumscribed by the sanctions imposed by his own personal views and feelings and by his society, as well as by the needs of his patient, the doctor needs to retain the maximum degree of flexibility in order to act as, and only as, his understanding of what he hears indicates. No amount of preconceived personal conviction or idealism about what the patient *ought* to do or *may* require can be allowed to divert him from any decision which may follow a careful consideration of the evidence gathered from his examination.

Such analogies with the medical profession need to be handled cautiously, for they only indicate in general terms how the social educator might approach his task. Within a large number of the personal relationships and social problems of a school or youth organization it is impossible to say why one event occurred or what the precise outcome of another will be – and any one of a very large number of prescriptions may satisfy the clients' needs. Nonetheless, though the diagnosis-and-response approach may not be exactly reproducible by the social educator, it indicates some of the ways in which he might work. For the client-centred adult in social education will need to accept that regardless of how certain he feels in advance about what any particular individual or group needs, some form of 'examination' may be necessary before he can decide what to do. And although he needs to make his interpretations only in the light of the 'evidence', the social educator will rely as much as the doctor on evidence which he cannot strictly see or feel: he will have to make some judgments based on inferred conditions of mind and body quite as much as the doctor does. Moreover, the social educator's interpretations will not concern merely the dramatic or bizarre: they will predominantly be about immediate practical issues of everyday occurrence, connected with the roles of other adults, the functioning of activity groups, the involvement of well-established members, the absorption of newcomers. An open-minded approach will be necessary at all times for the adult seeking to make a truly client-centred approach to young people.

It is important to note, however, that mere acquaintance with an understanding of human behaviour does not ensure that the practice of social education will be primarily client-centred. For, by itself, it offers no assurance to the society in which the adult operates, and which has legitimate expectations of him, that it will in general find the ways in which he applies his understanding acceptable. Nor even does it guarantee his clients that its employment will be appropriate to their expectations and needs. For such understanding is neutral in the sense that, in itself, it implies no special aims, inherent in it is no body of ethical considerations to indicate whether it is being used in accordance with society's and young people's basic ideas. Knowledge about how people function individually and about how they relate to one another can be put to ends very much at variance with those to which a worker's sponsors or his surrounding community subscribe. At one extreme, for example, it could be utilized to achieve a Fascist ideal, which would conflict clearly with the objectives of most social education in Britain today. Such an extreme example illustrates, without requiring any detailed definition of social acceptability, that understanding of the human sciences does not of itself give the social educator a guiding framework with built-in principles of work. Indeed, strictly, no such understanding has concepts of what is 'virtuous' and what is 'evil' contained within it and on its own it constitutes a quite sterile help for the practitioner.

In order to give it direction, to enable it to be applied acceptably and appropriately, it needs a set of occupational principles which will show the worker what is indicated by his responsibilities to his society in general, to his clients and to himself as a mature and independent human being. The social educator must fashion something comparable with the occupational principles which circumscribe the doctor's freedom of action and indicate his ethical responsibilities. The principles need to be sought deliberately and articulated explicitly. If he has only an unrelated understanding of human beings, without a clearly-stated set of occupational principles to guide his application of it, his task may well seem indistinguishable from those sharing his academic discipline, like, for example, the advertising practitioner or the lecturer in social science.

Such an occupational code cannot simply be imposed from without. It needs to be evolved by those in the field from what they have shown to be the best and most successful forms of practice. The assessment of this practice may well be more reliable and accurate if it is measured, again, against what can be learned from the human sciences. But if the principles are to be really appropriate, if they are to offer a guide which is truly helpful, they must be deduced empirically by practitioners from what they actually do. Establishing such an occupational framework cannot be an academic process carried on by intellectuals with no day-by-day knowledge of the actual relationships between social educators and young people formed amidst the pressures of society. It cannot be made up from a collection of abstract concepts and theoretical ideas. It can only come if workers themselves deliberately articulate what they know or believe to be good or proper conduct in their work.

This articulation is needed for two reasons. One is that although any individual worker who wishes to centre his approach on his clients must work out for himself the reference points he wishes to keep in sight, he cannot do this in isolation. A small group with varied experience is perhaps the best medium to bring out verbal and open expression of the principles. The other reason is that social education generally at present badly needs to become conscious of such principles, in order both to interpret its function to the public at large and to help new recruits to see how best their full or part-time efforts can serve young people and society. Only practitioners already in the field (again, whether full or part-time) can give meaning and authority to this process. Only if they join in the dicussion and give voice to what are the principles of their best work can a code of occupational practice be forged.

How can this code be deduced from practice? What, for example, are the guiding principles which derive from the fact that an adult serves young people to social educational ends within a democratic society? The contrast which we attempted to outline in Chapter 2 with what might have been expected of him had he worked in Britain seventy-five or a hundred years ago would indicate some of these, and a contrast with, say, China or the United States of America today would indicate some others. On what are his relationships with young people based? What can be learned by comparing them with the relationship of parent to child, of policeman to young offender, of young person to boy or girl friend? Or again, what principles are involved when a social educator relates acceptably with his sponsors, or with other community workers, or with parents of members, or with his own staff?

Though no simple or precise answers are possible, these are some of the questions which the following chapters assume to be fundamental. No code can be evolved which will be dogmatic or eternal, or even necessarily uniform. It will be useless to look to the most learned academic or to the longest-serving youth worker or teacher as if any of these could act as the fount of wisdom in this matter. But over the years, assumptions have been made and attitudes have evolved (especially in youth work) about what constitutes the 'best' actions, 'good' practice, 'proper' conduct of the work. A great deal is now acknowledged by implication as being right and wrong, correct and incorrect, acceptable and unacceptable. Certain very basic principles are discernible, often stated and widely agreed to; still others might be propounded if workers in the field reflected upon and examined what underpins and what circumscribes their work.

Thus the decision about what action should follow any 'interpretation' of a social-educational situation, if it is to be appropriate and acceptable, will need to be made as consciously as that interpretation itself and will also be subject to guidance from an analysis of responsibilities. The range of alternative decisions which may be more or less 'right' will be wide.

But again, too, by working within a frame of reference, the social educator will be more likely to react according to the realities of a problem or a human circumstance, and so select out of all the possible answers the one most fitting to what a client or clients need. The adult's responses are thus modified by reference to an understanding of human relationships which is broader, and to principles of guidance which are more reliable, than individual experience can offer. This understanding thus seeks to illuminate rather than to prescribe practice, and the principles reveal how wide is the range of possible lines of action and 'correct' responses. They do not remove from the practitioner, as any manual of suggestions or correct procedures of work seem to do, the pressing responsibility on him ultimately to make his own personal decisions about how to act or, on some occasions, to refrain from acting.

In order that his understanding and principles really affect his work and relationships, the practitioner will have to make continuous and deliberate reference to them and seek guidance from them in as self-conscious and detached a way as he can. Amid the pressures and uncertainties of his ongoing practice, the forging and perpetual exercise of a discipline by the use of such principles and understanding will be essential. By working consciously according to a discipline rooted in an understanding of human relations and in principles deduced from the best occupational practice, and by adopting the conceptual framework which the two together will provide, social educators will be enabled to take a somewhat more detached view of what happens when they encounter young people.

Many adults who work with young people may be suspicious of the deliberation and the calculation which this sort of practice involves. But warmth of response and personal concern for young people are clearly essential to any successful youth work or teaching. Moreover, no retreat from spontaneity is inherent in the use of a discipline, and the social educator, because he is a *social* educator, must be involved, must act and respond immediately and in a recognizably sensitive way. In fact, in the sense in which the word is used here, detachment has nothing at all to do with coldness or indifference. To stand aside from the complexities of a human situation and see it with some degree of objectivity does not necessarily mean that one is unmoved or careless of what may happen to the people so deeply embroiled. Such objectivity is rather a means of making more likely a fuller and more appropriate use of warmth and personal interest. Merely to have a sympathetic nature, to be sorry and feel deeply for people does not ensure that the service given will be the

K

one that is most needed by them. Warmth of response and personal involvement and concern can be misplaced and overdone if they are unchecked.

Thus, if he thinks in a detached way about an event, the chances of a worker's responses being carefully considered and of his actions being deliberately taken are increased. A degree of detachment helps to ensure that concern and human feeling are more relevantly and appropriately expressed, and is something of a safeguard against excessive and misplaced emotionalism and against too self-interested a search by the worker for personal satisfaction. It is in no way intended to imply indifference or condescension. It helps also to prevent each 'failure', each criticism and disappointment and aggressive action by a client from being interpreted too simply as a reflection on the worker as a person. It seeks to give him a greater strength to overcome apparent denials of his competence, and to be involved simultaneously with a number of personally testing situations.

Nonetheless it is understandable that an emphasis on discipline and detachment should cause concern to some adults. For, whatever their conscious and explicit motives, many (perhaps most) people are attracted into social-educational work, whether part or full-time, because they enjoy being with young people. They like being associated with their energy and liveliness and some of the adults are in great need of the satisfaction which they derive from their acceptance by and identity with teenage groups. Any suggestion, therefore, that personal involvement is not a necessary characteristic of successful social education will be resisted. So too will any suggestion that it may be right that the workers concerned do not find all their experiences personally warm and satisfying. Such defensive reactions, however understandable, do not disprove the importance of a carefully worked out and consciously applied discipline – a second, more detached and deliberate order of viewing human situations. Indeed they only serve to emphasize the need for it.

A second objection to this emphasis on a disciplined approach to social education is, often, that much successful work with young people has been done in the past without it, mainly on the basis of enthusiasm, dedication and intuitive insight. This is, of course, undeniable and the service rendered by many practitioners starting only with these qualities has still to be given the recognition it deserves. Nonetheless, such workers on the whole represent a select band of survivors, even more remarkable perhaps for the ability to survive, but very exceptional. What of the much larger number who have made up the astronomical 'wastage' rate from youth work in particular over the decades? And what of the number who have moved, frustrated, from post to post in search of a situation to suit them? Have these men and women all lacked the 'right personality', or might they have been able to offer much more to young people, as well as to find fulfilment for themselves and stability for their families, if their natural gift could have been nurtured, reinforced and made serviceable to them? Those who have survived have often taken ten or twenty or more years to gain the quality and reliability of their performance and, as they will be the first to admit, they have, in improving their skill, made mistakes costly in human or material terms. We cannot continue to afford such a lengthy learning period, if ever we could, nor is it necessary. For means not only must but can be found of short-circuiting the learning process by developing a reliable discipline to guide practice. The discipline which is needed is not a revolutionary approach, but a conscious formulation and expression of the best existing work. It is not alien, but has its roots in the best of what is familiar.

For among the most successful practitioners who have learned by experience there already exist the thought-processes essential and central to a discipline, in that they clearly recognize a particular event as an example of a general principle and act accordingly. What is most helpful is not a body of prepared reactions to however wide a variety of situations, but principles and understanding to guide and illuminate the adult's practice. The need is for a discipline, for reference-points, not pre-determined routes and preconceived patterns of action.

1. J. WAKELIN, in *Responsibility for Youth*, published by the Conservative Political Centre on behalf of the Bow Group, 1961, p. 19.

Chapter 7

Principles

The adult who is engaged in social education cannot be forearmed in the sense of having instruction given him in advance of a situation, such that he can say 'when I get to that point, I shall do so-and-so'. But he can be given, instead, the means of gauging for himself what to do at each future moment. Although he cannot expect to forecast situations and the dispositions of people in advance, and his preparation cannot therefore take the form of a supply of stock remedies and responses, he can be helped to develop the personal equipment to diagnose and prescribe at the time what he ought to do. The adult in social education cannot, as it were, be given a 'route card' which says, 'Proceed $\frac{1}{2}$ mile N, turn to SE, proceed 22 yds, turn L through $35°$ . . . etc.', but he can be offered some reference points, some help in knowing what his starting points are and an appreciation of the general line of movement, so that he can choose his own route according to the changing lie of the land and check his bearings as he goes. What then are the reference points which enable the social educator to assess what progress has been made and what needs to be done next? It will be argued in this chapter that they are the principles which should guide his practice, and that they derive from the three sources of sanction which affect his work.

One of the sources of sanction of a social educator's practice will, of course, be the society in which he works. Simply as a member of this, but also and more particularly perhaps as an agent with specific tasks to perform in his relations with the young, he will find guidance for his actions. In many ways our society's expectations are difficult to discern and to conceptualize. Many of them are imprecise and even contradictory. What exactly they indicate in terms of action by the social educator will often be far from clear, yet at any moment a social educator will have to take account of them. He will often have to infer or guess at the guidance which different sections of society are offering him, since it will frequently be left implicit: but guidance and expectation there will be from many quarters – from his sponsors, helpers and assistants, from the parents of his pupils or members and the neighbours of the organization, and from the law and other social institutions like the churches and the press.

A second source of sanction is young people. They too can and ought to provide the adult with many of the most important indications of how he should practice. Stated in this way, the principle sounds both over-simple and unreal, and much will be done to qualify it and to present some of the practical problems contained in it as this chapter proceeds. Nonetheless, it is basic to all social education and follows logically from what has been advocated about client-centred practice. The adult may need some help in distinguishing exactly what it is that young people's own developing maturity requires of him, but if he learns to discern their needs then he has an indispensable guide to his own actions.

Thirdly, however, the social educator will on many occasions find that his own personality is the sanction for what he does – and rightly so. He will have to interpret certain expectations of society, and his response to a particular member's needs will often be through his own ideas, feelings and abilities. Out of a variety of possible and acceptable actions which may meet the needs of a young person, the adult will probably think first of the one most compatible with his own hierarchy of good-better-best uses of time and energy. The precise nature of this source of authority may be extremely complex. The adult, for example, may decide to act in a certain way because his educational philosophy influences him consciously and explicitly – that is, because he believes certain actions to be educationally desirable for the young people he meets. Or he may be affected by equally conscious but more private and personal convictions – not so much by the belief that such-and-such an action is best for a client but by the conviction that standards and ideals which govern his *own* life must be applied also to his work, even though this unwittingly may mean some contradiction of his educational ideals. Or, in a less deliberate and conscious way, it may be the adult's emotions – fear, dislike, joy, frustration, tiredness, the need for achievement or recognition or satisfaction – which exert the major influence.

Again, these various strands of his educational ideals, his private conviction and his personal emotional need cannot easily be disentangled. Nonetheless, the adult worker will fall back very often on personal resource and discretion, and will always himself provide a source of sanction for any work he does in any human situation. However much he attempts to illuminate his decisions by an appraisal of the requirements of society and his clients, his choices will be influenced in important ways by his own personality, beliefs and needs.

The sources of sanction for the practice of someone who works with young people in social-educational settings can thus be defined as the society in which he operates, whose influence may be immediate or indirect, explicit or inferred; his clients; and his own personality and ideals. Separated in this way, they can be examined in more detail, and the principles which should guide the social educator in his practice can be deduced. Four of these principles are, appropriately, drawn from the source of sanction provided by the needs of the young people who are the clients.

Society

In saying that society provides a source of sanction for the youth worker and social educator generally, we must not forget that any society and its educational processes are in a constant state of interaction. The educational system, and the content of the education within that system, are partly a result of the society's view of its needs: but the society itself, and the priorities it sees in assessing those needs, are also partly a result of the education its present adults received. Educational aims are in part a reflection of a society's changing values and norms, just as a society's changing values are in part a product of the changing educational experience of its members. Social education – the education towards maturity for the society in which young people will live – is clearly especially affected by this influence, for its whole content and purpose are susceptible of modification as social changes occur.

But such shifts in influence will be felt only over a long period and at national or regional level. The social educator working in a particular locality will feel that society's sanction on his work varies not over a period of time so much as across the spectrum of sections in society with which he is in contact, and within the discordant range of voices through which society speaks. To which of these voices should he pay heed? It is tempting to refer him to 'the community', as an apparently warmer and more personal entity than 'society', but this is of little help. Some adults would find, in the area in which they work, a sense of community based on a neighbourhood and the accidents of housing: if such a 'community' identified itself with the aims and objectives of the agency – whether school or club – which sponsored the social-educational work in which the adult was engaged, he might then count himself lucky and settle on 'the community' as a source of sanction for his work.

But in most areas the worker will be aware of the cross-currents of 'community' which affect most individuals in our society and of the variety of loyalties and affiliations which most of the people near his club or school will feel. Many 'communities' exist side by side and within each other and any single person will belong to a number of them at any one time. He will simultaneously be involved in and committed to the generalized regional, national or even 'British' community, for example, and also more immediately and personally in 'subcultures' and in 'localities'; he will belong to and participate in a variety of domestic, occupational and social institutions which these larger entities contain. All of these groupings may attempt to influence and sanction those adults who meet and work with their younger members, so that the youth worker and the teacher will need to accept that a variety of sanctions might exist, some more specific than others. And because some of these various sanctions and expectations which are derived from 'communities' will differ from each other and even be in conflict, some of the actions indicated for the social educator will at times be barely compatible.

Many of the internal communal conflicts do express themselves in comparatively superficial ways – in clashes between local education committees and ratepayers' associations over whether public money should be spent on youth work, between churches and commercial bodies over what values and interests should be placed before the young, between youth work agencies and schools over dual use of buildings or whether pupils preparing for external examinations should attend youth organizations. Youth work in particular, because it is still a small and relatively unfashionable segment of our education system and because adolescents are a threatening and much criticized group in the population, often finds itself the focus of immediate and tactical communal engagements.

Often underlying these, however, are far more fundamental and long-term issues. For, as is shown by the examples quoted above, dominant social values and customs are formulated by and express themselves through a variety of channels, many of which are not immediately apparent. Nor do they always represent the mood or the intentions of most of those whom they are affecting and regulating at any particular moment. Thus in Britain today certain religious, sporting, artistic and even social values exert a quite meaningless influence on the educational system, since they are appropriate neither to the time nor to the places or lives in which they are applied. As a result, many schools embody a culture and advocate standards which can claim only a minority of adherents but which are purveyed as if they were self-evidently good and unquestionably right, and many youth workers have inherited virtually the same body of traditions. The social education which is given to young people in our society therefore, though it can claim to be sanctioned to some extent by 'the community', is too often affected by mere sectional interests which pass themselves off as expressions of communal expectations and guidance. Thus contemporary education tends to ignore or repress many influences on young people in their immediate and local environment simply because such influences lack a significant expression at national or regional level. Though now the traditional voices of the community speak less confidently and more discordantly, their demands and opinions press hard, and often with little opposition, upon the social educator.

In many instances, of course, this influence is amply justified. For undoubtedly the vested communal interests can still offer young people much help and so need to be acknowledged often by social educators as legitimate sources of guidance. The mere fact that their basic assumptions and standards are today apparently accepted unhesitatingly only by a minority and that these are being more openly questioned and flouted by the majority does not necessarily make them valueless. They frequently offer, regrettable as this may be, the only 'stretching' body of educational ideals, and they are part of the only comprehensive and coherent value-system available to us. Nevertheless, the social educator needs to be far more sceptical about the relevance today of some of the demands made of the younger generation by some parts of the community, and to allow far more freedom from customarily dominant communal standards and expectations. The young will not necessarily be harmed by this and in fact will almost certainly benefit.

In practice, this means that adults might be recruited for social education much more regularly than at present from among those who do not wish to identify with substantial parts of the traditional value-framework of the dominant elements of the community. And the provision of opportunities for the young to enjoy the educational and recreational facilities and interests of their choice might much less often be made conditional upon their joining approved communal causes and traditionally sanctioned activities. Wherever sanctions are irrelevantly imposed in the name of the community by somewhat self-interested sections of it, social educators above all, because of the nature of their 'subject matter', might examine what is being demanded of them and might look elsewhere for guidance.

One such source might more regularly be that section of the community from which the young themselves come and which has bred in them many of their most deep-seated and personally helpful assumptions. For customs and values of the dominant minority which so often hold sway in our social-educational agencies are frequently sharply at variance with those of the subcultures within which these agencies function. Youth work, as we have seen, was sponsored by men and women who themselves had few if any roots in the areas within which they established their organizations and who tried to transplant to these areas the values, attitudes and interests of their own social background, even though in reality this was no more than another, often antagonistic subculture. This spirit remains alive today in many of the voluntary organizations whose origins can be found in the nineteenth century, and also among the sponsors of many youth work agencies, statutory as well as voluntary, established more recently. Like many of the adults connected with our schools in various capacities, many social educators and their sponsors are quite unprepared to see any worthwhile values in the subcultures in which they work, and are extremely reluctant to incorporate any which they do see. This approach from the outside is not of course confined to social education and is to some extent inevitable and even desirable if any educational advance at all is to be attained. Where, however, the specific and essential end of the educational process is the development and expression of *social* mores and *social* skills, the attempts of outsiders to graft their own pattern of behaviour onto learners seems likely to create a less easily justifiable conflict. The consequence is the alienation of many young people and adults whose indigenous culture, within which they must continue to live, is being totally disregarded or scorned. Hence the failure of many, perhaps most, of the young actually to identify with any educational agency and with any wider community. Such lack of identification is certainly to be observed in a significant proportion of those young people who make no contact with social-educational agencies after they have passed the age of compulsory school attendance. And many of those who are in contact, either because they are still of school age or because certain of the provided facilities attract them to attend voluntarily, still look upon the framework of values surrounding the facilities as an alien imposition: neither they nor many of their parents regard the ethos of the educational agency as similar or even appropriate to that of the life they will live, so that educational values do not seem integrated with real values. It will never be possible to say whether social education suffers from too many examples of sponsoring agencies introducing values from outside the familiar environment of the clients. It may be argued that such an infusion of new ideas and views of life is inherent in the educational process. What seems inevitable, however, if the agents of the process or the sponsors of the agency come from different subcultures and purvey their own values, is that the client will be subject to tension and conflict.

For as educational experience develops a young person's ideas and talents, changes his interests and perhaps modifies some of his attitudes, so some of his links with and involvement in the milieu from which he comes will almost certainly be weakened. Indeed, the provision of new and broader opportunities, with the consequent exercise of untapped abilities and the release of novel modes of self-expression, can do more than loosen a young person's connection with his own background: they can put him in opposition to it. Educational experiences might lead the young person to contrast what he was before with what he has or might still become. It is often argued that, in a quite different area of our educational system, the grammar school needs to create this conflict in the lives of many of its pupils if they are to grow and develop at all. Grammar-school staffs can impart not merely history and physics but also a code of 'good' manners, 'respectable' sports and a 'proper' dress sense. Other secondary school staffs too may carry from their sixth-form and college background a whole set of assumptions quite at loggerheads with those to be found in the environment of their pupils, particularly if the teachers serve a rehousing area with seventeen-storey flats and young people who will earn as much at 20 as the teachers do at 50.

These subcultural differences may be regarded as a valuable and integral part of the educative process, and the conflicts which they set up may occur without ever being intentionally encouraged. But they may also be seen, with equal validity, as unwitting attempts to split a child or young person from his immediately local background, to substitute an alien, imported code and view of the world for that which is most meaningful, helpful and relevant to the young person. The experiences of school and club may both educate the adolescent *and* produce subcultural conflict. This will affect young people in various ways, because of the variety in the cultures of schools and clubs and in the behaviour patterns of the families from which pupils and members come: but there certainly seems no reason for social educators, any more than for other educators, to pursue without reservation the growth of young people's disenchantment with the conventional ideas and habits of their background.

The major conclusion to draw at present, however, is that 'the community' is on the whole an indecipherable guide to those whose purpose is social education. A great variety of groups may claim to be part of the community in which the club or school exists, and the guidance would include a motley assortment of precepts. 'Community' may seem a less difficult concept to deal with as a source of sanction than 'society', but in fact it is equally variegated and bewildering.

If 'society's' views cannot be represented by 'the community', what can they be represented by? One line of guidance is discernible which is truly authoritative although limited in its scope, and that is the law. The social eductor is of course subject to the normal legal obligations falling to any member of the community; he needs to remember also that he is liable, like anyone else, to be called upon to give evidence, and that he will not then be regarded as having the same privileged relationship with his clients as is accorded to a priest. There can be no doubt that 'society' gives the social educator all the guidance about his actions that is contained in the law of the land. He needs to respect the limits set by the law, not mainly because he is an example to the young and in some way especially reponsible for imparting a concept of legal right and wrong to them, but more because the law itself will expect him to be within its bounds. From the law, in fact, he will receive more than guidance – he will get direction.

In practice, because youth workers and some teachers meet young people in informal and voluntary relationships, some adults find that they cannot let even the law direct them strictly in their work and in their use of information. Like many other members of the community, including at times policemen themselves, they feel they must be left to some degree to judge a situation independently and to use their discretion. Their actions must be decided in part at least according to circumstances and personalities, even though legally there may be only one course permitted. And in practice too those responsible for enforcing and judging the law's requirements will often, though not always, try to allow them some room for such discretion.

Such a qualified endorsement of the law as a source of guidance in society may seem unnecessary to many youth workers and other social educators. But since society is made up of so many subcultures, and since many of these do permit and even encourage illegal practices, some of the adults involved are bound to be constantly on the borderline of whatever, in their district, is being perpetrated, whether it be under-age drinking, or drug trafficking, or car offences, or income tax fraud, or sexual or property offences. Many of them would deny even so that any problem exists. They would claim that young people need to know from the start that the adult will in all circumstances uphold the law, and indeed it is true that all relationships with the young must be founded on the understanding that the adult must, sooner or later, be bound by the law. It would be clearly scandalous if this were not the case: and experience suggests that young people have as little respect as 'society' for the adult who compromises his own position beyond the point which society will tolerate. But some of those who work with young people have found that, in some subcultures, in order to establish contacts which will be productive in the long term, they have had to ignore – though rarely to participate in and not to condone – certain minor and immediate offences. And society's law enforcement agencies – the police – have been at times exceptionally sympathetic in these cases, so that the social educator has been allowed temporarily to neglect what would normally be a clear sanction.

Apart from these extreme cases, however, the social educator must always be known to be 'on the side of the law'. He may have many reservations about the sanity or relevance of much of our law, particularly because his work enables him to observe how alternative codes of behaviour apply more meaningfully to those areas of life about which the inhabitants of his district care most. He, like any other citizen, may not feel bound automatically to report every single act known to him which breaks a law, and will often need to decide consciously and uncertainly what the desirable and correct course is. But he cannot, in his work, be other than an agent of society, and as such must expect to be treated as a strict upholder of its legal code.

For the rest, the social educator must cut his difficulties down to manageable size. If he is to use society as a source of sanction for his actions, he must resign himself to simplifying the problem. This may mean giving some areas and sections of society very little consideration and virtually ignoring others for much of the time. Such a choice, however, will need to be made not by evaluating all the possible sources of influence on the adult's work and then selecting what seems to him the most worthy, but by deciding on purely practical grounds which sections can impinge most on what a social educator must do. These may not seem to be especially worthy or significant in terms of the high ideals which the worker may have; but they will affect him most and so demand greatest attention. And when looked at in the light of such a criterion, it is undoubtedly the agency for which an adult works and the parents of his clients which demand and deserve continuous consideration.

To emphasize that parents are a sanction for the social educator because of their intimate responsibility for their children may cause some uneasiness, since a great deal of what some workers do and many of the actual educational ends which they pursue suggest that they regard the family as of less importance to the child than the school or even the youth organization. The home, they often seem to imply, ought to interfere less in the child's upbringing. This certainly seems to be conveyed for example by the unthinking insistence by many of them on uncompromising loyalty from young people to their club or school and on deep and uninterrupted commitment to its activities and values. The boy who does not arrive to play in a football match, the girl who joins a club or society but stops coming after two or three weeks, the group which uses a leisure organization 'as a convenience' are all in danger automatically of being categorized as unreliable or classed as failures. They may of course by their behaviour be giving some evidence of personal instability or deeper dissatisfaction. What is too rarely considered, however, is whether their 'failure' in such comparatively marginal spheres of their lives is, if looked at from another and more important point of view, merely a sign of their successful involvement in other spheres, and in particular in their families, which are much more intimate and meaningful to them.

It is true, of course, that in some places educators must overcome some seriously inhibiting domestic habits and values before the young can be helped to fuller personal growth and expression. In such a case it is as difficult for the educator to judge 'how far to go' when the values of the home itself are being called in question, as we have seen it to be if the values of the young person's whole subcultural environment are in danger of being eroded.

He may realize, for example, that the boy with an authoritarian father is discovering a measure of real independence and self-sufficiency in the club, and is beginning to jib against the restrictions imposed on him at home. Or that the young girl who has found new pleasure in visiting the theatre occasionally or a talent for painting, or who simply welcomes the opportunities provided by a youth organization for talking and thinking about herself, is becoming more conscious of and vaguely dissatisfied with certain limitations at home. Or that a boy's attitudes to aspiration at work, or to ways of being entertained and gaining relaxation, are being altered considerably, as also perhaps are his views and values in religion and morality. Whatever the worker's responses to such situations of conflict, he will certainly need to be alive to their possible existence.

In other areas of education the prestige and influence accorded to parental choice are sometimes doubted. When, for example, the age until which an adolescent should stay at school (after the compulsory period) is being decided, or the type of secondary or further or higher education is being weighed up, the views of the parents are often thought to be of little help to their children's future. One point of view maintains that as long as the length and type of schooling is a matter open at some point to parental choice, the system will, at that point, discriminate needlessly against a child according to his parents' limitations. It is an arguable point whether the rights of the child are safeguarded as well here as they have been by legislation in other spheres of our social services, since parents have the right of choice in matters affecting their children's education and the educators concerned are entitled and encouraged only to offer advice.

Yet it is not always justifiable to suppose that parents who do not choose what the educators advise either do not understand the educational system or fail to grasp the opportunities open to their child's potential. For although many parents clearly do make choices affecting their children's education which are reactionary in this sense, a large number of others must act as they do because they are deeply resentful of the values and ideals represented – or believed to be represented – by the educators and often particularly by the schools. Moreover, although it seems fair to criticize the parent who wilfully restricts the amount of academic or technical learning to which his son or daughter is allowed access, it seems unfair to complain of those who resist some forms of social education currently offered to their children. For whether the social education is purveyed alongside other education – in the extracurricular activities at school, or in college and university unions – or in youth clubs and centres, it may well be seen by the parent as sufficiently alien in values and content as to provoke his rejection or anger. He may even wish to withdraw his child from the scene altogether, despite the fact that to do so means withdrawing him or her from the academic or technical education as well.

For there is often much more than preference for early wage-earning behind a withdrawal from secondary school and an enrolment for further education on the basis of day-release from work. There is evidence, too, that while some sections of the population look askance at technical education, other sections prefer their children to study at a college of advanced technology than a university because of the social values obtaining. Nor is the withdrawal of young people from youth clubs by their parents an uncommon phenomenon, though perhaps in this case it is more common in some areas for the parents to attempt to influence the events about which they are concerned.

The conflict of values between home and educational agency may in some cases be desirable, in some cases it may not occur, and in other cases it may occur but be resolved, yet one general rule is surely inescapable. A social educator must be concerned with the way in which parents are interpreting what he is doing and how the young person is reconciling what he is learning with what he meets at home. He cannot act as if conflict will not occur, and he cannot dismiss any divergence of views by some parents of his clients as merely uncooperativeness or superiority or inverted snobbery or interference. For the social educator a knowledge of background, of parental expectations, standards and assumptions and of the subcultural pressures to which a member and his family are subject will offer some indication of how he should act. They will not be the only source of sanction provided by society, but the parents' views must be taken into account.

The other particularly significant means by which 'society' expresses itself to the social educator, and through which he may obtain sanction for his work, is the agency. Whether he is paid or not, full-time or part-time, the adult engaged in social education is doing his work under the aegis of some agency or enterprise constituted for the purpose; it may be an organization or a committee appointed to manage or be trustees of a club, or it may be a school or college.

All agencies whether they be schools or youth organizations will have some basic intentions and expectations, and all of them will therefore to some extent make demands of those who work under their banner. However basic and vague some of these demands may seem to be, however far removed from the standards and the immediate expectations of the young people themselves, however much they differ from the adult worker's own views, they represent to some degree the philosophy and the aims of those 'representatives' of society most closely concerned with the work being carried on. The members of the policy-deciding committee of an agency may be 'representatives' of society only in the sense that they are the worker's closest, most immediate and direct sounding-board. They may also be representatives in the sense of being a 'cross-section' of the community, or the appointees of the elected representatives of the residents. They may be seen by the clients and their parents as intruders conspiring to introduce an alien pattern, or as the socially-conscious and actively concerned people they often are. But whatever view others may hold, the worker will see his sponsoring agency as the major source of guidance in 'society'. It is the sponsoring agency which gives him the authority to act in an educative capacity, and it is the agency's policy to which he must pay closest attention.

Part at least of the agency's policy and purpose may be laid down categorically, perhaps even in writing. Alternatively, large parts may be formulated in only the most general way, and there may be many issues in which a worker will have to exercise considerable discretion when deciding what is expected of him at any moment. Again, between the two extremes and probably most commonly, the adult will have to work within a varying and complicated pattern of freedom, advice, persuasion, pressure and direction. Often, in his day-to-day work, he may feel that the indications which his agency gives him may inhibit and even prevent his carrying out what he sees as his obligations to that part of 'society' – the subculture within which he operates – with which he is most immediately and meaningfully in contact. At its most superficial this conflict may emerge over attitudes to dress or swearing or the use of furniture. Or it may be highlighted more deeply by differing assumptions about how courtship should be carried on, or how one behaves during a competition or sporting fixture. And the adult may often feel, also that he is being 'untrue to himself', or being asked to work in a way which contravenes his own convictions.

Some workers earn sufficient respect from their agencies to be able to interpret back to them, as the policy-makers, the sources and reasons for conflict, and some agencies' policy-makers may already be partly aware of them. To some extent therefore it may be possible to effect a compromise between different subcultural divisions and 'expressions' of society, or between the different sources of sanction for their work. In the day-to-day practice of his work any practitioner will have to take decisions himself based on the known or deduced policy of his agency and the other sources of sanction, but in the long term he has a duty to help his agency's committee in the formulation and modification of policy. His own advice must be based on this complicated interaction between the three sources of sanction, which include the agency as the most immediately influential expression for him of the sanction provided by 'society'. He must give his advice to the agency, taking account of their view alongside his other sources. If they ignore his advice he is bound to accept their decision (even if only temporarily until he can restate his view) or, if the strength of feelings warrants it, resign: for it is his sponsoring agency which gives him the authority to practise, and he cannot but be bound by them.

In looking, then, to society as a source of sanction, the social educator may have regard to certain general ideals forming the climate in which social education is conducted. He must expect to be treated as a person who is unequivocal in his support of the law, even though on occasions he may behave equivocally. He should not ignore the values of the parents and the subcultural environment of his clients But above all he must regard the agency under whose aegis he works as the most significant expression to him of the sanctions of society.

The Client

In our society there are good reasons why the needs of the individual clients should be regarded as sanctions for practice. Many of the social and political ideals which prevail among us recognize uncompromisingly the importance and integral worth of the individual person, young or old. Ours is a democracy in which each member is assumed to be both a participating and a benefiting citizen, which means that it is a democracy in more than a narrow constitutional sense. In social, economic and cultural matters, too, the primacy of the individual is acknowledged and he is accorded freedom for expression and enterprise. Such deeply entrenched liberal values indicate to all educators that their practice must acknowledge and support the personal beliefs and attitudes of each young person with whom their work brings them into contact and that it must aim at fulfilling his unique needs.

Some might question the actual extent of the influence of such liberal principles on our society's organization, and claim for example that, socially and economically even if not politically, individuals are too little

L

considered and too often exploited. From a number of different points of view it is argued that the individual counts for little because 'mass' society – urban living, the welfare state, mass communications, industrialization and so on – is undermining the personal and intimate nature of our existence and making each person's influence weaker and less respected. In some generalized senses these judgments may be true. But as we contended in Chapter 3, they are too rarely treated critically, and, in fact, in vital respects they oversimplify and so misrepresent our current situation as it is actually experienced by many individuals 'on the ground'. For on many very important occasions in their lives, individuals today seem to be required to act more independently, in greater isolation from social direction, protection or support, than at any time in the past. Individual members of our society as it is at present constituted are more and more being asked to take certain types of decision on their own initiative, and may well find these choices extremely exposing and demanding. An immense range of actions is now firmly in the domain of personal, conscious decision, and much less governed simply by authority, convention or unquestioned belief. We are reminded once again that ours is a teleological society, that less of our time, energy and money are now committed to gaining the basic essentials of life, and that, although our expectations of a standard of living go up all the time, we have increasing choice over what we shall take to be the symbols of this raised standard – how to spend our uncommitted time and money, what order of priorities we shall observe, what we prize most. In short, we can with considerable freedom determine what our values will be, both as individuals and as contributors to a subculture and to a wider culture.

In the past our society has been exercised to foster individuality, variety and independence of judgment in those who would lead, but now it is no longer sufficient to look for such characteristics in the education of an elite alone. The ability to take one's own decisions, to bear full responsibility without undue anxiety, to initiate without the permission of an acknowledged authority – these characteristics are needed by all members of our society, in political, economic, social and cultural contexts alike. They are virtually obligatory requirements on a personality who wishes to live up to the demands of society. Discrimination, choice, judgment are the tokens of the adequate, they are the normal equipment of the socially competent. Those whose education, especially social education, does not give them the opportunity to develop these characteristics fail to realize their potential and so fail to contribute as fully as society needs them to: the more serious cases become the 'inadequates' whose numbers swell our hospitals and clinics.

For all these reasons it is essential that 'workers' in agencies responsible for helping and developing members of our society should increasingly strive to take their lead from, to respect, to safeguard as much as is practicable the personality and potential of individual clients. In this way they can best support them and give them confidence in making their own choices. The focus must more and more come to be on the special circumstances of each of those clients, his or her individual wants, needs, values and interests. More and more, therefore, the sanctions operating on the social educator must be dominated by the sanction provided by the needs of the clients.

The agency, of course, helped by the interpretation given by the worker, must be ready to define its own policies more flexibly if it is to take account of the changing needs of clients. In the long term, such flexibility is well evidenced: agencies which once gave clothing and soup now offer sailing and vehicle maintenance. But there are still agencies which have to be forced, struggling, from one decade to the next, which still cling tenaciously to the minutiae of policy arrived at in one social circumstance as though they were abiding dictates.

The worker, too, must increasingly see his personality not as dominating the work he does but as a tool at the disposal of his clients, to help them achieve their own purposes and to contribute to their development. This often requires an adult to overcome strongly personal and irrational responses to the young. For whatever intellectual statements may be made it is only too easy for him to underestimate what is implied by the 'individuality' of the young. When confronted by behaviour which refuses to follow the norms to which he has become accustomed, the adult worker may frequently be justified if he condemns it as impoliteness, irresponsibility or lack of self-discipline in the young. But he may also be using such terms to shield himself from that challenge and threat which the young in general are likely to present to him. He may use such comments to excuse himself from granting to the young people in his practice adequate licence for self-expression and self-realization. But the shield may be one which he needs also for much more immediate and personal reasons. He may adopt it because he is, in fact, extremely unsure of himself and his own work and individuality. Or it may be one which he has automatically thrown around him because of the methods used by the organization or movement through which he works. Or again, he may behave so formidably or be so withdrawn that he is insensitive to the challenges and divergences being expressed around him. In this case he is effectively though not deliberately allowing the sanction of his own personality to influence his work too greatly.

Thus, just understanding divergence and individuality is not the whole part of tolerating and encouraging it. Many adults can be intellectually prepared for an understanding of adolescent idiosyncracy and independence, but still remain incapable of coping with it, still react to it as if it were a rebellious affront, still make a response based on fear or defensiveness. Again, many adults develop an understanding, even an expectation, that adolescents will act in a challenging manner, will be 'wayward' and want to find their own answers for themselves. These adults then give the impression of resignation to this, of 'fearing the worst': they behave not with joy at the emergent independence of an individual, but with sorrow at a creature needing discipline. They are emotionally unable to accept that the end of the adolescent's dependence creates a replica of their own human individuality. Such adults have presumably grown to depend, themselves, on seeing adolescents as dependent figures, and are threatened rather than assured by their release into free, fully-fledged integrity. Such personally defensive responses by social educators are incompatible with an intention to seek guidance in young persons' individuality, and cannot guide genuinely disinterested and client-centred practice.

What principles do need to be observed, then, by adults who meet young people in social-educational settings and who wish to ensure that they observe their individual requirements? Firstly, respect for any person as an individual implies acceptance of him (or her) as he is, merely as a human being. It is not enough, for example, to think of a person with whom one is working as 'butcher' or 'orphan' or 'fiancé' or 'centre-half' or 'artist' or even as 'pupil' or 'member'. He may play all these roles at different times and with different people, but to think of him as any one or two of these is to do less than justice to him as a full, whole human being. It is because he is a young human being that he has a call on the worker's attention, not because he can fulfil any or all of these roles which bring into play only some aspect of his personality. For the social educator this means accepting young people as young people, unselectively, simply because each of them is a member of the social group whom the adult is intending to serve.

There may well be severe practical limitations on how many and which young people a worker can receive into his organization. These limitations may follow from his own personal abilities and skill, from the expectations of other young people, or from the requirements of society in its various forms. Like a doctor who may be forced to exclude some newcomer to the area from his already full list of patients so an adult who works with young people may in practice have to turn away some potential clients. But a doctor's code of occupational principles and ethics means that he is not entitled to refuse medical care to some people because he judges them undeserving of it. This acceptance by the medical services of all sick people because they are sick, represents a fundamental principle which is based on an acknowledgement of each individual's significance and therefore right to good health. It is a principle which services to young people might also recognize as inviolable and of primary ethical significance. Admittedly, an adult may need to say, in effect: 'I cannot at this moment in my present circumstances work with that young person; but I agree that he expects and requires and thus has a right, because he is a young person in a society operating a service of social education, to consideration by an adult prepared or at least designated by society as a social educator'. What cannot be his starting point, however, if he has genuine concern for the individual, is an assumption that some young people are not worthy of any social educator's concern, even though they may indicate that they would welcome some such service. If the principle of acceptance were acknowledged, no young person could be left outside the appropriate services *simply* because of some attribute – what he is or where he comes from or what he looks like. If provision were truly client-centred, only considerations of practical possibility – resources, staff, funds, etc. – could deprive a client of the help he sought.

At the same time it must be noted that model-centred social education presumably will always have a place. In particular, in a society which contains denominational schools in its education service, and church as well as agnostic adoption and other services in its social welfare schemes, there is no reason to suppose that model-centred youth work will be squeezed out. The Youth Service will not be wholly client-centred of course until there is a client-centred provision available as an alternative to any young person not wishing to be serviced by the model-centred provision in his area. Even then, however, we need not anticipate the demise of those agencies or adults who wish to serve a sectional purpose, to work in a model-centred way, and who are prepared therefore to select for servicing those young people who, in a genuinely voluntary sense, are willing to join the organizations they sponsor. No doubt, too, again for very practical reasons, some institutions will find it easier to serve certain categories or groups of young people or accidentally will find themselves doing so. But, in principle, youth workers, like social educators in general, need to see themselves as agents appointed or permitted by their society to act in the interests of the young of that society, whoever they may be. The mere facts that the young are within the appropriate age and social group and are demanding some help from the society should be sufficient reasons for them to be able to find acceptance somewhere within the social-educational services.

It follows from this that the adult, whatever his own personal beliefs and values, is not in a position, in so far as he is a designated social educator, to allow his own attitude and response to a young person to be affected by his approval or disapproval of that young person's behaviour, beliefs or values. He may privately judge that this or that action is wrong and be extremely shocked and critical. And he may also, as would any citizen, recognize that this or that action is illegal and that therefore he must make his own attitude clear and even perhaps inform the police. But there is the obligation on him by virtue of his occupation, part-time or full-time, to take the individual young person as he is or might become and to seek to discern from this how he, the adult, ought to behave as a social educator: this means that he cannot allow his actual practice to be directed or overtly and consciously influenced simply by *personal* considerations of what is proper. In the same way, patients qualify for a doctor's services regardless of the private judgment made of them and their conduct by any particular medical practitioner. The latter's personal judgment of their worth is not supposed to interfere with the professional services he makes available to them. Such non-judgmental attitudes need also to characterize youth work practice.

An adult's respect for an individual's independence and integrity also implies that he will need to circumscribe very carefully his influence on the decisions which young people take when determining various aspects of their way of life. A social educator may help a young person to see what decisions are possible, what the range of choices is and what are the consequences of the alternatives. But in the end he has to demonstrate in practice the principle that each young person must be free to go his own way if his personal feeling of independence is to develop and, once developed, remain unimpaired.

Adults have recourse to many subterfuges of thought and argument to conceal from themselves this requirement on their practice. It is easier, but in the long run a disservice, to give directives and so to protect young people from the burden of responsibility for their own decisions. It is almost as easy to ensure, by the selection of some facts or the omission of other alternatives, that the 'choice' made is acceptable to the adult: indeed, without scrupulous care in putting forward possibilities which he personally considers disastrous or unthinkable, it is possible for the adult quite unintentionally to influence a young person to make what would be the adult's choice. The ultimate sophistry of the adult is to argue, 'Ah, but young people like you to have a firm line, even if it is only to kick against'. This is often merely a device to save the adult the much more difficult task of helping a young person come to his own decision, but often it is a quite unconscious propagation of immaturity. For young people can choose between two possible, but educationally undesirable, responses to an adult's directive or prescription: either they can accept it and reinforce their dependency on authority, which is always much easier to some than outgrowing it; or they can reject it, giving the cynical adult additional evidence that they want something to kick against and reinforcing the reflex in the young person which has to reject merely to prove his non-dependence. The educationally *desirable* response, of hearing the adult view, examining it, weighing it and finally coming to the same or a different conclusion in the light of the young person's own judgment, is liable to be a long time in developing unless adults are prepared to follow the difficult non-directive, non-authoritarian, path. The hypothesis that young people want a firm line is a self-validating one until the adult meets an adolescent who is mature enough to demonstrate his independence of view, and is able, without any help from the social educator, to rise above the dependency-or-rejection reflex. But since the social educator ostensibly does wish to help adolescents to maturity, he must avoid the stimulus which triggers off this reflex, and work whenever he can in the much harder but truly educational non-directive way.

This does not mean that the adult must not have his own views, nor that he should not state what they are. It simply means that he should not, except for some other pressing and overriding reason which is rooted in the sanctions governing his practice, in any way circumscribe his clients' need for self-determination, for accepting responsibility as far and as often as possible, for as many aspects as possible of their own ways of life. The adult may see no point in expressing his view at all. Certainly such reticence will leave no doubt that the burden of responsibility lies with the client. The client may resent this as an apparently unjustified suspension of guidance: but to help the client attain the maturity of decision-making, the worker must bear with the resentment. If the adult does express his view, the way in which he does it must indicate an expectation that it will not be accepted by the client simply because it is the worker's. The inflexion of voice, the phraseology, the facial expression or the gesture which conveys this must depend on the locality and the people concerned: but the idea must *be* conveyed that the worker will not be personally offended if the client decides differently. And this must be conveyed, of course, without suggesting that the worker does not care what the young person does, since this would be neither the truth nor part of any service to young people. The worker does care about the decision; but, unless other principles based on other sanctions prevail, the worker cares most that, by now, the client can determine this matter for himself.

The adult is clearly far from passive, therefore, if he adopts this principle of self-determination for his clients. And certainly at those points where society makes demands or where the worker feels that he must allow the demands of his own personal convictions to prevail, then action may have to be taken which does prevent the young person from self-determination on this occasion, and so effectively overrides at that point the sanctions on social-educational practice provided by the needs of the client. This does not detract, however, from the general rule that once the worker has ensured that all the relevant issues have been aired and that all the possible opportunities have been made apparent, young people need to be left to use their talents and determine their behaviour in their own way in their own time. If he truly recognizes and respects the individuality and integrity of each young person, he must grant them the maximum degree of self-determination compatible with the other sanctions which bear upon him.

It follows also from a recognition of individual value that the relationship which an adult builds up with a young person must always be founded on trust, and on the young person's knowledge that what passes between them will remain a matter of confidence. This trust is not the same as that which the young person may have in the worker's judgment, in his reliability as a fellow-mountaineer or as driver of the club's mini-bus. This kind of trust will develop, no doubt, and should do so, for although it is a form of dependence and can be an inhibiting factor in development, it can also, properly used as a basis for the mutual respect of mature people for one another's individual strengths and weaknesses, be an element in the relationship which enables the young person to grow. But the trust which is under consideration here is that which observes the confidential nature of the interchange between one human being and another whom he helps, a part of whose personal life he is privileged to know. The relationship need not be solemn. There may, indeed one hopes there will, be fun and joviality, and an easy and sociable contact between 'worker' and 'client'. Unrelieved intensity and seriousness are not in the least necessary and in fact in the informal and recreational settings in which the adult works they are likely to be a hindrance. None of this, however, means that a working relationship should be taken up light-heartedly and treated in a casual, gossipy manner. If an adult is working with respect for the integrity of young people, humbly and sensitively, they will reveal, both indirectly and by intention, what are to them important and even intimate aspects of their personalities and circum-stances. As we have already admitted, it will not always be possible for a social educator to treat what he learns as a result as completely confidential since, at times, the law may require him to reveal it. There may occasion-ally be other principles which prevail and force his hand because they too have wider reference or greater sanction at this point. Nonetheless the principle, the guiding ethical consideration, is that in recognition of the young person's independence and integrity the adult's relationship with him must be a confidential one. The vast majority of what is imparted will not as a rule be passed on – not even necessarily to a parent, to an employer or to a fellow worker – without the permission of the young person himself. Even if it seems that information needs to be passed on for the young person's good, or for the good of society by giving it to the police, there will be very few occasions indeed when that needs to happen without the young person's permission, or at least his knowledge. The redirection of someone else's life, or any part of it, without his having an opportunity to decide for himself about it, is treatment reserved among adults for criminals and some of the mentally sick. The adult who manipulates an adolescent's life by infringing the confidentiality of his relationship can only do so for very pressing reasons indeed.

Acceptance of a young person simply because he or she indicates some desire to be served and belongs to the section of the population which these particular adults have been designated to serve; an attitude which, as far as is humanly possible, withholds judgment of that young person; an avoidance of any imposition, however subtle, of standards or patterns of behaviour which he ought to be determining for himself; a relationship founded on confidentiality – these together indicate how an adult might guide his practice in the interests of and with respect for individual clients. Together, they ought to ensure that, where this is appropriate and the most important sanction, his practice will be best designed to safeguard and further the personal needs of each young person.

We must reiterate, however, that the needs of the client are not the only sanctions operating on the worker in his practice of social education. Society, and his own personality are also important sources of sanction: the principles which guide his practice must include not only acceptance of clients, non-judgmentalism in respect of their values, self-determination for their behaviour and confidentiality in his relationships with them, but also recognition that he holds a position on behalf of society, represented particularly by his sponsoring agency, and acknowledgment of the involvement of his own personality in his work. Here again, in fact, the social educator is not unlike the doctor, for example, in having sources of sanction outside the needs of his clients. In a case where a doctor believes that contraception for an unmarried woman is advisable, or abortion even for a married one, he may find his hands morally and/or legally tied. The principle of care for each individual, and the body of ethics which arises from this, comprise only a part of the framework which guides the doctor's practice just as they comprise only a part of that which guides the social educator's.

There is no doubt that to practise even in a client-centred way is extremely difficult, without having to bear in mind the other important sanctions, so that it is doubtful if the social educator will be accomplished in such practice straight away. In the first place, he must develop the habit of constantly recognizing that young people are first and foremost 'other people': and, as Dr Josephine Klein succinctly puts it, to recognize other people always as both 'other' and 'people' is a characteristic of a person of considerable maturity.[1] The social educator will probably find himself listening more and talking less, questioning more and stating less, explaining more and suggesting and advising less. He may need to accustom himself to the idea that he will feel less often that he has 'helped', 'moulded' or 'moved' young lives, and that frequently he will just not know what his correct role is or whether he has had any impact. But, in fact, his impact will still need to be very considerable, if not so directly measurable. He will have to make a very positive contribution, and this because his concern is to meet the *needs* of clients, and not merely their *wants*.

It is this distinction which, under the guidance of the other sanctions provided by society and by his own personality, transforms the social educator's practice from a series of responses to his clients' whims and wishes, into an educational process based on personal and social relationships. Of course, such an adult is available to offer some of the means by which young people can achieve some of these opportunities and experiences which they are conscious they are seeking. But at the same time he is committed to providing facilities and personal help which will enable young people to identify and satisfy much in themselves which is as yet unrealized.

If wants are known and explicit, needs are less consciously felt or directly expressed. If wants are those expectations which young people are aware they have and which in words or gestures or actions they make obvious, then needs are more deep-seated potentialities, not superficially or immediately recognizable and requiring some external stimulus if they are to be realized. If wants are those drives or urges for which a person thinks he has found a satisfactory answer, then needs are those which are either uneasily sensed and experienced by the person yet not satisfied, or those whose existence is communicated to a sensitive observer by other forms of compensatory or repressive behaviour. The social educator interprets this in an endeavour to find a medium of expression for the young person which meets the need.

On the whole, youth workers for example would say it is comparatively easy to know what young people *want*. When they join a youth organization, they are clearly looking for the opportunity to play a game, act in a play, or dance, meet friends, talk about their mother or their boyfriend, laugh, relax, refresh themselves after a day's work. What are less easily or satisfactorily definable are their *needs*. Too many adults seem to assume that these can be reached only if in some way they probe young people's personalities profoundly and therefore act as though they have extensive psychological knowledge and psycho-analytical skill. Few youth workers or teachers have such knowledge or skill and ought not to take on roles which imply they have. What they can assume, however, is that young people have talents which their activities so far have not yet fully released. This implies that the worker will move amongst the young people who actually join his organization, establish relationships with them which they are willing and pleased to acknowledge and then, through a sensitive appraisal of and insight into the sort of person each of them is, begin to identify more realistically how he or the other adults in the organization might act in order to meet the need for development. They start by meeting the young people as people, by being concerned to know and understand the personalities standing before them, and to discover what in these is as yet unrealized and untapped, and what are likely to be the conditions necessary for members to extend the range of their experience, voluntarily, in directions of their own choice. In these ways the members will gain a greater and acceptable sense of achievement and recognition in society. The worker, then, in seeking to meet clients' needs in this sense, is playing some extremely positive, dynamic and skilful roles which are quite the opposite of the withdrawal and servile accommodation to every whim and wish that are often imagined to be the inevitable result of 'meeting needs'.

The worker who attempts to discern the needs of his clients in order to use them as a source of sanction for his work places himself, of course, in several dilemmas immediately. In the first place, how sure can he be that the 'needs' he sees are not, in disguised form, what he, the adult, wishes young people to do anyway for other reasons? He has to guard against imposing, albeit unintentionally, his own values and interests under the illusion that he has carefully assessed his clients' 'needs'. It is only too easy to assume that the image one has of what one would like young people to be is made up of what they need, and easy then to attempt to model them according to it. In any case, even if the adult is striving to identify genuine needs, he needs to do so humbly and to be aware of the presumptuous position which such a procedure implies for him – unavoidable and justifiable perhaps, but still a presumption. For he is starting from the assumption that he may be able to help young people discover much that is 'good' for them which they might not discover if left to themselves. Not all adults would claim to be able ever to make such a diagnosis of need on the part of a fellow human being, and this is why the adult engaged in youth work is particularly reliant upon the guidance from his various sources of sanction.

A second dilemma implicit for the worker in the process of assessing need is the possibility that he may find himself attempting to achieve more and to go further than young people anticipate when, voluntarily, they join a youth organization or other leisure group. Since young people are not compelled to join and since they do so in their leisure hours usually for reasons of relaxation, what they expect their membership will entail would seem to be a major, some would say the paramount or even the only, consideration in assessing what they should be offered. There is of course no necessary conflict of interests simply because young people come for enjoyment while the agency and the worker seek to educate them socially. The range of possible experiences is wide enough to enable both interests to be served simultaneously for most young people most of the time, and, as Mr John Parr reminds us in *Enjoying the Club*, education, especially social education, is no less educative if it is enjoyed.[2] Nonetheless, it is important to ask how far an adult is entitled to go in seeking to have a deeper and more extensive influence than the clients themselves sought when they allowed the original relationship to develop. Is he entitled to look for needs and concentrate deliberately on satisfying them if this is not what the clients originally came expecting?

And what if an individual's wants and needs do clash – if, to put it crudely, what a young person wants is not, in the view of the social educator, what is good for him? In part, the adult's dilemma will be resolved by reference to other sources of sanction, and in particular those embodied in society. For some at least of the expectations of young people cannot be satisfied because the law, parents or his agency will not permit the adult to act in the ways necessary for this. However, these will never offer a solution to all the problems raised on a particular day, and a social educator may be left sometimes with a clear choice between wants and needs. Is he to assume only the role of provider, or does he also see it as legitimate to play the roles of trainer, developer and stimulator?

Certainly no adult would seem to have the right to deny young people all that they know they want, simply in order to achieve what he feels they need. There are however many adults who behave as though they do have such a right. Perhaps they have too narrow a view of what is educational. Perhaps they suspect anything enjoyable of being frivolous and non-educative, and resolve their dilemma by avoiding as often as possible what young people want in case they enjoy it. Perhaps it is that what young people want and enjoy, although quite legal and generally socially acceptable, happens to seem strange to an older generation which, as a result, is irritated and discomforted by it. Alternatively, perhaps the adult reaction may follow from their own feelings of guilt about mere pleasure and indulgence in relief and distraction, and their inability to allow that there may be very adequate cause for some people to spend time on these things. Perhaps, again, some adults in social education cannot tolerate the characteristically short-term nature of any of young people's wants and objects of desire and attainment, and uncomprehendingly dismiss them as unworthy.

If such guilty feelings *are* the motives for some social educators' insistence on continuous purposeful and self-improving activity while young people are in their organizations and for the antagonism to so much that young people simply *want* to do, they seem in themselves inadequate. The adult in social education should accept that part of his work will be to help young people get what they want and should lose any sense of shame he has about it. After all, the community pays for similar types of 'pastime' for those young people who, because of greater intellectual capacity and more favourable home backgrounds, go on to higher education. Society even rationalizes this provision of pleasure-giving facilities by pointing to the social intercourse and experience – that is, the social-educational opportunities – which a university or college union makes possible. There is no logical reason why it should not do the same, with or without the rationalizations, for the rest of the same age-group.

To suggest, however, that clients' wants must be given due place as a source of sanction for a worker's practice is not to say that wants are all-important. We argued in Chapter 3 that young people ought to be regarded as having some requirements which are special to them, even though these by no means separate them completely from the remainder of the population. If only because they, to a greater degree than older and more set personalities, are capable of becoming more than they are at present and can stimulate society in new ways, they deserve at least some special attention. Many people, whose job brings them into a servicing relationship with another adult, feel that they can see 'just what he needs': this may be partly self-delusion, but even where it is not, the 'worker' frequently knows that the person whom he is servicing will never be able to have his needs met because he is no longer flexible enough to embark on the new experience which would be involved. Young people still have the flexibility which is necessary, and may be helped to retain it longer simply because an adult helps them, through new social-educational experiences, to exercise it more. It is for these reasons that the social educator is a necessary special category of adult, able not only to help young people achieve their wants but also, and probably more important, to facilitate a fuller growth and realization of potential than they might otherwise achieve. As Ray Gosling has already argued, it is not the function of a youth organization to offer only 'a juke-box c/o the Ministry of Education'.[3] The commercial bodies can already offer these facilities adequately, so that, for this end, there is no reason to provide communally-subsidized facilities or to attract and train adults to run them. To justify the establishment of a public service, arguments are needed as well as (though not instead of) those based on young people's *wants*. These stem from the fact that adolescents, as yet incompletely shaped, with abilities not yet fully tapped and possibilities not yet fully expressed, with aspirations still capable of realistic growth, have *needs* which a skilful adult can enable them to fulfil.

The Personality of the Worker

The third source of sanction for social-educational practice is in the personality of the adult himself. However much guidance he can obtain from sources outside himself, his own convictions and feelings will remain ineradicable influences on what he does. These personal factors will include some which are vital in the fulfilment of his purpose and which ought deliberately to be strengthened and deployed; and they will include others which will be hindrances in his work as a social educator. If these personal factors were not influential and often valuable, if it did not matter what attitudes, aptitudes and feelings were brought by educators to their work, then any selection processes would be irrelevant. Any adult would be as valuable a recruit as any other. Clearly this is not so, and indeed without certain basic and well-established personal beliefs and attributes, the desirable social-educational ends and roles could not be adopted. The contribution of the social educator must be made in personal terms: his personality is, as is pointed out elsewhere, the tool above all others which he will use in his practice. It is a tool which he puts at the disposal of an educational purpose, a medium through which he seeks to practise, with guidance from sources of sanction outside as well as within himself. He needs to develop, therefore, the facility for seeing his actions always in the light of the full range of principles relevant to his work. He needs to become literally 'self-conscious', not in any embarrassed or inhibiting way, but in a way which makes him always conscious of himself as an agent whose actions have their justification not in his own inclinations but in the processes of social education he is there to assist. When he makes decisions and arrives at conclusions he must do so deliberately and consciously: he cannot simply act and react. As far as possible his practice will need to be guided by carefully calculated and considered responses to people and situations.

Many of the decisions to be made may be small: whether to type a letter to a young person in hospital and risk some apparent coldness of presentation, or to handwrite it even though the personal nature of the approach may be misunderstood by the recipient; whether to remind the members' secretary to write up the minutes for the next committee meeting, or leave the chairman and other members to take her to task if she fails them; whether to insist for the club or school's good name that a full side be fielded for a particular match, or allow the team itself to deal with absentees and with the league's fine. Some of the choices will be bigger, affecting people's lives deeply (including the worker's own), and involving human joy and sorrow. Whatever their magnitude, however, it will be the adult who has to make the decisions and to make them deliberately and consciously. He will have to look forward and enquire 'what will the consequence be?', or look back and wonder 'was that the right (that is, the appropriate) action to take?', and in answering he will need to look to all his sources of guidance to help him.

The adult who seeks to guide the use of his personality in this way is of course undertaking a greater burden than anyone who constantly relies on his own convictions and feelings alone (or, for that matter, than anyone who relies *only* on the sanctions of his clients or of society). He may be active on many more fronts, be responding to many more facets of every situation. If he is silent and inactive, his very silence and inactivity will more frequently be a positive, preconsidered response. His involvement, though more objective, will be absolutely greater because it will call upon more of his energies and faculties. He will be more conscious of the full weight of responsibility which is the proper experience of those whose work affects, often intimately, the lives of others.

Such self-conscious use of himself will mean that the social educator recognizes the possibility of separation on some occasions of his personal philosophy or convictions from the practice which he undertakes under the guidance of his sources of sanction. Thus in some areas of his work he sees that the beliefs and standards which he holds to be right for his own private life cannot automatically prevail in guiding his work: the sanctions of society and the needs of the client may override them. He does not merely prepare himself for the occasions when the standards by which he conducts and judges his own life will not be appropriate and simply transferable to the lives of the young people with whom he is working. He recognizes also that his wish to use all relevant sanctions to guide his work implies unavoidably that he cannot use the standards and propositions or beliefs on which his private life is based as the only point of reference for his practice as a social educator.

Moreover, this separation of the responses made in private and those made in social-educational practice must extend to the adult's feelings as well as to his beliefs. To feel a care and concern for the welfare of others is of course no less dispensable for a youth worker or teacher than to have a personal philosophy. But just as a personal philosophy on its own is not an adequate guide to action for a social educator, so the indications given by his emotions are not necessarily valid or appropriate either. His anger at a blow thrown by one member at another, his frustration at an injustice shown by one person to another, his fear, his sorrow or his joy are not in themselves reliable guides to what might next need to be done, however strongly felt they may be. Because personally he may *feel* that such-and-such ought to be his response does not automatically make it correct for him as a youth worker or teacher.

It may of course be that the action called for by the reference which he makes to all his sources of sanction coincides with what his own beliefs or emotions urge upon him. But this coincidence is misleading. His action, even though it is what his philosophy or feelings tell him to do, is not justified on those grounds: his personality alone can never be adequate justification for his action while he is working with young people. An action which is part of the practice of a youth worker or teacher, even if it is co-incidentally called for both by his personality and by all his sources of sanction, is justified only by the latter. It is therefore to be seen as an accident and an exception if a social educator's personal philosophy, values or feelings give him guidance which can properly form the basis of his practice. The *rule* on which he should base his expectation is that these personal attributes will not give guidance which can be accepted unchallenged for his practice in social education.

Many youth workers and teachers today would agree, would define their purpose as allowing young people to develop individually and would argue that they therefore do not canvass their private beliefs in their work. Many even who believe that their own philosophy embraces essential truths (whether revealed or rationally deduced) which they are convinced young people would do well to acknowledge, still maintain that they do not use their educational roles for proselytizing. Similarly, social educators and other teachers would agree that their personal emotions and moods, including their strong feelings of care and concern for young people, should not be allowed free rein in influencing their practice.

M

Such workers have thus clearly come to terms with the need to separate the dictates of personal philosophy and emotion from the guidance which principles offer to their practice. But many adults would resist the idea that any such separation can exist, claiming that they cannot be two-faced, deceptive, insincere. They would say that they are always the same, that, for example, wrong is always wrong, certain uses of time always wasteful, certain pursuits always harmful, and that they will always say so and act against them, even in their work with young people. As private individuals, they are entitled to believe these things and behave accordingly, and this no one would deny. Whether, however, society has empowered them to use their public positions to do so, or whether they are then most likely to help young people to develop more fully and individually, is another matter. The sanctions of society – both as represented by the clients' parents and by an educative agency – and of the clients' needs both suggest that social educators above all need to accept the existence of the separation. To do so involves them in no way in being 'untrue' to their 'real' selves since, like any other human being who must live within a variety of situations and accept a variety of roles, they have no single-faceted 'real' self. Most of them would consciously accept that there is no deceit in acting differently in certain ways in their capacity as husband from the way they behave when they assume the roles of parent, church-warden, personal friend, chorus-member in the local operatic society, collector for a works' charity, voter or youth worker. Even more of them would agree that the expression of their 'true self' which is concerned with being lover or political propagandist has no legitimate place in their educational work. Why, therefore, in fulfilling the roles which this latter demands, should they assume that it is correct and even necessary to act as expounder of a personal morality or purveyor of personal recreative enthusiasm? It would seem that attempting to limit the impact of these elements of personality involves no greater untruth to oneself than restraining one's political or amorous urges, or carefully judging how one should act in all the other, often conflicting, areas of one's social existence.

This separation of private values from occupational principles clearly has another important consequence. It means that an adult cannot be regarded as suitable or unsuitable for social-educational roles *simply* because major or dominant sections of our society approve or disapprove of his personal behaviour. The groups of people responsible for selecting the workers in any agency, area or organization cannot allow themselves to be attracted to or repelled by a prospective social educator merely on the grounds of his or her domestic behaviour, social life or political or philosophical allegiance and ideals. Indeed much valuable work in social education has been and is being undertaken by adults whose private values many members of society would judge to be 'wrong'. For if the adult's function in social education is not simply to inculcate his own personal standards and attitudes in young people, then these are clearly not the only criteria by which to assess his suitability. Instead, the probable quality of his practice will need to be judged by his capacity for working according to principles derived from the several sources of sanction, including ones external to himself. On the other hand, while non-normal behaviour and values are not in themselves disqualifications to practise as a social eductor, they are as likely as normal behaviour and values to be an indication of something which does make an adult unsuitable for such work.

The adult who acknowledges the separation between his personal beliefs and the practice to which he is guided in social education is bound to experience a number of tensions in his work. These arise as he becomes a more thoughtful and deliberate social educator, and their existence may be an index of his attempt at sound practice. Such tensions may broadly speaking be traced to four sources. The first occurs because it is never easy for the adult to decide whether he is openly stating his views on some occasion because he is truly required to do so by the needs of young people or by society, or because he wishes at that moment to justify himself or impose himself and his views selfishly on others. In a similar way, he can never be certain whether he withholds a personal statement because the principles of his work genuinely require him to keep silent on this occasion, or out of cowardice or uncertainty.

This tension is all the more prevalent because adults in social education need to be people who have ideals and attitudes of their own which are clearly worked out. For there will be many occasions when the adult *is* required by the principles of his work with young people to make his own personal view explicit, when he is required to demonstrate by word or deed where he stands or what his values are. In social education the adult's own feelings and thoughts are integral elements in the learning experiences of the young people he meets, and the adult must be ready, without relying on clichés or having recourse to saying 'because such-and-such an authority says so', to restate and defend much that makes life coherent for him.

His personal beliefs are called upon also in a less overt and direct way, for they provide him with a platform of private assurance and support from which to act publicly for long and exhausting periods. Indeed, an adult ought to be helped by his training to strengthen this platform, to become more certain of what he does believe to be right and good for himself. Everyday happenings in social education can be exhilarating and satisfying but they may also provide a fundamental challenge to the sensitive and humble adult, demanding some clarity of personal view, much resilience and great resourcefulness. Essential to this is a confidence and inner certainty (which are not the same as arrogance) based on a personal philosophy as clearly worked out and as reasonably explicit as the adult can manage.

The adult's emotions, too, will become fully engaged in his practice. Because his impetus to be among young people is in part altruistic, based on feelings of concern and caring and on sympathy, he cannot fail to become emotionally committed. This does not imply any false sentimentality or indisciplined abandonment of self-control. But there must be feelings which will stem from an awareness of and solicitude for the condition and potentiality of fellow human beings, and these sensations and emotional responses are bound to constitute an important element in his work.

This tension, however, this uncertainty about whether he can trust his own judgment and feelings over stating or withholding his personal views, is not the only one which the adult will experience. For there is a second kind of tension inherent in the interaction which must occur in the mind of the worker between the three sources of sanction. Thus although the agency is likely, in society, to be the major source of guidance, what it requires or suggests will almost certainly conflict at times with what some other source of sanction indicates, whether this be the client or the worker's personality. Tension from this source will of course arise with greater or less frequency depending on the general compatibility of the views and inclination of the agency, the clients and the worker. A certain degree of discrepancy is to be expected, for example, between the wants of the clients and the views of the agency and the worker, and the skill of the latter lies, as we have said, in meeting their needs in such a way as to serve the ends of all three sources of sanction. But where repeated conflict arises between the views of the agency and the worker, he needs to ask himself seriously whether he is in an agency which can allow him to make the best use of his skills, and the agency itself needs to question whether this particular worker is best able to implement their view of their task. (This is assuming of course that neither the agency nor the worker is wishing to centre the work on some particular model: if either is model-centred in approach then clearly it is important to ensure that the other has the same model in mind.) There may be other elements, too, in society which create a conflict in the mind of the worker who attempts to conduct his practice with regard to all three sources of sanction. In particular, the parents of the clients may have expectations of or for their children which differ profoundly from what the adult feels he personally ought to do.

There is a third kind of tension which can arise in the mind of the worker. For he may find on occasions that his interpretation of the guidance he gets from the needs of his clients also creates much soul-searching. For example, because he wishes to respect fully the integrity of the individual and to develop what is essential to his or her uniqueness, the adult may sometimes be forced to repress firm ideas and strong feelings of his own, and to condone or even support and encourage behaviour which personally he finds distasteful or believes would be wrong for himself.

The young person whom he is committed to accept non-judgmentally and to allow to be self-determining may choose to live in a way which is within the law and which, after full consideration of all the facts, the young person believes to be most satisfying and fulfilling for himself. Yet the adult may judge it privately to be fruitless, wasteful and even dangerous or immoral. Certainly an adult in this position will try to ensure that the young person has truly given full consideration to all relevant facts, to make available new information and to suggest possibilities and alternatives which have been overlooked. But if the young person concerned is not going to harm society or others, in the end the adult may be required to help that young person act in a way which is contrary to the adult's own private beliefs, standards, interests or feelings. Whether it emerges in his support for a musical activity whose product he thoroughly dislikes or in help given to two young people whose intimate relationship he considers to be morally dubious and personally destructive, he may be able to demonstrate his respect for the individual only by standing aside from or even by lending support to behaviour of which he personally disapproves. Extreme cases may occur only exceptionally. It will not happen often that an adult is faced with condoning by implication (or at least, refraining from condemning) actions or attitudes which are neither illegal nor severely damaging to others, but which nonetheless seriously contravene his own private code. Moreover, if he is faced with such a decision, he will, as in the case of conflict with an agency, be able to contract out of it by making it clear that he personally can have no part in what is to be done. If he does this, however, he may need at least to re-examine his ability to practise with acceptance and without judgmentalism.

Finally, there is another particular tension to which the adult in social education will always be subject, and it arises out of the fact that many members of society invest him – in their own eyes – with an authority as educator, and yet often his clients' needs can only be met if he uses that authority as rarely as possible. In social education, if it is client-centred, the end itself is that the client shall take the responsibility for being there and for doing whatever he does, alone or in a group, while he is there. The social educator hinders his purpose whenever he uses the authority which many members of society regard him as having, because he impedes the assumption of responsibility by his clients. In particular, in youth work and work where attendance at all is optional, he runs the risk of the clients departing in protest at his limitation of their freedom. This may be good, if it means that the adolescents have matured sufficiently to need the agency and the worker no longer, but the worker will always be anxious not to produce a *premature* departure by some of his clients in response to the unnecessary limitation by him of their freedom to make their own decisions.

The adult must accept of course that he is going to have to use his authority on some occasions, and therefore restrict the development of his clients' assumption of responsibility for their own lives. This is part of his role as educator, part of the clients' experience and learning. None of us, in any case, has absolute freedom, and the adult's imposition of limits will both be understood by young people most of the time, and be similar to many other limitations with which they are already familiar. The adult who does not accept that he will need to impose his authority from time to time will not only be deceiving himself, his agency and the rest of society, but he will be incomprehensible to his clients as an unfamiliar phenomenon in their experience.

And yet the adult will not wish to exercise his authority very frequently, because this will impede too greatly the experience he wants his clients to have. Some authority he will have to exercise, but to a considerable extent he can both enhance the learning of his clients, help them to assume responsibility, and reduce the number of times on which he has to impose his view if, as a general rule, he utilizes the processes of the groups in which his clients meet. This is no easy way out for him, for the sanctions of his own personality, the needs of the clients and the expectations of society upon him must still be balanced. But the group or groupings of young people into which his clients fall will, given experience and freedom, raise spontaneously many of the issues which the worker has in mind himself as a result of his consideration of the principles guiding his work. If there are not, among his clients, voices which represent what is sanctioned by their own wants *and* needs, by society and by his own personality, then he can introduce relevant ideas into a group's interaction (although, even here, he need not do so from a position of authority). It is not the intention now to discuss the details of group processes. It is important to point out, however, that in grappling with the tension between his own undeniable authority and his clients' need to assume responsibility for their decisions, the worker must consider the use of their groups, as much as himself, as legitimate regulators of his clients' freedom.

It is clear, then, that the worker must experience a variety of tensions if he practises self-consciously, since he himself is an important source of sanction for his practice. He thus offers to himself for guidance not only his own personal convictions and values, but the fruits of the immensely complicated process of reconciling this guidance with that given by society and by his clients. The adult, engaged in this process, is the inevitably isolated figure whose function is to make decisions affecting other people's lives.

How can this isolation be made easier? What aids can he have? What can help him discern more accurately and work more effectively within the interplay of society, client and self? How, in other words, can his judgment be informed, given a basis on which to juggle this variety of principles? We shall in the next chapter examine three areas in which a deepened and increased understanding can illuminate the principles we have suggested and provide the data on which the worker can weigh one against the other.

In summary, then, the principles are: acknowledgment of the social and educational purpose of his work, acceptance of his clients, a withholding of judgment about their values, maintenance of their freedom to determine their own attitudes, observing confidentiality in his relationships with them, and a recognition of the worker's own personal involvement in the process.

1. J. KLEIN, *Human Behaviour and Personal Relations*, National Association of Youth Clubs, 1963, p. 18.
2. J. PARR, *Enjoying the Club*, The Fifth Methodist Association of Youth Clubs' King George VI Memorial Lecture, 1965.
3. R. GOSLING, *Lady Albemarle's Boys*, Fabian Society, 1961, p. 19.

Chapter 8

Understanding

In the previous chapter we described and discussed the social educator's sources of sanction, the areas on whose authority his work must be based, and we put forward our view of the principles which he needs to observe in his practice. However, these principles comprise only a part of an appropriate frame of reference. For the social educator also needs the help of some form of objective understanding which is empirically based. If he is forced to use only his own innate and intuitively acquired understanding of human relations and is dependent only on the knowledge available to him through personal experience, he has an insight which is valuable, and indeed much more valuable than is often suggested, but which on its own is inadequate because it is narrow and unrepresentative. It has the admirable but limiting uniqueness of individuality and need no longer be relied upon so exclusively. For there is now a body of evidence about human behaviour available to him which has been collected in many fields, tested and ordered, and which can inform and illuminate his practice. This evidence needs, admittedly, to be conveyed in ways which enable the social educator to see its significance, and not presented as the self-validating academic system which it sometimes appears, unrelated to daily life and circumstances: this is a matter of training method. But the evidence is there, and is more reliable than unrelieved personal experience, because it is more widely based, evaluated and organized.

Three areas of knowledge seem especially relevant to the social educator's work. One is his own personality: he can be aided in deliberate efforts to heighten his understanding and awareness of himself. A second is the field of human behaviour and concerns the factors which move human beings to individual action and above all, in this context, pattern their responses in small groups and in communal institutions. And a third lies within the area of business management: because many of the roles which the social educator must play demand administrative and communicative action, he ought to increase his insight into the processes which this sets in motion. These are the themes which will be pursued in this chapter.

Self-Awareness

Because a worker's own personality and philosophy are especially significant factors in his social-educational practice, it is vital that he seek to understand them. If, in any worthwhile way, he is to appraise and control the relationship between his working practice and his private reactions, then he must have some knowledge of what sort of a person he himself is, what his needs are and what his beliefs and values are.

The aim is not to eradicate the subjective element in his work, since this is neither desirable nor possible. Indeed, it is for the very reason that his personality is so integral to his work that he needs to increase his self-awareness. It can be crucial for his practice to know where his personal feelings and beliefs are strong, what kind of relevance, if any, they have to his work, and how they might most fruitfully be deployed. Equally he wants to know where they are not relevant and how he can limit their impact. Because in social education the worker's personality is so organic an element in the learning process, because it is perhaps the major tool for the work, the worker cannot afford to use it indiscriminately or unthinkingly.

Thus self-awareness is a foundation-stone of a social educator's practice. By carefully developing his knowledge about himself, he can come to understand along what lines some at least of his practice needs to proceed. But what is being asked for is certainly no deep and elaborate piece of psychoanalysis. Such an exercise is known to be helpful for some work in close contact with other people, and is a necessary preliminary for other such work, but certainly it is not called for from youth workers and teachers. The development of self-awareness is not greatly concerned with a profound explanation of *why* a person is as he is, of the childhood and infantile origins of some of his characteristics, of the suppressed drives revealed in some of his behaviour. It is concerned far more with how he actually behaves in various situations and under differing conditions, with the effect of his personality on other people and with their effect on him.

Nor does self-awareness involve an adult in self-condemnation. Discovery about oneself is liable, as we suggest in our discussion of training methods, to be surprising, exciting and occasionally painful, but it is not intended to be an exercise in self-denigration. The adult needs to recognize that there will be times when he feels guilty about traits and feelings which he thinks he sees in himself but which he would prefer not to have. He needs to be helped to see, therefore, that self-awareness is a constructive process and that value judgments are usually irrelevant. For much that we see in ourselves cannot be given high or low value in any absolute sense. The terminology of the psychologist, with specialist meanings and conveying no value judgments, is misused if a layman invests it with an emotive force in the belief that it implies approval or disapproval.

Guilty responses to self-examination, therefore, offer no platform on which better practice can be built. Self-awareness is intended not to undermine personality but to provide a basis for clearer understanding of what is there. The purpose is not to blame, doubt, inhibit and eventually change oneself fundamentally, but to help the personality which already exists to adapt to the demands which work in social education will make on it, and to enable the responses made to be based on wider understanding.

What has to be recognized, however, is that most adults have developed, almost as part of their adulthood, various devices of thought to protect themselves from noticing certain traits which they happen to regard as 'weaknesses', and various devices of behaviour to prevent themselves exposing these. The development of self-awareness will seek to decrease both 'wishful thinking' about 'good' qualities and this curious 'shame' about 'bad' ones. Self-awareness implies the acceptance of oneself without comment or qualification of this kind, and a highly-developed sense of self-awareness will dispense with any hierarchy of 'qualities' as absolutely good or bad. The self-aware worker will assess his qualities not as 'strengths' or 'weaknesses' unrelated to any particular purpose, but as helpful or unhelpful in attaining his objectives as a youth worker or teacher. The process of increasing his self-understanding will give him confidence in himself that is well-founded confidence, so that he demolishes some of his illusions and self-deceptions and comes instead to a more realistic appreciation of his effectiveness as a social educator.

The adult involved will probably wish to leave some aspects of his personality unexplored, since not all his life and behaviour are relevant to his practice. He will probably feel, not without some justification, that there is much in his personality which needs to go unacknowledged if he is to go on living coherently and securely outside his youth work or teaching. This reservation is quite acceptable, if the worker wishes to make it: on the other hand, it cannot be overstressed that any aspect of his life which he chooses to consider and to try to understand will contribute to his working skill as a social educator. Increased knowledge about himself in any respect and in any context will add to his knowledge about and his confidence in his abilities as a practitioner. Moreover, because the evidence available to him about his own daily behaviour and its causes is so much more complete than any he can have about any other person, the careful evaluation and interpretation of this evidence will give him the best chance of understanding the behaviour of others.

Far from being required to dig deeply into the long past of his behaviour, then, the self-aware adult will have tried to know and to deploy with care and deliberation those aspects of his own behaviour which, in an immediate and obvious way, affect his work as a social educator. What happens when he meets, talks with and reacts to other human beings, how they respond and something of what they feel about his impact, how he influences or moulds a situation, how he measures achievement and deals with failure – reflection on some of these sorts of questions will help the social educator to know himself a little better and to know how to use himself slightly more appropriately in his relations with young and old. He will need to look for and examine both spontaneous and passing moods and reactions, and more long-term attributes and tendencies. The man who records and then plays back his voice in order to improve the tone, modulation and dramatic quality of his speech, will not indulge in fundamental self-analysis in order to explain why his performance was as it was, and he will not, if his aim is a practical and constructive one, simply be self-condemnatory. He will want to grasp more fully as many essential features of the way he speaks as he can, in order to modify and perhaps reduce certain habits and to emphasize others. The adult who puts himself to work in social-educational situations needs similarly to try to 'hear' something of his personality, and for precisely the same reasons.

Ways in which the adult might attempt this development of self-awareness will be discussed in the next two chapters. It may be worth emphasizing at this point, however, some of the areas of human behaviour which are most likely to affect an adult's work in social education, and which he needs to look for in himself.

In the short term, tiredness and disappointment are perhaps most common, with their possible consequences of short temper, irritation and reduced forethought or concern for others' feelings. Some people will need no special training to recognize these tendencies in themselves or to discover the need to try and control them. At times, however, such conditions may work indirectly and express themselves unexpectedly so that if an adult has made himself aware that he is likely to be affected by temporary mood or emotional disturbance, he may be better able to prevent some of the consequences. If a man arrives at a club tired after a hard day's work, for example, or a woman has left a sick child at home, both may be tempted to vent some of their discontent or to relieve their anxiety on those most conveniently at hand, whether it be by loss of temper, complete withdrawal or an attempt to dominate a conversation and turn it to their own ends. Naturally, in ordinary life all humans use one another in these ways, and all adults are familiar with the need to let another 'blow his top' or 'sulk in a corner': this is well and good. However the social educator who uses the situations and clients of his practice for these purposes cannot be having due regard to *all* the principles which govern his work. Admission to himself that he could try to use his social-educational situation for his own ends in this kind of way, that he is on occasion likely to display qualities unhelpful to his clients' social education, may do a good deal to reduce the frequency and effect of such behaviour.

Self-awareness can also deepen understanding of more permanently and extensively influential personal responses and, in particular, can bring perspective and detachment to work in which an adult has become too deeply immersed. Too great an involvement in a project is almost bound to lead an adult into sinking too much of his emotional capital into it, so that he will almost certainly be in a disadvantageous position from which to view much of what is happening. Pride, need for achievement, compensation for frustration or failure elsewhere in life may infect his work. The altruistic purpose with which he set out in social education may become partially or wholly lost to sight, submerged, if he is not aware of his own reactions, amid a welter of compensations and personal release.

In coping with the dilemmas and choices which occur every day in his work, the risk is ever present that an adult will unintentionally allow emotions to affect his practice unduly, to the detriment of young people themselves. By greater understanding of himself, the adult may be able to some degree to limit this. If he is able to admit that he has publicly staked much on the success of a dramatic production and would find it hard to deal with a flop, he is less liable to drive the young people involved harder than they are prepared for, or to make them pawns in his personal face-saving game. If he is able to acknowledge that the talents and manner of one young person threaten him considerably, he is less liable to react aggressively towards him. If he is able to grasp, and to accept, that he finds letter-writing a bore, then he is less likely to procrastinate so long that important arrangments are not made, or, perhaps better, he may ensure that someone else's talents are secured for this job. If, most fundamentally of all perhaps, he is able to admit that, although he enjoys young people's company immensely, this should not be his sole justification for being with them, then he is more likely to be able to show acceptance of individuals who are for some reason unattractive to him, he is less likely to be deeply shaken that some young people have, in his eyes, 'let him down', and he is less likely to depend on young people to fulfil his own needs.

Moreover, the development of self-awareness cannot be simply an exercise in directing adverse criticism at oneself, since equally it causes the adult to locate and confirm to himself those talents and personality traits which are of positive value in his practice, whether these be in the field of play production, coping with aggressive behaviour, administration or working with society's 'rejects'. Undue modesty, as often as undue confidence, may hinder the social educator since he may fail, because of it to offer a young person the particular help or opportunity he needs.

Self-awareness is not a precise study, like letter-writing or play production. It is, however, an area of understanding through which progress can be greatly helped if the worker is familiar with the semi-precise studies of the human sciences. The general principles observed in human growth and development relate to his own past and current development and behaviour; the general concepts devised to describe the social interaction of one human being with another refer to his own relationships with other people; the general patterns which have been descried in past and contemporary societies make up the background against which to see his own life.

The terminology of the social psychologist and the social scientist will enable the worker to describe more precisely the facets of the image which he is constructing of himself as his self-awareness develops. He does not, of course, need a mastery of the whole scheme of social psychology before he can use its concepts, any more than anyone needs a degree in French before being able to speak enough of the language to make the best of a holiday in France. It is sufficient to say that the worker's self-awareness will develop as fast as he finds words to describe its facets, and many of those words will be derived from the human sciences. His grasp and understanding of the scientific words will be sure only when he learns to apply them precisely to facets of his own – or in some cases other people's – personality. The ways in which he may be able to break in upon this spiral of increasing understanding are discussed in later chapters, but it is encouraging that many other words of a non-scientific nature have always been current to explain categories of human behaviour.

The social educator seeking self-awareness can, then, draw on these sources to help him describe to himself the various facets of his personality. If he achieves, in due course, an image of himself which corresponds more closely with that which others have of him, he will have done well indeed. What he is particularly concerned to develop, however, is an awareness of the unique combination of ways in which his own personality may help or hinder any social education in which he is involved.

Human Behaviour

The second area in which the social educator needs to deepen his understanding is one which interlocks at many points with his awareness of his own personality. The understanding of human behaviour, particularly in the context of the society in which he and his clients are living, not only offers valuable help to a worker who is seeking to understand himself. It is also a field of study which itself directly informs and illuminates the worker's principles.

As we have suggested, the human sciences claim no *complete* understanding of human behaviour. Even in the field of non-human behaviour and of the physical environment, the ability to describe and explain what happens still remains imperfect. Where human actions are concerned, the imperfection is often considerably greater. The complexity of so many of the situations, the disguised nature of so much of the evidence and the uniqueness of each of the participants make certainty impossible. Nevertheless, because examples have been collected and collated from the widest variety of sources, many generalizations can now be fairly made about how and even why people behave as they do. The experience of past practitioners in educational and related fields has made a significant contribution to the accumulation and organization of this knowledge. So too, perhaps to an even greater extent, has the work of empirical researchers, who have compared like with like and have contrasted unlike phenomena. Human behaviour may not be reducible entirely to laws, but greater understanding of it need not today be left just to chance and can be deliberately increased. It is not our task to describe or evaluate this understanding in any detail, but its general nature is worth outlining.

Those involved in social education must look for guidance and sanction in their work, as was argued in the preceding chapter, not only to their own convictions and feelings, but also to individual clients and a variety of elements and subcultures in society. They must therefore first see and then be able to comprehend the guidance given to them by these sources of sanction. Some of the indications will of course be obvious, and will thus require no special knowledge or insight. But on many other occasions the worker will need to act as interpreter for his clients or for some section of society, perhaps his agency. Either of these sources of sanction may know they want something of him, but may not be able to articulate it. Alternatively, he may recognize that they have a need which they have not turned to him to fulfil, and again he will hope to be able to articulate it for them. Or, not uncommonly, they will be demanding something which he will see to be unrealistic, and he will need to try to trace their demands to their sources and suggest a practicable alternative solution – again a process of interpretation. To be able to perform such interpretative functions, the social educator must be acquainted with some of the existing knowledge about the way in which human beings behave in society, and about the structure of his own society in particular.

To take the latter area of understanding first: at a very practical level, any youth worker or teacher will be very familiar with the need to understand the society in which he works. Concern about a boy's distraction from his studies because his sick mother needs his help in the house, or about a girl's employment at a firm whose heavy work is too tiring for her, will bring the social educator into contact with home-help, welfare and youth employment services. The adult is demonstrating his own as well as his clients' dependence on the society surrounding them, and demonstrating too that he needs to understand this society and its organization. Here then is one area of understanding with which the adult must have contact. It is also one which can be systematized, and may be acquired less haphazardly, more economically and more completely than by accidental practical contact. A worker also needs to understand adequately how the domestic customs and assumptions of his own social class and geographical area differ from those of the young people he meets, and of how this difference may affect their educational attainment, vocational opportunity or recreational interests. He will again be greatly helped if he deliberately sets out to acquaint himself with what has been discovered empirically about these matters. To say, however, that the adult needs to know something of, for example, sociology or anthropology, or the social services does not mean that he must be *told* in a long series of lectures what others assume he wants to hear. Nonetheless it is unquestionably true that without some insight into what these sciences have revealed, without some careful acquisition of understanding about a society's institutions, values, purposes and internal subcultural and class variations, the social educator's vision is likely to be unnecessarily impaired and his practice in consequence unnecessarily less effective.

An understanding of the way human beings behave in face-to-face relationships or in groups is of equal importance with this understanding of the structure of our own society. The adult may only *suspect* that there is more involved in the individual behaviour he is encountering than meets the eye, but cannot know how to interpret what he sees unless he has some grasp of the general principles now known to underlie much human interaction. Again, mere exposure through lectures and books to knowledge of individual and social psychology will not automatically supply answers to specific situations. Some deeper and disciplined insight into how human beings behave will nonetheless make the adult's perception of these situations broader, more sensitive and more flexible.

However, if the adult is to respond in this way to individual young people, an understanding of *individual* psychology will not in itself be enough. On most occasions, he will not meet his clients separately, as if they formulated their behaviour while in isolation, but will meet them while they are in contact with and responding to other people. The social educator will thus be forced to take into account the effect that people have on each other's behaviour. Almost by definition, in fact, because he is *social* educator, he will need to consider individuals as a part of a social context. In particular, he will be bound to think of each young person as one who is interconnected with many others, as a participant in groups which are sufficiently small to allow personal, face-to-face relationships (however superficial or transient) to develop among all members. Individual behaviour is almost inevitably modified by the presence of others, so that knowledge of the patterns of this influence, if and where they can be discerned and described, can be of immense help to the social educator.

N

To say that the adult will contact individual young people in their groupings does not mean of course that the individual is less important than some impersonal group force, or that his integrity must be sacrificed in order to serve this. The group has no existence independent of the human beings who form it, and it is not being invested for some ideological reason with a significance greater than that of its 'components'. Nor does it follow that, because an adult is called on most often to work with groups of people, he will never have to work intensely, on a one-to-one basis, with individual young people. If he is well known and trusted, some of them may well need him from time to time to listen, support, counsel, encourage. On a more casual level, too, the contacts he will have to make will be very personal, since in all his work his purpose will be person-centred. The social educator needs to be able to apply the principles outlined in the previous chapter to a situation in which he is dealing with only one young person on his or her own. The growing concern in social and other forms of education with the use of counselling and the skills of the case-worker is in no sense misplaced.

From a purely practical point of view, however, those involved in social education are bound to be in touch with young people mainly in groups, as this is what resources of staff and finance in both the Youth Service and the schools will dictate. The practical possibility of an adult in these circumstances being able to form an intense person-to-person relationship with more than a small number of the young people he meets, and to use such a relationship as the principal medium for his work, is slight even if it is desirable. Social educators in the future may do an increasing amount of case-work, but for most of them working with young people in their groups will be a necessity.

There are also sound educational reasons for doing this. For, in order to achieve a full human existence, people inevitably congregate for some part of their lives and so acknowledge their mutual dependence. The complexity and fluidity of this mingling is essentially and distinctively human, for the depth of interpenetration is made possible by the precise tools of communication which only human beings have. Young people especially can be expected to exhibit this need for dependence and self-expression through contact with others, since much of the relaxation and learning which they seek is most fully achieved, not privately and in isolation, but by means of group experience. Many – though of course not all – of those in their teens will, of their own accord, act collectively in order to gain *individual* satisfaction and fulfilment. Before ever coming to clubs or organizations, they will have joined together, and not only in search of 'mere' pleasure, but also for the security which identification with others brings, for the acceptance, and for the recognition. Once in groups, they will be required to adjust to the personalities of others, to comply with expectations and standards which already exist, to contribute positively and acceptably to any modification of these, to play a variety of roles and take part in the various forms of activity which a group will create. In fact, in groups of their contemporaries, they will be able not only to increase their enjoyment, but also to learn and develop much of that social skill which, we suggest elsewhere, characterises 'maturity'. Their very membership of groups, far from undermining their individuality, can thus be a means of expressing it. The setting may be a 'mass' one, but what is gained from it will be very personal to each participant in it. The provision of conditions for individuals' involvement in group situations in order to help their growth and achievement is therefore a primary task of the social educator.

Teachers of certain subjects may sometimes be able to achieve some of their purpose by working as though all the essential lines of communication radiate from them to each of their individual pupils, on the grounds that it is on contact with the teacher that the learning of the pupils depends. However, when *social* skills are being learned, the main medium for the individual becomes the people with whom he most associates, and the adult is only one of these. At moments, the lines of communication may seem to the adult to radiate from him to all the young people in any particular group or, more likely, to one or two of them and thence to and among all the others. Usually, however, the learning of the young is far less dependent on such a direct contact with an adult, since there already exist among group members some of the most vital stimulants to individual growth and development. The interrelations present the social educator with an appropriate vehicle for his purpose, which is concerned much more with the *social* progress people are making than with the practical or activity progress. And his clients can accept the use of such a vehicle, since it is entirely familiar to them and they are integral to it, and his use of it in no way implies a diminution of concern for the individual.

The teacher or youth worker involved in social education thus starts both with the belief and also with some empirical proof that the young can teach each other and that he, the adult, has skills which are mainly concerned with easing, increasing and occasionally supplementing this process. In consequence, he is bound to seek a deeper understanding of how this intimate involvement in relationships with others influences and changes individual behaviour – and of how individuals contribute to group development, existence and disintegration. However, because the behaviour of groups is influenced in vital ways by the ideals, assumptions and conventions of the wider society in which they live, and because much of the available understanding of group relations has been gained in North America, social educators in Britain need to use a great deal of the evidence with care. For example, they need to bear in mind that members of our society today are not generally accustomed to integrating into a common culture a large number of disparate groups of people relatively recently arrived from many different backgrounds. Consequently, among individuals, there is less experience of joining a group whose pattern of behaviour is quite unstructured. It is expected, usually with justification, that a recognized procedure and ethos will already exist. Those who join a group which lacks these norms of behaviour are demonstrably less ready than are members of a society whose institutions are less deeply rooted to 'contribute from scratch' to the development of 'purpose-built' procedures for the group. They have learned by experience to feel more comfortable if they can carry into each new group a pre-formed idea of how they will behave. As our society at national, regional and local levels increases the rate at which it devises new structures with new purposes, and as more new opportunities for cooperative uses of leisure arise, its members will no doubt grow in their adaptiveness, their readiness to devise group norms afresh in new groups.

Whether or not these changes occur, however, the social educator can certainly utilize American experience if he makes allowances for cultural differences. Moreover, it would be wrong to imply that no knowledge is available based on British social relationships, since a good deal is. From all sources, in fact, much now is known about membership of groups and interrelationships within them. Much is known about the taking of the lead in situations, how 'leadership' evolves, how it is exercised and how it relates to those who 'follow' and to their expectations and aspirations. Much is known of these aspirations, of values and required standards; of morale and cohesiveness; of the effects of the external environment on internal group behaviour; and so on. It is not our intention in this book to describe this knowledge in detail, or to show precisely how the British social educator might use it. But its availability needs to be noted.

Insight into the behaviour of individuals, then, and into the structure and operation of society, together with this knowledge of group processes, constitute the second of the three areas of understanding important to the social educator. Because this understanding of human behaviour is so essential to his appreciation of young people, it may be said to be the vital area for informing and illuminating the principles on which he works.

Management

In general, social educators will see themselves as practitioners in human relationships. Many of them will have agreed to work in youth organizations or in the social-educational work of schools because they enjoy being with young people and because they wish to help them. It will therefore be accepted by many social educators without demur that it is necessary for them to try to improve their understanding of people and relationships and their own part in these, although some practitioners will disagree about the emphases to be given to each of the aspects. Because, to them, people count, they see the face-to-face contacts which they make with individual young people and the humanity and feelings which these contacts generate as the core of their work.

It is true that a great deal of time *is* spent with people if one works as a social educator. But youth workers and teachers both find that, if they are to fulfil all the obligations upon them, they have to devote a significant proportion of their time to work which does not directly involve them with their clients. This other work, which includes all the procedures which service the actual involvement with the clients' needs, may broadly be described as administration or management: this comprises a third area in which understanding must be deliberately sought.

The actual proportion of the social educator's time likely to be spent in this way is difficult to calculate, but a certain amount of evidence is available. In September 1961, Virginia Kent and Simon Pratt carried out a postal survey of over 200 full-time youth leaders and produced a report on their working hours.[1] They admitted that the detail of their findings could not be taken as wholly reliable. Nonetheless, their report contains some significant indications of how much time may have to be devoted to administration by some social educators.

Kent and Pratt asked the youth leaders they surveyed how much time each week they gave to 'essential administration'. The following is a summary of the answers:

14 leaders	0 – 6 hours
60 leaders	6 – 12 hours
62 leaders	12 – 18 hours
54 leaders	over 18 hours

TOTAL 190

Some of these figures may be surprising. Certainly they suggest that the traditional conception of what the *youth leader* does might need some revision. For they make clear that the time spent by 61 per cent of these leaders on essential administration was probably as much as or more than that which was spent actually in contact with members, if one assumes that their clubs were open 5 evenings a week for 2½ hours or 3 hours each evening. In addition, some at least of a further 31 per cent of the leaders seem to have been spending hardly any more time in face-to-face contacts with young people than they were on administration. The fact that the leaders themselves thought that so much time was needed for administrative tasks, even though some of them may have had a good deal of scepticism and reservation about the importance of these, makes the figures even more interesting.

Obviously the weight of administration will vary considerably between one practitioner and another. Although Kent and Pratt were concerned only with full-time youth leaders, their very basic study suggests that any adult needs to know a good deal about administration and management if he has ultimate responsibility for an agency, or for a department dealing with the social education of the adolescent within a larger agency like a school or settlement or community association. Presumably any helper or assistant also, even though he does not bear full responsibility, can only make his fullest contribution to the work of an agency if he has some degree of understanding of such administrative skills and if he exercises this understanding within his sphere of work.

There are two factors which must not be overlooked at this point, since both could exaggerate the problem. One is that many adults who undertake social-educational work part-time may well be employed in their full-time occupations in the management of enterprises of one kind or another, and may therefore have a good deal of understanding already which they can transfer. If this is the case, it is necessary only to ensure that they are aware that the distinctive overall purpose of the social-educational agency may in some respects require them to follow administrative and management procedures there which differ considerably from those appropriate to the business enterprises in which they work during the day. The other warning note is that the time which Kent and Pratt found their youth leaders to be spending in administration may be quite in excess of, or below, what is necessary. For not only are some clubs seriously inefficient due to under-administration, but some leaders spend *too much* time on administrative work. In some cases this is because they do not make the most economic use of their administrative time, due to lack of understanding: in other cases leaders may be said to retreat behind a shield of administrative duties when they find the human relations demands of their work too overpowering.

However, both the findings of the survey and the experience of many practitioners do give some indication of the proportion of working time likely to be given over to administration. Its volume should not really be surprising, since work which requires the adult to cooperate with and to maintain liaison between parents, sponsors, clients, educational, social work and commercial bodies, the press and many interested parties will inevitably have many administrative elements. The adult's efforts to discern individual needs and to help in seeing that these are satisfied will also require him to work for some of the time in an administrative capacity, perhaps at one stage removed from contact with the individual young people who are benefiting.

He can of course ignore this or treat it as an unfortunate chore to be carried out as quickly and skimpily as possible. And since so many adults select themselves for social-educational work because of (to use an over-worked phrase) 'an interest in people', some chagrin at finding themselves dealing with administration is understandable. Nonetheless, a positive attitude to these responsibilities is certainly essential, since the efficiency with which the adult discharges them has a direct bearing on the strength and fruitfulness of his human relations. At a very basic level, a failure here will almost certainly react unfavourably on young people's respect for, trust in and willingness to cooperate with him. A boiler which is not turned on because the youth worker forgot to inform the caretaker that a group would be meeting; a grant not made because a form was not sent punctually to the education offices; a public event inaccurately reported because a newspaper was not invited to send a representative – all these may damage, however slightly, an adult's relationships with his clients and so impair their educational development. In individual cases, where a young person is in difficulties or has particular talents, the reliability of a worker's administrative skill can be crucial, whether he needs to enlist the aid of a social worker, a commercial organization or a football club.

The social educator, indeed, is at times the manager of a small business enterprise. His functions may include something of public relations representative, secretary, buyer, accountant, wages clerk, personnel officer, clerk of works, security officer and many others. His main focus will remain on people, but in many aspects of his work he will rely on 'impersonal' systems, on structures, machinery, organization. And far from trying to pretend that this is or ought to be otherwise, he will need to be ready for what it involves and be helped to achieve it. Many adults will be unable to function fully in their human relations roles if they are not prepared for their administrative duties.

In part, this assumes that ideally they will need to possess or have easy access to equipment such as typewriters and duplicators and to some secretarial help. However, the fact that they may have to manage their own organization also means that they must gain greater understanding of the underlying processes of management generally. Here, as in all the other spheres of understanding which we have discussed, they cannot attempt to make themselves experts, fully in command of all the theory of business management. However, since there are today some systematized bodies of knowledge on how this sort of management is best carried on, those social educators whose responsibilities are likely to justify it need to look deeper than the merely superficial functioning of a subscription book and a canteen stocktaking. These are important, but less so by far than the fact that the adult must relate successfully to sponsors who wield ultimate authority over him, to colleagues who work around him and depend on him, and to staff – secretarial, perhaps, caretaking and even catering – who are responsible to him.

Depending on the size and complexity of the human enterprise in which he works, the adult will encounter more or less of the 'normal' problems of communication, status, identification with the organization's goals, and so on. Again, because his is an agency which is concerned above all with the *social* lessons of education, these problems will have a special significance. Many of them will not be incidental offshoots of the main purpose, but central to his task. How the members' committee relates to the management committee or to the caretaker, whether the coffee bar makes a profit, how its accounts are done and who does them, who answers letters, what the cleaner thinks of him and of the young people will all be key factors to the success of his enterprise. And all will assume some insight into the administrative processes going on around him. In particular, they will require him not just to apply his understanding of himself and of human behaviour to his relations with young people but also to use it to illuminate his contacts with adults. In his role of manager, he will need to acquire some understanding of the functioning of human institutions in general so that he can gain some insight into the particular institution for which he is responsible.

It is clear, therefore, that for the social educator there is no hard and fast dividing line between his administrative tasks and his 'work with people', and that his oversight of a building or his secretarial arrangements need to be as fully influenced by insight into underlying processes (most of them human) as do any other parts of his work.

Here then is a third area where a deliberate search for a deeper and disciplined understanding is necessary. The adult does not need to become an expert in this or any of the fields outlined. Unless he is ready and able to do so, the adult does not have to absorb three vast bodies of academic learning. One of the major themes of our chapter on training will be that the understanding must be built on the experience which all adults have in the fields to be covered. No adult is entirely ignorant of himself, his impact on others, of human behaviour, of our social structure, or of the management of a piece of business. There are many instances each day where he is seeing or participating in some of the mechanisms and processes dealt with in the human sciences. There are many methods of making him alive to these, of making these elements in his experience accessible to him in the form of an understanding which will help him to practise social education more certainly. What we have been concerned to establish in this chapter are the three major areas which this understanding may be said to cover.

1. V. KENT and S. PRATT, *The Working-Hours of Full-Time Youth Leaders*, September 1961: an enquiry sponsored by the Goldsmiths' Company.

Chapter 9

Forging a Discipline

Social education, by its very nature, may require an adult to act spontaneously without opportunity for lengthy reflection, and yet it is important that he avail himself as often as possible of the sources of guidance and illumination which are embodied in his purpose, principles and understanding. In this chapter we shall suggest two devices which will help him to do this.

One is through the written or tape-recorded description of the events of one session or meeting of a social-educational agency, and of the adult worker's impressions and interpretations of them. The other is through the regular discussion and evaluation of his working experiences with someone who is uninvolved in the events themselves but is skilled enough to enable the adult to see his own behaviour and obligations more clearly. The two 'tools' we thus suggest are recording and supervision.

There are two ways, therefore, in which the word 'discipline' may be applied to these procedures. In the first place it may be said that to put into words, regularly each day, a description of the events of a club or class or group meeting, and to follow it by an interpretation and perhaps at some later stage by a discussion, constitutes a discipline in itself. By simply carrying out the exercises of recording and supervision, the worker is disciplining himself always to reflect upon the session just passed, and always to discern how the general principles apply to particular events.

But there is another sense in which the social educator needs to have a discipline. He needs to make the principles and understanding so much a part of himself, impressed and ingrained in his mind, that they affect even the spontaneous reactions which will make up so large a part of his practice. The ebb and flow and the unpredictability of adolescent life, and especially the life of adolescent groups, are perhaps the most dominating factors of his work. They impose on him an often inescapable obligation, not only to act, but to think and act quickly and firmly. Thus decisions often have to be taken, and even longer-term policy to be stated or implied, immediately and on the spot, without opportunity for preliminary consideration. In any case it would clearly be extremely damaging to their purpose if social educators constantly withdrew from face-to-face contacts with young people in order to give themselves time to choose their words and actions deliberately.

The social educator who regards himself as a man of action does not mean that he only has to act, never to think carefully about what he is doing. But he *is* constantly 'on the spot', under the microscope in a situation and set of relationships unusually free of structures and laws which confirm and regulate his behaviour. This is as it should be of course. But in view of this the adult must look for a long-term disciplining effect from the retrospective thinking which recording and supervision entail. They must not be an empty exercise in being wise after the event or being wildly hypothetical about the future.

In time therefore the adult must absorb into his personality what he learns from such reflection upon his experiences. What he discovers as a result of these devices must be incorporated into and reconciled with his existing philosophy and habits of thought and feeling, so that he loses some of his self-consciousness about it. When this has occurred, what he has learned from reflecting deliberately on his past practice will affect and pervade many even of his spontaneous reactions in the future. The process may be called one of internalization: it is vital if the adult's daily practice is to benefit from and reflect the principles and understanding which we have described.

It is this internalization, this constant awareness of the principles and understanding relating to practice which is the second sense in which discipline can follow from recording and supervision. This is very far from the habitual repetition of identical responses day by day. It is primarily an opportunity to establish a constant frame of mind which brings some regularity, consistency and unity to the work. The ways in which the adult gets used to thinking in the security of his retrospective reflection will begin to extend themselves into the immediate responses which are required of him outside this apparent ivory-tower, in the quickly-changing world of club or school. Even as he goes through an incident with some young people, chords may be struck in his mind and feelings so that, without his realizing it or doing it consciously, he is referred back to his principles and his understanding.

The process of internalization is best begun in the early stages of an adult's training in social education. Certain kinds of recording can be introduced into the initial training which he undertakes, though at that stage they will have a training purpose and will not necessarily be the best kind for him to use as a practitioner. But training is not a once-for-all process and the careful reflection which recording entailed in training is equally indispensable in practice. The forms of recording used by a worker in post may differ, but if he once gives up the habit, which recording inculcated in him during his initial training, of subsequently referring events back to basic principles and empirical understanding, then a hardening sets in and the practice itself becomes stale habit and conditioned reflex. Spontaneous reaction becomes token rejoinder, the social educator becomes a performer, polished but responding mechanically to every situation. Nothing is seen as new, everybody is 'just like' somebody else, every situation is believed to have had its exact replica some time back. 'Internalization' is arid unless what is internalized is constantly exercised on the practice of the day: it is, like training, a never-ending process. Indeed, it is the major part of, some would say another word for, training. For explicit training procedures, helping practitioners in intensive ways to internalize the guiding principles and the understanding which illuminates them, are really only a part of the long-term process which may be described as forging a discipline.

Recording

Recording, as we have suggested, is to be regarded as a device for instilling a discipline in the thinking of the practising social educator. Some suspicion has been directed at it in the past, partly because it takes some of a practitioner's time. That it does take time is undeniable, but to see it as simply another task, to be added on to the many tasks already part of the practitioner's work, is to place it in the wrong category of thought entirely. Recording can only justifiably claim a part of a social educator's time if it directly helps him to carry out his main purpose better. Its function is to add certainty, dependability, insight to the tasks which the practitioner has to undertake anyway. It is intended to ensure that conscious thought and greater coherence are brought to the existing content of his practice. It is an integral part of the discipline, the mental processes, which need to underpin all social education if it is to attain the highest standards most consistently.

It is true, however, that much of the evidence of the value of this type of recording is derived from American experience and that not all of this evidence can be assumed uncritically to be relevant to Britain. For if, in the U.S.A., those who work with young people are responsible for smaller groups than their British counterparts, or more often receive skilled supervision of their practice, or have available more secretarial help, then the forms of recording which they have developed may need considerable adaptation before they can be applied in this country. The work load often carried by British social educators, the advantages and difficulties inherent in the fact that most youth workers and an increasing number of teachers are occupied only part-time in social education, the isolation of so many of them (especially youth workers) from other practitioners, the almost complete absence of regular supervision of the kind described below, and the shortage of secretarial assistance all suggest that it would be too optimistic to expect to transplant an American system unchanged.

There is, of course, an objection to any form of recording, other than that which is strictly demanded for administrative purposes, on the grounds that it is unnecessary because the required reflection can take place 'in the adult's head', during regular 'thinking' periods: committing to words any form of record thus becomes superfluous. No matter how deliberate and conscientious this reflection by thinking may be, however, it is extremely difficult to maintain 'in one's head' the degree of coherence and logical progression which is possible on paper or tape, and the worker is unlikely to gain so clear a picture at the end of the process of what has already happened or what his next move might be. It is always difficult to consolidate recollections and thoughts unless some confining framework of expression is imposed on them. Recording ensures that haphazard and disjointed memories, feelings and attitudes are more completely connected and more clearly arranged so that future practice can emerge more deliberately from past experience. The process of recalling the details of a situation or series of events, reflecting on their origins, repercussions and significance and then writing down or, less satisfactorily, tape-recording these thoughts, brings a clarity and orderliness to the planning and direction of practice which are difficult to achieve on one's own in any other way.

It follows inevitably from this that recording depends on the worker's ability to recall events, to interpret them according to his understanding and to evaluate them according to his principles. Thus the quality of his recording depends to a real extent upon the range of his vocabulary, especially in the relevant fields of study. This does not mean, of course, that the social educator can never achieve high standards in his practice without mastering some of the vocabulary. It does mean, however, that these high standards cannot be attained so certainly or so consistently, because it is through the vocabulary that he is enabled to manipulate the principles and understanding which relate to his practice.

More precisely, therefore, two main gains may be looked for from recording. Firstly, the actual activity of committing to paper or to a tape the thoughts which are in his head acts as a stimulant to a worker's memory. Some of his experiences will, of course, dominate his thinking anyway and will be recollected with little special effort. Other events will have been so transient or, perhaps, uncomfortable, that they will be lost to him forever. But all such introspection is highly selective unless it is rigorously controlled, and the adult will forget or unintentionally suppress much that could be significant for his practice if it were brought back to the level of conscious awareness and consideration. Many small encounters, snatches of conversation or gestures may unwittingly not be recalled. A calculated attempt is needed, therefore, to prevent anything significant being lost. Written or spoken records, by acting as prompts to the memory, do guard against such loss, and do increase the chances of recalling some at least of those words which have been heard but not listened to, some of those incidents which have been seen but not noticed. Pen or microphone thus in a sense become channels of communication with a worker's own past experience.

The second main value of recording on paper or on tape is that the notes or spoken recollections, however abbreviated, offer a basis on which to carry out a planned search for the lessons of immediate past practice and for appropriate future action. By attempting, as far as is ever possible in human affairs, to make objective descriptive statements about his work, an adult will have done something towards separating fact from opinion. On the basis of these statements he will be better able to consider the meaning of his experience and offer himself some interpretations of it and some tentative projections of what ensuing lines of action might be. Such interpretations and projections will often, because of the obscurity and unpredictability of much in human relationships, need to be in the form of questions: 'Is this necessary?' or 'Would X like that?' Few firm answers may be available and none ought to be faked for reasons of tidiness or self-esteem. Even to be so tentative, however, will serve the diagnosis-and-response approach which was advocated earlier and will make easier and more likely some regular reference to the relevant principles and understanding.

Recording, then, is not an end in itself. What is more, its prime value does not lie in the material product of what is finally written down or spoken into a microphone. What matters most is the process of thinking and analysis implied in translating an experience into words on paper or tape, and the studied reflection which can take place once experience is committed to words. It is the challenge of expression which helps to ensure that the thinking and anlysis go on, go on consistently, and go on more certainly than they might if the practitioner just had regular private 'thinking periods'.

It is the self-imposed, daily routine of expressing past experience in words which is thus important. The justification for recording is not that the worker may reread it in two months or two years and so jog his memory about past events, though it may be used to help him draw together experiences and reflections encountered over time, and so provide a better perspective of the long-term movement of an individual or a group. Recording what has recently happened is justified by the opportunity it gives the worker of applying his principles and understanding to immediate past practice, taking stock, and planning future work.

This however still leaves unresolved the practical problems, especially of finding time for recording. Under the pressure of the variety of demands already being made on youth workers and teachers today, it *is* often difficult to fit in the period needed for recording. Even if it is acknowledged that recording is not just another task of the same order as restocking the canteen or counting the football jerseys, it still does require at least a valuable thirty minutes of an already crowded working day. Moreover, the length and complexity of the sessions during which an adult is with his clients poses another problem. For if he is expected to record in full all that is remotely interesting or potentially significant in an afternoon or an evening's meeting, he is likely to be faced with a mammoth task. The events and relationships of the highly informal situations which he is continually meeting are subtly interlinked, often completely without order and utterly confusing to the thoughts and emotions of the adults involved. From among these fast-moving and chaotic circumstances, the social educator has to extract some order and coherence. He will have to record many incidents of which he is part, many reported to him, and many which he simply observed. Unlike, say, the social case-worker, he will be involved much of the time with many clients at once and not just with one alone or with two who are jointly discussing the same problem: and he will have to operate without the structure which a case-work interview imposes. Inevitably and necessarily, some selection and some abbreviated written or spoken form will have to be achieved if the task is not to take on unmanageable proportions.

The actual form of recording by which the adult may best be helped to introduce discipline into practice must itself develop as experience is gained of different systems. The concern here has been to sketch the justification for and uses of recording, and the objectives it is designed to attain in the work of the practitioner.

Supervision

The second device for instilling discipline into practice – supervision – is sometimes misunderstood either as a prying interference by an outsider or as the general administrative and personal surveillance and even pastoral care exercised by a headmaster or youth officer over a teacher or youth worker. This latter oversight is of course essential, and the support derived from it is valuable particularly to new entrants to social-educational work.

But supervision in the technical or specialist sense in which it is used in relation to the improvement of a practitioner's discipline in his work is a different process. The supervisor's concern is not to inspect or to administrate: he is there to enable the practitioner to attain the highest possible standards of work by his – the practitioner's – evaluation of it. Moreover, a worker's relationship with his supervisor is on almost all occasions as confidential as a worker's relationships with young people. The supervisor will be strictly bound not to act upon any information he acquires, whether about the worker or a client of the worker, without the explicit permission of the person concerned, and only on the gravest grounds will another principle prevail over the one of confidentiality. This may raise some problems if the supervisor both knows the identity of the client under discussion (and this is rarely necessary) and is in a position to contact him or take initiatives intended to affect those affairs which have been discussed in confidence. Problems may arise also because the supervisor will have obligations to the law, or because, on occasions, he is forced to consider those sanctions originating in the requirements of individual young people or their parents. But such exceptions will be very few. In general, the supervisor's confidentiality towards the worker will override all other considerations.

This will be essential if only to ensure that the worker feels able occasionally to include in his discussion with his supervisor material which he knows in confidence from his clients. In such cases, the worker will rarely if ever need to name or otherwise to reveal the identity of the client involved. Even if he does so, however, he would not infringe his principle of 'confidentiality', since the supervisor is in effect no more than an extension of the practitioner's most important working tool – his own personality. The supervisor thus becomes a part of the mental equipment with which the practitioner reflects upon his work: his only use of confidential information given to the worker by a client will be in helping the worker to decide what he should do – if anything – in the best interests of the client.

A confidential worker-supervisor relationship will be necessary also because it will have an importance for the worker himself. For if the worker cannot be sure that he can speak to the supervisor in confidence he will be unable to examine his work openly. He must be certain that the recording and subsequent verbal discussion will not be used except to enable him in his work to maintain standards which are the highest possible for him. When, for example, he feels that something reflects on his success or weakness as a practitioner – and at times it may – he may be reluctant to divulge it if he fears it may be used in any way to jeopardize his own position. Wherever possible, therefore, the supervisor needs to be a figure not identified in any way with the organization or structure sponsoring the agency in which the practitioner works. He needs to have, in the mind of the worker, an independence of all authority-hierarchies to which the worker may regard himself as answerable, and to be identified only as a resource-person for the worker, helping him to exercise the discipline relevant to his practice. The less he is confused with authority in the worker's mind, the greater is the mutual confidence between the two likely to be, and the more productive will their work together become.

Supervision therefore is in a sense a neutral process. No automatic assumptions of superiority are built into it and no value judgments

o

inevitably made. It is not concerned to measure the success of the worker's practice for any outsider, though the worker himself may use the process to test what he is doing and may be led to judge of his own accord that some of his previous actions in his work were mistaken. Nor is it intended to lead the worker to certain objectives simply because the supervisor judges them to be desirable. It is concerned mainly to raise 'open-ended' questions which will probe what a worker has done, search out what may never otherwise have occurred to him or what he might have avoided, help him to articulate what he had not realized he knew and refer him continually to all the main elements in the frame of reference surrounding his work. At times, to achieve these ends, the supervision may need to go beyond mere questioning and indicate or suggest possible alternative responses or interpretations, but even this needs to be done in a genuinely open-ended way. It ought not to attempt to impose ideal solutions from outside the worker's experience. The supervision will not be helped if the worker feels he needs simply to defend what he has done, since this will probably lead him to resist some of the central questions and suggestions. But it will not be helped either if the supervisor attempts to insist on answers to problems for which he has no actual responsibility, because this too will upset the balance of his relationship with the practitioner by endangering the latter's sense of authority in matters concerning his work.

Really thorough supervision will thus throw all the contours of the worker's practice into relief and enable him to see himself and the effect of his work with his clients in a new light. He will be helped to examine his own strong and weak points as a practitioner constructively and so will be given a greater chance to develop his own skills and insight further. Because this will serve in the long run to support and encourage him in his whole approach, the supervisor must be seen as a supportive and not a dominating figure, in no way reducing the worker's responsibility and sovereignty in his practice.

The basis of the exchange between supervisor and practitioner is usually the latter's recordings. It is these which give the necessary form and focus to supervision. Occasional, even regular, chatty sessions following no planned course and lacking continuity between one meeting and the next are not enough. A careful control of time, so that vital issues of immediate past experience may be considered, is essential. Thus, through the recording, the supervisor could help the worker in the two most vital areas of his discipline – recall of the detail of what happened, and interpretation of this so that future action can be considered. It is in this sense that supervision is an extension of the recording and recording itself, though still helpful on its own, is far less so if it is never subjected to the supervisory process. For through supervision, through the need to *talk* as well as to think and write about his experience, and through the extra dimension which an uninvolved but skilled outsider can supply, the purposes which recording serves are much more likely to be achieved.

In the absence of the specialist supervisor the social educator will gain much from the help of a skilled 'other person'. For while supervisory skills do exist as an expertise of their own, any person *not* directly involved in the worker's practice may be able to help him considerably, provided that he is prepared to be bound by the principles appropriate to supervision. One practitioner may, for example, be able to help another practitioner by playing the supervisory role, and may then exchange places and be supervised himself. Clearly such an arrangement will produce an experience markedly different from supervision by a specialist supervisor. But another mind, aware of the guiding principles and understanding relevant to the work and acting upon the recorded experience of a practitioner, will stimulate a good deal more reflection than will the practitioner unaided and alone.

Supervision between two practitioners of equal experience and similar function is clearly a second best. But where there is a disparity, as for example between the trained and disciplined worker and one who is relatively inexperienced, the 'senior' partner can take the other a long way. Two examples may be given of such a supervisory relationship. One is in the large agency in which the worker with ultimate responsibility helps his assistants to reflect in this way on their experiences during the recent session or meeting, and so spreads his own skill somewhat wider. The other is in the practical element of many training courses, where the worker in an agency holds supervision sessions with an adult temporarily attached to his agency as a working student. The relevance of supervision to both initial and continuing in-service training may be clearly seen in these two uses.

The worker-supervisor relationship is a delicate one which needs to be entered upon by both parties with forethought and preparation for its demands. But properly developed and used, it can be most productive. The value to the worker should be seen in increased self-confidence, detachment and understanding. It should be of special value to newly-trained entrants into the field, in particular those who are full-time or fully in charge of an agency's work, since it offers a means of tangible and very personal support in the face of immediate and often unanticipated pressures and uncertainties. The confusing and frequently depressing effects of the early days of full-time work or of undertaking full responsibility might thus in part be offset. So too might the resultant risks of weakened ideals, of reduced willingness to look for guidance outside oneself and of increased emotional involvement. Far from being an unjustifiable luxury, in fact, supervision might be seen as an essential means of preserving and strengthening the existing working force. If supervision were available to more practitioners, especially new entrants, many more of them might grow more easily and fully into a realistic grasp and acceptance of the highest standards of social-educational practice.

Supervision is therefore both a means of initial training and a device to help the practitioner in post to keep his internalized principles and understanding under constant review. It might even, in some circumstances, be seen as an alternative to longer or more frequent courses since it saves plant and money. Moreover, as a training medium, it connects theory with practice much more closely than can most training programmes. Because it has educational as well as practical advantages for training, it will be considered again from that rather different point of view. For our purposes in this chapter, however, we need to emphasize the immense practical and immediate contribution which it could make to the work of the social educator day by day.

'Group Work' and the Practice of Social Education

What we have attempted to do in the foregoing chapters is to find a language and a set of verbal concepts and descriptions which will embody the principles and essential nature of social education. We have not referred to large numbers of 'techniques' in this kind of education, nor suggested that there are any which are extractable, communicable to others and then repeatable in their predigested form in ensuing circumstances. We have argued that it is possible to construct a framework of aims, principles and understanding within which the social educator can operate. Thus we have tried to present ways of thinking about practice, of guiding and evaluating the behaviour of the adult in social education, so that he may determine his responses for himself in each situation in the light of his objectives and the various sanctions bearing on his work.

The phrase 'social group work' has been used increasingly in recent years to describe various approaches to social education not unlike the discipline outlined in this book. There is some value in having a shorthand phrase by which to refer to the core of the discipline relevant to social-educational practice, but some caution is called for over the adoption of this particular one.

For the word 'social' in this context seems to be used by different people for three quite separate reasons. The first is that youth work and many other forms of social education takes place in an informal atmos-phere which is intended to encourage the participants to be 'sociable' – to meet voluntarily and socially in order to enjoy themselves. The second reason is that this form of education is understood to be one which, more than any other, helps young people to make contact with and learn to participate in the various elements in 'society'. And thirdly, there is the suggestion that social education needs to be identified more with the servicing ethos of social work than with the controlling or instructive ethos of teaching. Each of these interpretations of the word is of course valid, but since 'social group work' is used as a shorthand phrase it is uncommon for it to be defined, and much confusion can easily result. Each person who hears it or reads it or uses it gives it his own meaning one day, and then finds another day that its context implies another, apparently sensible but different meaning.

Because the phrase 'social group work' derives from the terminology of American social work the third of these meanings, with its reminder of the parallel skill 'social case-work', creates even further confusion. In the first place this arises because the phrase 'social group work' in American writings is widely, though not exclusively, used to denote a skill with small constant groups of people attached to a particular worker for regular meetings, often of a therapeutic nature. But a second confusion arises from the view of many educators and social workers in this country that the skills of social work have little in common with the skills of the educator. The approach of the social worker can still be seen as exclusively suited to a remedial, saving process, designed simply to prevent those (in some way) 'below par' from growing worse, and to help misfits and deviants to become more acceptable members of the community.

In practice, however, social work and education are not so far apart as a superficial examination would suggest. Organizational divisions do exist, but more out of administrative convenience and historical accident than because of any philosophical or even practical difference. Moreover, they tend to disguise the fact that there is a similarity of purpose between the two fields. For, to help individuals from maladjustment to greater adjustment (as in customarily attempted in social work) is not essentially at variance (either in principle or purpose) with helping individuals from normal adjustment to greater self-expression and fulfilment. The *starting* points along the spectrum of possible client behaviour, need and 'normality', may differ but the spectrum itself and the direction of hoped-for movement are always the same, and the ideal end-point applies in general terms to both processes. Seen in this way, social work and education become merely two ways of describing services which our society makes available to people whose stages of personal development happen to differ.

However, not only is there an affinity between the purposes and principles of social work and education: in order to achieve their aims and apply their principles, the two fields are also increasingly using the medium more usually identified with the other. For many workers in both fields accept that, to create opportunities favourable to clients' growth and self-realization, it is possible to work, either through the single relationship of client with worker or through a network of relationships in which the worker joins a number of his clients. Both the face-to-face interview and the group are now seen as suitable media for furthering a worker's purpose. Thus, social workers, like probation officers and those who work in Family Service Units (that is, those normally designated social 'case' workers in this country), are increasingly meeting with their clients in group settings. At the same time, schools are recognizing that some of their educational ends may be more fully attained if 'welfare workers' or counsellors meet pupils and parents individually and offer additional aid; and some forms of remedial teaching and some of the educational approaches to the handicapped, as well as the most helpful of the tutorial counselling in some schools and higher education, are all reminiscent of case-work. Thus, the media being used at a practical level less and less reflect the administrative division of social work from education and increasingly bear witness to the similarities of their purpose.

Nonetheless, because the word 'social' has other connotations, it is likely to go on causing confusion where the phrase 'social group work' is adopted and might therefore be dropped from it completely. Indeed, to resort simply to 'group work' as a shorthand description of the core of the social educator's discipline has advantages of its own, since it refers to all that needs to be referred to in this discipline and no more. Its focus is on work with people in groups by a practitioner who has a heightened perception of their interaction and relationships. Thus, the phrase 'group work' calls attention to the uses of this same understanding in a variety of settings. It points to the links between social educators and many other practitioners – doctors, industrialists and teachers, for example, as well as social workers – who are using or could use 'group work' in the settings in which they work. They, too, must have a conscious understanding of human relationships without the social educator's emphasis on adolescent characteristics, and will apply 'group work' according to additional principles relevant to their own setting and objectives.

For 'group work' does not imply any particular set of aims, nor does it presuppose any special methods or sanctions. The person who wishes to use it can do so in any field, although he must assume that certain sanctions will operate in that field, that a set of principles can be derived from those sanctions and that the principles will need to be illuminated by his understanding of human behaviour.

Chapter 10

Training

Improved Performance and Greater Confidence

Attitudes to training for social education vary considerably. The most negative one assumes that it is completely unnecessary to train anyone for work with other people. According to this view, those who lack the innate abilities required will never be 'taught' them, while the rest, who already possess them, know all that they need to know about getting alongside young people, understanding them, influencing them – 'for the good' of course – and giving them what they want and need. Thus training is seen as irrelevant: either an adult has 'got what it takes', or he has not, and no amount of training can alter this fact of life.

Although such an attitude betrays a quite inflated faith in 'flair', it does call attention to the fact that there are certain traits and characteristics and certain basic general principles of life which are prerequisites for work as a social educator. As these traits cannot be acquired by training, there needs to be wider recognition at the stage of the recruitment of adults for social education that careful selection procedures are necessary, whether paid or voluntary workers are being sought. It cannot be assumed that any adult who expresses willingness or interest in working with young people is automatically suitable, and any shortage of recruits cannot properly be met by accepting all-comers. In fact a considerable disservice will be done to the young if any 'interested' adult is allowed to select himself for social-educational roles simply by coming forward. A determined search for the appropriate personal characteristics seems fully justified.

It can be admitted without qualification therefore that educators of the type described in this book cannot be built from scratch by a training programme. This, however, is not an argument against training, for it is by means of training experiences that an adult's existing personality and ability with young people can be developed and made more effective. It is possible, for example, to short-circuit some of the errors which new practitioners are liable to make and to support the hesitant or unsettled beginner so that he has as good a chance of survival as the newcomer who finds his feet quickly and unaided. It is possible to strengthen the average practitioner, to make the uneven worker more consistently good, to revive the experienced hand should he tire. It is possible to extend and deepen for any worker the skills and values appropriate to his social-educational practice. Training is certainly no substitute for the 'right type' of personality, but it can support and supplement capacity which is already there.

However, more influential today than those who reject all training as unnecessary are those who agree that training has a value but who give the meaning of the word too rigid and restrictive an interpretation. There are many, for example, who see training simply as purveying a collection of tips and techniques, of guaranteed gambits for dealing with youth group situations. There are others who are satisfied to use training only as an inspirational process, on the uplift of which the worker can, for a shorter or longer period, face all circumstances regardless of their nature. Still others see training as consisting of a statement by an expert of what are believed to be the qualities of leadership in the hope that this will enable the trainee to develop these qualities himself. All these groups see training as necessary, but assume that it consists very largely of the conveying of facts and information which authoritative teachers already possess.

This particular interpretation of training undoubtedly fulfils some of the justifiable expectations and at least consciously felt needs of many of the adults who enter social education. Their plea is often for 'sound techniques' for handling young people. This is often understood to mean that they are demanding help in acquiring a competence in the type of prescribed patterns of work and preconceived procedures which were criticized in Chapter 5. What they seek are information and skill in something which will act as a bridge between themselves and the young – in coaching a game, perhaps, or in instructing in a hobby or in passing on a corpus of knowledge related to a faith. Adults properly feel a certain unsureness among a large number of young people (as do young people among a crowd of adults). It is good that they should admit this and aim to deal with it by seeking a vehicle of contact. It is to be expected and healthy that they should look for ways of increasing their confidence and boosting their morale. But, as we have tried to show throughout this book, to seek confidence in these ways is entirely to miss the central point of social education.

Because adults have traditionally based their social-educational approach to young people only or mainly on skills in the externals or superficialities of a human situation, that is on the activities and hobbies which are the vehicle or medium for human leisure-time relationships, it has been naturally thought sufficient for them to be trained in these skills. This type of preparation has been expected by itself to provide them with ready-made openings for forming relationships with young people and for finding a stable and important place in their lives. Sometimes this expectation has been a product of the adults' intention to mould young people according to their personal model, or the result of the false conviction that all young people simply want to learn the skills or gain the knowledge which the adults have. But by concentrating chiefly on the adults' ability to teach, instruct or inculcate, such an interpretation of 'training' certainly does not encourage the release of as much of the adults' personal potential as is required for genuinely client-centred social education.

Of course, there are many adults who enter teaching or youth work because of an interest in and an innate flair for working with people rather than things, and such forms of training are quickly dismissed by them as superficial and irrelevant. Workers like these are, and often feel themselves to be, 'right' for work with young people because they are spontaneously capable of making contact with them over and above the transmission of the externals. They give a low priority to such forms of training, not out of a belief that they do not require any appreciation of the externals, but because they see – often intuitively – that while the externals are being imparted personalities and relationships are being developed, and that this is of even greater social-educational value. It is with these human elements of a learning situation that they feel most concerned and personally best equipped to deal. They are aware that their strength lies in their ability to communicate passages of their life-experience to young people, rather than subjects, hobbies or activities.

Training in the personal relations processes which are so crucial anyway to any form of genuinely social education is of course quite possible. Adults in social education, even the 'naturals', can be helped considerably to realize their spontaneous and unformulated abilities to the full and to transfer them if necessary to a variety of different working situations. Fortunately such training is becoming more readily available as it comes to be recognized that social educators can no longer be expected to rely solely on their knowledge of how to produce a play, control a committee, or impart the externals of religious faith.

Unfortunately, however, many of the methods which have been commonly used in training adults in activity skills and the rest, and which may well be appropriate there, are too often automatically applied to courses whose content has changed. Human relationships training in social education has often received treatment more appropriate to an impersonal process involving the accretion of certain barnacles to the superstructure which the trainee presents. The implication has been almost that the trainer can effectively *tell* adults what constitutes human behaviour and human interaction.

The use of such methods to convey this kind of content is strikingly at odds with the experience and the values of many who work in the field of education. It certainly makes no allowance for the tensions and complexities of the social educator's practical situation, in which he will almost certainly be quite unable to make use of human relations knowledge transmitted in this non-involving way. Yet those who carry out training are frequently tempted to offer, to anyone who is being prepared for a new experience at whatever level, nothing beyond a portfolio of information arbitrarily chosen in advance by the 'trainer'. Some colleges of education preparing students for work in a variety of secondary school settings still give evidence of this misapplication of method, as does some of the training for part-time and full-time youth leaders. The implication is, whether the information is presented by lecture, pamphlets or books, that there exists outside the student an authoritative source for the skills he needs to deploy in his human relations work.

Too often therefore training methods continue in use as though it were effective to convey the human relations content of a course in the same way as the knowledge and skills of an activity or the facts and ideas of a faith or organization. Bombardment from the outside is still too common an approach. So accustomed have adults become to this kind of training, in fact, that many of them prefer it to any method which suggests that they, personally, must be the starting-point, that they must in some way act as the origin of some of the material which will enable the training to take place. It is of course much easier for the trainee to be offered a situation in which an authoritative statement is made, since the trainee needs only to accept or reject it or any parts of it which he separates out. Indeed, some adults thoroughly enjoy frequent training experiences of this kind in which their personal involvement is limited. This, however, is no guarantee that they have been given an adequate grounding for their work with young people.

It is true, of course, that few, if any, programmes of 'training' are completely authoritarian, least of all perhaps academically authoritarian. Most allow for discussion – a most important safety valve if this system of preparation is used. It is true also that the initiates will be very selective about what they actually take from the portfolio, and this is good as well as inevitable since otherwise indigestion would follow and their own very personal requirements might never even accidentally and peripherally be touched. Again it is true, as we have argued already, that the adult does need to deepen his insight into human behaviour and to search deliberately for understanding which has been carefully and empirically tested by himself and others, and which can therefore illuminate his own personal practice. Trainees need, therefore, to be brought into contact with the authoritative insights of the human sciences, and some information-giving will be necessary for this and other purposes in every course of training.

However, it is doubtful if this need be as great a part of the course as many sponsors of training make it. It seems unlikely that adults learn best by choosing, from portfolios of material which are presented to them by others, those facts and ideas which they find palatable and for which they can stay awake. Nor will they be adequately prepared for the human situations they are most likely to meet if the whole process is treated as a non-personal, completely objective one of passing a set of facts and ideas from one point to another. To allow social educators to think that training in human relationships can be reduced to an indoctrination in externals does not seem to be a sound way either of initiating these educators into the roles they will have to play, or of serving the young people in whose interests all this is done. The development of an awareness of the principles, understanding and discipline required for such roles and such a service would seem to demand much more than the mere exposition of subjects like 'Personal Relationships in your Club' or 'Preparing your Pupils for Marriage'.

As the content of training for social education must primarily be concerned with human relations, methods must be employed which are especially appropriate and effective for communicating this. No human being is entirely rational, and this advantage needs to be utilized in any training for human relations; no adult is without valuable first-hand experiences of personal relationships, of adolescent joy and depression, of social and work situations, of family life and so on, and again these experiences must be deliberately tapped.

The adult we are concerned with is training not to propagate the structure and dogmas of the 'Youth Service' or of 'teaching', but for human and social intercourse with young people. He will need to become acquainted with structure and organization, just as he will need to know something of the fruits of academic disciplines. But the social educator's training needs to involve him or her personally in the process. Because his feelings and personality will be at least as integral and essential a part of his responses in his practice as will his knowledge and ideas, his training will need to speak to his needs, to seek and to adopt approaches to learning which elicit his commitment and engage his experience and feelings.

And so, in training adults for the aims, principles and disciplines of social education as advocated in this book, there needs to be less concern with presenting constructs and patterns of ideas and facts put together by the trainer or based on some external authority. More positively, there need to be more opportunities for the adult undertaking the training to express what lies within his personality, and to utilize the understanding and experience which he already has. A trainee's life-experience is at least as significant for his work in social education as anything which the trainer can add or introduce, and it needs to be recognized as such.

But deliberately to utilize the general experience of human relationships which the adults already have, and to help them become conscious of where it is relevant, is only to fulfil a part of the purpose of training. For each adult trainee must also be encouraged to increase his understanding of what sort of a person his experiences have made him, and of the ways in which they influence his behaviour among young people; training must then go further still and enable the adult to release and make available to young people the fruits of this experience in ways which are acceptable and applicable. If by these means training connects with and indeed grows out of the trainee's previous experience, it can enable the adult to gain that confidence which he might have expected to find by acquiring 'sound techniques'. The social educator has a right to expect that his training will give him grounds for confidence, since like any worker in the field of human relationships he is liable to be repeatedly exposed to overt or implied criticism and challenge.

Social, intellectual, or emotional, these challenges are likely to occur in his practice as a social educator to an extent which he would not tolerate in his private and social life. In his own adult social club, for example, the individual who is rebuffed several times in a week, or who finds himself constantly at odds with most other members, might reasonably consider changing his group of friends. In a youth club or other social-educational setting, however, the adult may have to be proof against many of his approaches being ignored or failing. He will need a confidence which overcomes rejection and estrangement, and the hurt and tension which they engender. He will need to see these not as personal slights against himself but more often as the working out of some need by young people quite regardless of the individual personality whom they are using merely as a convenient object. Thus, if he is to achieve through training the confidence which he hoped for, he must first develop his capacity to recognize and yet remain detached from feelings and attitudes which he will not be able to eradicate but which are not necessarily reliable guides to appropriate practice. And this will mean that, rather than depending on 'sound techniques' conceived and validated by someone else, he will need both to accept his own impediments to good social-educational practice and to acknowledge those personal attributes helpful to such practice.

Growth in self-understanding needs to embrace also an examination of the worker's own attitudes to young people, his means of communication with them, and the place to be held by his own experience and beliefs in this communication process. Growing self-knowledge will help the adult trace his own profile, to see it in relief against the background of society and the profile of others. From this, training will need to develop a conscious statement by the adult of his interpretation of his life-experience and of the philosophy which this has given him. It will need, too, to force him into comparing his own outlook with that adopted by others and into an appreciation of its place in his work with young people. The intention here is not, by questioning and demands for re-examination and explanation, to doubt the validity for the trainee of the ideas which he has worked out for himself: rather, the intention is again to prepare the trainee for the pressures on his own self-assurance and on his personal beliefs, assumptions and ideals which his work will bring. For many young people themselves are enquiring, challenging, doubting and un-committed, and many sponsors of social-educational agencies will have legitimate expectations of his work which are contrary to his own. The social educator, whether part-time or not, needs to be equipped to meet the uncertainty and crises of self-doubt which will inevitably result at times from his practice. Discovery at leisure of the contours of his own attitudes is likely to reduce panic and loss of self-assurance under stress.

But the aim of training goes further here. For re-examination and re-statement of this kind, during training alongside others, can help the adult to see that his own experience and the lessons he has derived from it are truly personal and individual. Courage and self-assurance are needed to face the fact that his own interpretation of his life-time, his attitudes and his standards are not necessarily typical. Again, no one will want to deny that they have validity for him, and for many others whose orientation now is similar to his own. But by a mixture of confrontation with the life-experiences of fellow-trainees and systematically-derived factual in-formation introduced at appropriate moments, training can help the adult *feel* the equal validity of contrasting attitudes which stem from the undeniable life-experience of others. Most of us claim that we are ready to accept the other man's point of view, that we are not prejudiced. Yet first most of us need to become fully conscious of the flimsy, unsubstan-tiated nature of the constructs we place upon events, to become fully engaged in trying to explain, justify and support the interpretations we make of people and situations. Only then, perhaps, can we go beyond mere intellectual tolerance and appreciate with any reality of feeling the equal worth as a human being of that 'other person' over there. Some adults may not need any specially created opportunities to gain this appreciation. Most do however, and they include some who feel par-ticularly strongly that they themselves do not. And for those adults who wish to serve the community by working with its young people, it cannot be left to chance whether they have this prerequisite to the work. Training can create a clearer understanding of the untypical and highly subjective nature of one's own point of view, and in this way may make it less likely that a practitioner will attempt to impose, however subtly and indirectly, his own interpretation of life on the young, and then reject them and their attributes because they reject it.

Yet there will be much in his life-experience which will be of potential value to young people and worth presenting to them so that they have the opportunity to adopt it. In order to communicate any part of this to them, or indeed to communicate anything at all to them, he will need to understand their situation and condition. Communication is clearly not established unless at least two people have taken part in the process – a transmitter and a perceiver. But since the adults represent a society which recognizes the advantages all round in communicating with young people, then the onus for successful communication lies upon those adults. They must initiate and seek the most effective means: this requires them to transmit what they wish to be received in a way and at a time acceptable to the perceivers.

This is not a degrading process for the adult, merely a courteous one. It is the effort we all need to make if we wish to be well received and understood by fellow human beings. Adults in social education do care that young people understand and receive them well on behalf of the society they represent, so that training needs to prepare these adults to recognize how and when to communicate the elements which need to be passed on from their personal interpretation of life.

However, if adults are really to gain a respectful, sensitive, appreciative response, they will first need to acquire from training a humble and sensitive appreciation of the situation of the young people involved. Such an appreciation is unlikely to be acquired if the training aims merely to present young people's general position in society – to offer a snapshot of adolescence. As was argued in Chapter 5, the generalizations inevitable to such an approach give the adult an apparently finite, descriptive image to hold on to, unless they are supplemented by study of particular groups of young people in their own personal situations. Generalizations can be no more than parts of a backcloth to the more personally-involving central and major parts of the training process. There is immense danger in allowing generalizations to be used as stereotypes on which the adult can comfortably and uncritically base a series of unvarying approaches.

The kind of understanding which the preparation of the adult must aim at is a far more intuitive and particular one: a grasp of 'what it must be like' to be a young man or woman in a particular situation known or describable to the adult. This offers a truly finite idea to hold, while mounting a real exercise for imaginative insight. The characteristic which is being demanded of the adult – that of sensitivity, of feeling for – is certainly one of those which are 'natural', which need to be sought at selection. However, if present or latent, sensitivity can be developed and, by deliberate cultivation, made more readily available and more often effective.

The effort in training must more and more, therefore, be to increase an adult's awareness of his own traits, attitudes and values: and it must be set more and more in the context of the realities of human nature and existence, especially the realities of the life of the kind of young people with whom the adult is to work. Such training will aim at exploring and making available to adults their own experience and beliefs; at making them conscious of the assumptions and the principles which underlie their approach and response to young people; and at enabling them to discover gaps in their understanding which may need to be filled by material from authoritative sources outside themselves. It is at this point, therefore, that training may need to make adults more aware of the sanctions which guide or dictate how they should behave and, increasingly as their training proceeds, of those areas of understanding – of individual human behaviour, of human behaviour in groups, of the management of human institutions – which were seen in Chapter 7 as necessary sources of illumination of their practice. Together, these must become more readily available to the trainee so that they can be used to improve working practice.

An Integrated Course

It is not the intention in this book to advocate any particular training 'method', since almost any training process will require the use of a combination of 'methods', and no single 'method' is inherently better than all others for achieving all purposes. It is not even possible to be dogmatic, in relation to one particular purpose, about any precise combination of methods guaranteed in all circumstances to be correct. For the order in which different methods should be applied, and the proportion of each method in any combination, have to be determined by the needs of each individual training situation. In certain important ways the trainer stands in the same relation to his trainees as the social educator to *his* clients: preconception and predetermination are hindrances, limitations on the range of possible ways of effecting training. If, for example, the trainer finds that one factor – the students, the subject-matter, the premises being used, the expert or resource-figure – is the same in two succeeding training operations, he cannot assume that the method used in the earlier one will be appropriate in the one which comes later. Permutations even of the factors mentioned above are one reason for this: the subject may be the same, but different students or premises may indicate a change in methods. There are many other variable factors not mentioned above, and these too may indicate a change in methods – the weather outside the premises, the time of day, week or year, the stage of the course, the political, economic or social situation as it affects social education, some widely publicized aspect of the behaviour of young people themselves.

It is clear then that the trainer can have no guaranteed method to suit

P

all circumstances but that he needs to undertake a careful appraisal and analysis of his task. We shall not attempt to elaborate in any detail the principles by which he should assess the situation and gauge his line of action, but it is likely that they will derive from similar sources of sanction to those which operate on the social educator.

For, firstly, the person responsible for organizing and carrying out the training operation must consider the expectations of the society in which he works and in particular of the agency sponsoring his efforts. He must consider, too, the personalities of the trainers, whether these include himself or not, and see what it is about them which will help, and what it is which will hinder, the training process. And again, most important of all, he must consider the needs of his clients (the trainees) – both those of which they are conscious, their wants, and those which he judges them to have. In taking account of trainees' needs, the trainer will wish to display acceptance and a 'non-judgmental attitude' as we have defined it elsewhere, and he will want to exercise confidentiality in his relationships: when he considers trainees' right to self-determination, however, he cannot simply adopt the approach appropriate for a social educator to *his* clients. Of course most if not all trainees are self-determining in the sense that they come voluntarily to be trained and so clearly have the right to withdraw from the training experience. But the *content* of their experience cannot be left to their choice within limits as wide as those which young people enjoy in social education. Almost any course of action chosen by young people can be used to aid their social education, and indeed the very exercise of choice is itself integral to the process which sponsoring agencies hope to encourage. Now it is true that the general ability of the adult trainee to make responsible choices is extremely important, and indeed the training of a social educator is much more effective if he is given the maximum opportunity for participating in decisions about the nature of his training. But training for social education is training for a particular skill or set of skills, and the purposes of a training operation can be attained only by a more limited range of approaches than can the purposes of social education, so that the trainer will be justified more often than will an adult social educator in his relations with young people in allowing his other principles – and in particular that of his agency's expectations – to override a trainee's right to self-determination. No principles derived from other sources of sanction are, however, going to conflict with the overall need of the trainees, which is of course an improved performance as social educators. In assessing, therefore, the combination of training methods to be used in each particular situation, and in taking into account the sources of sanction on his work, the trainer clearly needs to give major consideration to the effectiveness of the training in increasing each student's ability to fulfil the demands made of him in his practice. The question which the trainer must put to himself, therefore, is 'what experiences will *these* trainees find most helpful in raising their standard of performance as social educators?', and in answering this question he must be guided by the appropriate principles, and not by any preconceived ideas as to the supremacy or uselessness of particular methods.

Whatever the precise answers in any particular case, it is clear that in general terms any process which meets clients' needs 'starts where the trainee is', and that this is achieved most pertinently if the trainee's own experience is made the basis of the training. If he is encouraged to articulate his own personal experience, the training process can grow out of the concepts familiar to him, by connecting each new concept onto what he already knows in an order meaningful and significant to him.

An efficient way of achieving such meaningful connections is clearly through discussion groups in which trainees help one another to establish the relationship between successive concepts and choose the path of the discussion according to the ideas which seem to them to relate closely to the ones most recently expressed. The trainer's job lies in selecting for emphasis certain facts and ideas whose interconnection trainees have discovered for themselves but which, because of their importance to the training which is going on, need to be given special attention. The trainer may help also by offering additional information which may link with the connections already established through the trainees' discussions. Such an approach certainly exemplifies the assumption that students will learn not just, or even especially, from the 'staff' but also from one another, and pays full tribute to the lessons which can emerge from the trainees' own experiences.

However, the trainees themselves may not recognize the richness of this store. They may well have been led by successive previous educational experiences to underestimate themselves as a source of learning and so may have come to a training course expecting to be told or informed by experts. Initially, therefore, they may doubt the value of an educational process in which the trainer frankly acknowledges the narrow limits of his own proper competence and authoritativeness. The trainer may thus meet a good deal of resistance to what amounts to his attempt at sharing with the trainees the responsibility for improving their own performance.

This will be especially true because not everyone feels comfortable in a group which expects his participation on equal terms. Some adults fear to disagree openly in case they cause a breakdown in relationships and therefore prefer to conceal any opposition they may have to the views which seem to predominate in a group, or to the views of a trainer or someone else seen as an authority. A discussion group will encourage them to see – and the trainer will be able to help this to become apparent – that conflict can be contained quite adequately so that a frank expression of views becomes easier. Other adults are diffident or inarticulate and may feel that their learning is being inhibited by a training process which relies heavily on group discussion. It may of course be argued that, since it is an essential part of any form of human relations work to communicate with other adults, training should make some attempt to develop the social educator's ability to do this, and discussion groups offer opportunities for achieving this which more didactic approaches do not. But even the adult who never articulates his views is usually active in a group. He is frequently formulating his own opinions in his own mind, and he will certainly be matching his own attitudes with those expressed by the members of the group who speak out. The person who remains quiet but deeply attentive during a discussion may find himself, no less than those who speak, being strongly challenged, forced to ask himself: 'Where do I stand on this?' 'Do I agree with that?' 'What do I know about this?' Clearly those who do speak, who do put their views at risk, who do expose and attempt to defend themselves are making apparent the steps by which they learn. The others, though achieving less noticeable advances, may still be gaining in ways which are to them equally important.

Quite apart from the fact that discussion groups in training for social education encourage the meaningful connection of ideas in trainees' minds, they have the further advantage that in them a number of adults interrelate and interact with one another, and so are provided with a living experience of the processes and mechanisms which adolescents will experience in their schools or clubs. The trainee is prepared for his work not merely because he can learn from the communicated ideas and wisdom of other practitioners but also because he can share an experience with them. For example, it is on the vehicle of such an experience that an individual's self-awareness can grow, since it can help him to perceive the ways in which he differs from others. It can therefore enable him to gain a more accurate picture of his own identity, partly as this is reflected in the comments of others about him and their reactions to him and partly because he is made to draw out and so to become aware of hitherto unidentified facets of his own personality. These benefits of the use of discussion groups may be less tangible than the exchange of views, but they will be of special value to social educators since they derive from the students' opportunity to accept, work within and understand the human relations processes of which, in a group, they themselves are part. Because the job for which they are being trained will demand that they involve and at times reveal their personal philosophy and qualities, it is clearly wise to avoid where possible in that training any approaches which isolate and protect students from the direct experience of such involvement and revelation. Work done very largely through groups *entails* people's personal, emotional and intellectual commitment and thus envelops them in some of the forms of experience with which they will eventually be concerned in their practice. It is impossible to deepen anyone's appreciation of human stresses and emotions simply by telling him about these: indeed, this is the surest way of depersonalizing the content of his training and so removing from it that element which he most urgently needs to understand. To be relevant to his future need as a social educator an adult's training must immerse him in relationships which make demands of him, and this means asking him to become a member of a group small enough to allow face-to-face relationships to develop among all its members. It may be noted also that this in turn requires that there be someone attached to that group whose skill and functions are not rooted in what he knows but in how well he is able to make each person conscious of the nature of his experience both in other situations and, if possible, in the group itself.

The discussion group, then, both promotes the meaningful connection of idea to idea in the students' minds and offers them an intense personal experience of processes and interrelationships which is extremely important to their practice. There is a further advantage still which relates in particular to the organization of any given course of training and which affects the choice of training methods appropriate to the needs of any group of trainees. For discussion in groups can lead the trainees on a course to identify for themselves the areas within which they have need of resources of knowledge or expertise outside the group. Such a procedure enables the students to undertake a share in the planning and direction of their own course of training, and they really can participate responsibly in the improvement of their performance. The members of the group can well indicate, after discussion and with or without the aid of the trainer, the ways in which they can next advance and can thus effectively help to regulate the direction and pace of their learning. Many training organizers do of course retain some flexibility in their programme to enable them to respond to the revealed needs of the members. Indeed organizations like Workers' Educational Association branches owe their continued existence to this possibility of member-involvement in planning each succeeding course of study. But elsewhere within the education service there have been many pressures on trainers to concoct, before ever meeting their trainees, a neatly dovetailed programme of speakers, subjects, dates, times and places, and trainees' potential for identifying their needs has been ignored. This seems particularly unfortunate when, as in the case of training for social education, the trainees are adults, and when the trainer may well be aware of the injustice he is doing to the trainees. They in turn may either (if charitable or uncritical) accept that he has more authority and greater expertise than they, or (if not) resent the offering of material whose relevance they have not had the opportunity of discovering for themselves.

The discussion group, then, apart from its other advantages, can indicate to the trainer the needs felt in the group for the introduction of outside expertise into the course. The trainer must also bear in mind the differing requirements of individuals for information or ideas not available to them from the group. He will of course be able to satisfy some of these himself, just as he will meet some of the group's common needs by contributing to the discussion some of his own knowledge and experience. But he must be ready to put other resources at the disposal of trainees according to their individual requirements, and in order to be able to do this he will have to consult with each of them individually about what they believe to be necessary for their training. The individual, no less than the whole group, in fact, must be allowed a share in the planning of a training experience if it is to be genuinely helpful and appropriate.

For there is clearly a need in any course of training for the information and ideas which the external resources of 'straight teaching' and reading can bring to bear: the difficulty is to ensure that the principle of 'starting where they are' is not violated by the introduction of these didactic media into the course. Books and lectures, as the two major forms of didactics, thus clearly need to be at the disposal of the student when he is ready for them, so that what they offer really does 'connect' with what is already familiar to him. In social-educational training the use of books and lectures will be especially necessary to set the scene and give the background to the core of the training, and to give information on a number of subjects which students can acquire in no other way or by means which are too cumbersome and time-consuming.

Books are the most flexible form of didactics because they can be read at times, places and speeds to suit the individual, and each person in a training group can have his particular needs met from whatever range of resources is available in this form. But as far as possible a book needs to be suggested to a student as a consequence of an expressed interest or to follow from some work already undertaken. To recommend books to the trainee before any incentive to use them has been created means that the requirement to absorb material comes *before* any understanding of how and why the material is relevant. Books and booklists imposingly recommended in advance become a forbidding foundation to a course of study or an unexplained but obligatory supplement to a lecture, thus implying a demand on the student's time which is disproportionate to his interest. Because no internal motive to read such literature is present, most of it introduced in this way is often not read at all.

It is complementary to this principle that the trainer should utilize if possible any reading to which the trainee has been drawn of his own choice. For such reading may have already connected well with the individual's own thoughts and ideas, or may encourage some discussion and interpretation by the trainee's group or by the trainer himself in order that the fullest use can be made of it. What the student has chosen to read himself he must have been motivated to try to understand, and for the sake of the student the trainer will want to make the most of what has been read and to make it connect as fully as possible with what was already known.

Thus external resources in the form of the written word are of immense value if they come at the right time for the trainee in his training process and if what they offer is integrated by him or for him into the training experience as a whole. The other major form of didactics – the lecture – can equally be integrated into the course if each one is introduced at the appropriate time, although it has inherent and ineradicable weaknesses. For no matter how careful its timing or the interpretations by which it is supported the lecture is fundamentally unsuited to certain purposes, such as the teaching of attitudes and feelings. Nor can anything prevent it emphasizing the status of the lecturer at the expense of the trainees, and so robbing them of a share in the responsibility for that part of their training: the lecture, in fact, is only appropriate where the subject-matter is such that the statements of an authority figure are truly more meaningful than the views of the trainees and where the trainer available really is such an authority. Moreover perhaps the most important weakness inherent in the lecture is the strong possibility that, however good the supporting notes given out before or after it is delivered, however skilled the use of audio-visual aids, however careful the speaker's preparation, the listeners' attention will wander: periodically they will become passive, they will 'not hear' that which threatens, and they will often assimilate only the anecdote, the joke or the unfortunate mistake.

Nevertheless the lecture will frequently be a justifiable part of training for social education, and the trainer who fails to use it to its best advantage will be robbing a course of a great deal. As with a book, however, using a lecture to the best advantage requires that the students come to it at a time when they are ready for it: it must relate to their real needs, and come *after* their incentive to receive it has been created and *after* the understanding of the place of its content in their training has been developed. The trainer cannot genuinely anticipate the likely needs of trainees very far in advance and any arrangements which he makes which do so will inevitably distort their early discussions, by guiding them towards what they believe is expected of them. For as they examine the planned teaching programme they will almost inevitably assume that, because 'the staff' in their wisdom have stated that this is what their training should contain, they have in front of them a sovereign definition of what their needs are. That they have much to contribute to such a definition will probably in consequence never occur to them.

The integration of lectures into the course as a result of trainees' discussion and identification of their needs is bound to raise some administrative problems. In the first place, the trainer cannot book all his resource-figures six months ahead, since he will not know so far in advance what the trainees will need nor when exactly they will need it. Some anticipation of need, some booking of lecturers in advance may be unavoidable; but it should be as little and as flexible as possible, for as short a time ahead as possible, so that the course is committed to as few narrowly specialized outside speakers as is compatible with its achievement of its purpose. The necessity of some advance booking should not be turned into a virtue as it so often is: for there is no great virtue in a succession of lecturers forming a regular circus and passing before a group of trainees between the arrival and departure times of the local train service.

The administrative problem may be partly overcome if the lectures are given as part of residential training. In a full-time residential course lasting many months, when most of the potential lecturers or resource-figures can be on hand the whole time, there should be little difficulty since most of the course can be arranged so that the lecture-topics grow out of the discussions of the trainees. However, even in the short-term residential course, if a small team of three or four resource-persons is assembled, then even those whose training is part-time may be offered the chance to have lectures which follow upon their own identification of their needs. On some such courses the trainer is able to define the group's discussion within certain broad limits, so that only one resource-figure whose expertise lies within this general area need be asked to stand by. Even in the non-residential parts of training courses, however, it is possible quite often for the resource-person to be a local resident who can be introduced into the training *after* the students have had time to cover at least some of the ground themselves, and feel the need for his assistance.

There is a second administrative consequence, however, of an attempt to introduce the lecture at a stage meaningful to the students. For the lecturer cannot prepare what he has to say without reference to the areas of discussion covered by the students. This may mean that when he does meet the students, he has to explore with them precisely what they expect from him before he makes his contribution. It is difficult for a lecturer to arrive with tidy notes, unless someone, probably the trainer, has been able to interpret very fully to him in advance the requirements and expectations into which his expertise should fit, and indeed ideally no lecturer should be satisfied unless he can know something of his audience beforehand in order to go some way to meeting their particular needs. In fact, the careful integration of this kind of didactic element into training fully repays the trouble which it causes to the administration of a course, since it makes it much less likely that the resource-person will waste time and effort telling the group what they are better able to learn from one another or by other means. It ensures too that he offers his ideas and knowledge only when members of the group have had a chance to discover their needs. Their motivation to learn from him is strong because they are at the point where their own resources, but not the subject, are exhausted.

Many people in training courses, and not least adults in training for social education, have a great need to discover again what they already know and put in order what they have previously experienced. Thus, though there is an important function for didactic forms of training, these need to come at points in the training experience when the students are 'switched on' for them, ready to perceive what this book or that lecture is trying to communicate. Otherwise they meet the resistances and resentments which ill-timed attempts at 'straight teaching' are bound to produce. With careful discussion and gradual identification of needs, however, the books and the lectures can be fully integrated into the trainees' experience, so that each section of the course properly 'starts where they are' and connects with what they already know.

Active Participation

The assumption which underlies much of the consideration given in this book to training for social education is that adults will participate actively in an expression and interchange of ideas and information. Whether discussion centres around psychological or social matters or the practice of social education or the wider personal experiences of the participants, its vitality has been assumed to be central to the training process. Perhaps it is appropriate at this stage to enumerate some of the ways in which such discussion can be stimulated.

First, discussion may be based on an exploration of the areas of social-educational work which the adults in training find difficult. Trainees asked to define problem areas in which they need help will usually be able to compile a list quite easily. Such a request may seem at first sight to be more likely to be effective where the adults concerned already have some experience of working with young people. However, much of what needs examination will be concerned with human relations in general rather than specifically with the principles and practice of social education, so that any group of adults has experience which is relevant. In any case, the complete novice can usually identify needs fairly readily. Where the group of adults contains both some with experience in social education and some without it, there are special advantages. For not only can the 'old hands' teach the new but also the questions and blank spots of the novices can help the others to a clearer and more explicit realization of what they already know.

A second way of stimulating discussion is to encourage trainees to examine and define the various functions which they perform or will perform in their work with young people. Such an exercise is the beginning of a job analysis and has a good chance of making students more flexible in approach, since it may cause them to see the inadequacy of the rule-of-thumb guides to action on which they may have unthinkingly depended previously. It may help them to realize, in fact, that these rules are helpful for the fulfilment of some of their functions but not all, so that, as they delve deeper and gain experience, they may be able to define roles that they have to play at different moments – facilitator, instructor, counsellor, disciplinarian, a figure to rebel against, intermediary between agency and clients, and so on. In this way they may discover for themselves the sanctions which impinge on their practice, and they should certainly go a long way to unearthing the principles, perhaps unconscious but nonetheless effective, underlying their work. Even an adult who has no experience of social-educational practice can still seek and may even establish certain reference points and guidelines for his relationships with young people. Indeed, in any group preparing for educational roles the principles of work of those participating need to be aired, whether in the form of projections into the future or of extrapolations from the past. Contributive, student-involving methods clearly offer an excellent setting for students to put into their own words what they see their own positions to be.

Such an exercise is frightening to some adults. But many others, even if at first they are uncertain how to articulate their assumptions, or unwilling to unveil their principles, or fearful to admit that these exist or to face what they might imply, will later acknowledge the value of eliciting them from the tangle of recollected behaviour and anticipated practice. It will certainly require great skill on the part of the trainer to persuade students to go back and still further back on what they have actually done or what they might under certain circumstances do in the future, and then to get them to explain why they act so, what implied values underlie their actions, what attitudes, expectations, considerations are consciously or unconsciously taken into account in the process. Nonetheless what is involved here can prove to be a crucial part of training: if students can make explicit just for themselves the principles on which their practice is or has been based, they can undergo a most moving educational experience which is infinitely more valuable than the mere communication to them of similar information and ideas by others. Students' learning is thus advanced via a shared experience of uncertainty and exploration, an interpretation with skilled help of what that experience has made explicit and a deliberate relation of it (again with guidance) to the students' own future work with young people.

A third basis for discussion among trainees is the enquiry into selected fields – selected in the early stages, perhaps, by the tutor but probably later, as their sense of their own needs and position becomes more acute, in conjunction with the students themselves. Whether the enquiry be conducted through books, or by talking with people in the community, or by observing the human geography of the area, or by each student simply seeking the views of others, the engagement of students in their learning will become inevitable. Moreover, in this way, the student's judgment can be utilized, his interpretations evaluated, his generalizations tested and his factual knowledge perhaps increased. Intellect and feelings, prejudices and imaginative insight can all become involved so that the student can grow in understanding of himself, of his personal philosophy and of the circumstances in which these must operate. Moreover, as it is important that the 'enquiry' should not be a deception put over on students by the trainer, the latter must not only be concerned to engage the students in an operation which gives them material for an exchange of views, but must also value the actual data which the enquiries produce. For enquiries are not a gimmick to get the social (or any other) ice broken, but must, at whatever stage of the course they are introduced, be relevant to the students' training needs.

Nevertheless, it needs to be recognized clearly that an enquiry of this sort, conducted as part of a training programme, can rarely claim to be a genuine piece of scientific research. In fact, few trainers would put it forward as such, but the adults who have carried it out may tend to over-value its results, as may many others if the results are in any way disseminated. Moreover, to emphasize the importance of making any project realistic is not the same as saying that the group's experience can be evaluated only in terms of the significance of its results to interested outsiders. This is emphatically not the case. Nor is it true that the value of the project can be assessed only by the group's estimation of the tangible end-product, since there may be other justifications for the exercise than the answering of a specific question or the reaching of a specific conclusion. To think merely of the completion of the task and to demand only that it be obviously and accurately brought to a solution would be to underestimate once again the importance of the human relations dimension of the trainee group's experience. Some of the most valuable gains of working on a project – or pursuing a discussion topic for that matter – can be measured only in personal terms and in terms of the processes and human interactions within the group. Despite the dangers inherent in this particular approach, however, it is possible for a small group of adults, by *means* of it, both to increase to some extent their store of information and to provide raw material which can act as a substantial basis for discussions both inside and outside the training course itself.

If all the members of a training group enquire into the same topic, findings may be subsequently compared and pooled. But some topics may be covered by only one or two members of the group, turns being taken meeting by meeting, so that those members become the resource-persons for the group on their special study. The responsibility of becoming the group's expert on a theme adds another dimension to this special form of enquiry, since the preparation and presentation of a 'paper' on which the group is dependent for its learning requires careful organization of the findings. The importance of making clear the sources of information and ensuring that the results are not quoted out of context is thus stressed very strongly and the student's experience of contributing to the learning of the group is enhanced.

A fourth way of providing the raw materials of discussion and exchange within a training group is to ask some of the trainees to retail something of their recent experience in working with young people. Whether this is done by recall or by recording, the contribution for discussion purposes of passages from recent working practice promotes an interchange of views of vital concern to the group. Care must obviously be taken to reveal no details to a group of trainees which would break the confidentiality of a worker's relationship with a client: such matters as would do so must be reserved for the private supervision meeting with the trainer alone. Nonetheless, the retailing of practical experience – which will occur anyway informally – is such an important source of stimulus to discussion that it cannot be seen merely as one possibility among others or simply as a means to the end of encouraging interaction in the training group. For talking and writing about the practice in which a trainee is engaging is essential to his training, which must explore his current practice for the lessons it contains. It is comparatively simple and convenient to allow people to go through a series of incidents or events and assume that experience by itself is a great teacher. No doubt it often is, and certainly without actual experience very little that is presented theoretically can come to have its full or true meaning. But if it is unexplored and un- explained many potential lessons of an experience may be missed.

The practice which is the basis for such reflection and examination may have occurred in any of a variety of settings, and if it is forming a part of the training provision it may be arranged in a number of different ways. It is perhaps most valuable if the trainee can be introduced to social-educational settings which he does not already know, so that he can gain greater insight into underlying affinities and the common relevance of general principles and can thus achieve a broader perspective. If each student can be asked to undertake work in a series of different agencies, he will of course be better able to reflect on the similarities and differences, but such wide variety of experience will usually be gained only by means of short periods of work in each setting. Even more helpful, therefore, and perhaps more likely to be possible is regular, though not necessarily frequent, attendance at the same social-educational agency so that each return visit enables the trainee to see a little further into its life and to highlight new facets of its organization and relationships. However the adult will not always be undertaking a special practical work project in connection with his training. Quite often training will proceed through on-going experience in an agency within which the adult is carrying at least some of the final responsibility for the work done.

Under whatever arrangement the practice takes place, however, it is possible and important for the elements in his work to be made explicit for or by the trainee. The human content of each situation, and the significance it has for him, should not be taken to be self-evident. It needs instead to be given verbal expression so that, through articulation and the differentiation of one concept from another, the processes and inter-relationships may be brought to a level of conscious awareness and appreciation. This may, of course, be achieved by recording-and-supervision of a kind resembling that advocated in Chapter 9 as a basis for a *practitioner's* working discipline. Recording by a trainee similarly needs to fulfil two functions – a recall of the *process* of what actually occurred, so that the detail of a situation can become available for examination; and a diagnosis of the significance and meaning of this process for future practice. Similarly, the supervision of a student in many ways resembles the supervision which an actual practitioner may receive, since its purpose is not to judge or to offer ready-made solutions but to question and so help the adult to enlighten *himself*. Whether as a student or as a practitioner, therefore, the adult concerned can use recording and supervision to increase his understanding of his own and other people's behaviour and of how he might respond to them in the future. In both cases reflection on and a disciplined reconsideration of what has occurred in the past can heighten self-awareness, illustrate the relevance and nature of empirically tested information and make clearer the existence of a body of circumscribing principles.

Because recording and supervision *are* always means of linking theory with practice and so of improving the latter, it is possible to see them always as training tools, whether they be employed 'in post' or as part of a 'course'. Nonetheless, there remain important differences between their use by a practitioner as part of his daily work and by a trainee who adopts them for training purposes, whether he is operating in an agency for whose programme he carries some ultimate responsibility or in one to which he is temporarily 'attached' for learning purposes. For a student should be able and should be encouraged to concentrate his attention in recording on only part of what he has encountered, perhaps one process of human interaction or one half-hour, and use it subsequently therefore as a learning situation requiring intensive and detailed study. He can extract this from the whole of an afternoon's or an evening's events, because as a student his primary concern is not so much to deal with an occurrence but to elicit from it the lessons relevant to his training. Thus his recording in training may well be more detailed and more fully descriptive than that of a practitioner, and the subsequent discussions he joins in or the supervision he receives will be concerned almost exclusively with revealing general points of principle and illustrating broader areas of knowledge from which deeper understanding can be derived.

The verbalization and examination of recent practical experience can be done in two settings. One is that of the training group as a whole, where trainee practitioners are encouraged to discuss their observations and work with a group of fellow-students whose previous experience and background are varied and who are prepared to pool their understanding in order to discover what is common to them all. The aim here is not only to work through description and interpretation but much more to search for implications and for the relationship between one experience and another, to initiate the scientific process of comparing like with like, and to discern what from this emerges as a general principle. In this way, a foundation can be laid for systematic thinking about attitudes and approaches to young people and so for a comparatively objective frame of reference and a personal discipline of work.

The other setting for the verbalization of the experiences of social-educational practice is of course the supervision meeting when the trainer works either with a student alone or with a small group of students jointly searching the practice of one of their number for principles and insights. The purpose then is less the *interchange* of experience and interpretations, as with the group's discussion of an individual's practice, and more the deliberate and disciplined reflection under the guidance of the trainer. Practical experience is again the raw material of discussion, but the active participation and expression of views by the student is clearly at its greatest and most intense in this setting. None of the other possible stimuli to discussion is as pressing, as searching or as engaging of the whole personality of the student as is supervised reflection on practice.

The group or individual settings have their own advantages and disadvantages. If the examination is carried out by the group, the need to phrase questions and formulate attitudes to someone else's experience will stimulate a still greater growth in each student's consciousness of his own assumptions and ways of working. It may lead him to discover, also, that others start from very different positions and so may act in very different ways. On the other hand, there is a danger that other members of the group may adopt censorious or judicial attitudes, or that the individual whose experience is being discussed may think they have. There is a risk, too, that students may 'opt out' of the discussion when it worries them or touches their uncertainty, just at the point in fact where they have most to learn, since they have the excuse that it is not *their* practice which is under review. For these reasons, as well also as for reasons of confidentiality, it is often advantageous if student and trainer can analyse the former's experiences in private and so make possible the emergence of much that could not be aired or evaluated in a group discussion. In either case, what one person has encountered and how one person has interpreted this – in writing or on tape – becomes a case-study to be examined in depth, so that the student whose experience it is will gain by being brought to state explicitly what he saw, heard and felt, and how he viewed this. Thus can those lessons which are contained in experience but which are not immediately apparent be deliberately and meaningfully 'taught'.

Finally, it must be noted in connection with the 'practice' which provides raw material for this form of active student participation (and indeed with training in general) that it is not permissible to do anything in the name of 'training' which uses any young person as a guinea-pig any more than it is permissible to act against his interests in social-educational practice generally. Indeed any good course of preparation will be designed, as we have seen, to help students define a set of occupational principles and so to prevent just this kind of denial of an individual's integrity.

Adults in training for social-educational work, then, may be offered a variety of sources of raw material for the discussions which will be the anvil of their training. Whether the expression and exchange of ideas surrounds problem areas, a simple job analysis, enquiry topics or recent practical experience, it is through verbalization and examination in partnership with fellow-trainees that the adult has the best chance of discovering and evaluating his own attitudes.

The Tutorial Function

So far in this chapter, the word 'trainer' has been used to describe anyone, whatever his precise function, responsible for the training of social educators. In fact, however, there is a considerable variety of functions implied here, even though at times they may all be fulfilled by one, two or more people. Some of these functions, though essential to the overall training operation, are not directly concerned with the students' learning and involve the trainer in providing premises, recruiting and selecting participants and measuring their attainment, considering which (if any) resource-figures are required and ultimately evaluating the course itself. Other functions do bring the trainer into immediate contact with the situations in which learning is occurring but rely heavily on the traditional assumptions about didactic approaches and require the trainer to act as lecturer or instructor or demonstrator of approved 'techniques'.

There is, however, yet another range of functions to which we wish to pay special attention and which will at times demand that the trainer play what might be called 'tutorial' roles. These follow directly from the fact that any trainer's competence to speak authoritatively is limited and that, though he may have an understanding and even a vision of where students can get to ultimately, it is they and only they who can know where their knowledge and experience stand at the outset and whether they are prepared to allow these to be extended. The trainer's tutorial role enables him to help students build up confidence in their own capacities and ideas and to share with them much of the responsibility for directing and carrying out their training.

Though, sometimes, such tutorial functions will be fulfilled with individuals, mostly they will occur among groups and always they will be

Q

directly concerned with the actual learning processes which students encounter. Thus if the students and the trainer in his capacity as tutor are able, jointly and progressively, to put into words a dialogue about present felt positions and possible future advances, students will grow in that self-assurance which is an essential basis of true learning, the training content will be more closely tailored to their individual needs and their learning will be stimulated in ways which might otherwise be missed.

Such a role is more, not less, difficult than the didactic and other roles which the trainer will play, largely because it leaves so much to be decided by the tutor at the time that he is actually in the midst of the training situation. In working within a course whose detailed events and paths of activity and discussion are not under his complete control, it seems inevitable that at times he should feel a strain which would otherwise not exist. Since the right to make decisions is shared with the trainees them-selves, and since they may not know for certain what decisions need to be made or how to make them and be explicit about them, the tutor will necessarily be uncertain also for much of the time and such uncertainty is bound to be uncomfortable. Hesitant, sensitive progress is, in fact, inherent in all conscious working relationships between human beings, so that a tutor will need fully to accept before he starts that he may be anxious and uneasy for large parts of the training periods and that while playing his tutorial role he will be feeling his way the whole time, trying to act according to circumstances and people's reactions. The tutor will find himself continually having to make deliberate decisions – about what to say, when to intervene, whether or how to introduce an idea or a piece of information, how to treat an individual student – and yet can have no advance guarantee that the choice he makes will turn out to be the right one.

The tutor does not of course need to appear to be omniscient or infallible. Indeed, if he is to maintain an integrity in his relationship with his students the tutor will find himself frequently acknowledging that they have delved deeper than he has and now know more than he on the topic in question. At the same time this acknowledgment will be a source of encouragement to the student because he will see that tutors have their limitations, too, and because it will remind him of his share in the respon-sibility for his own training. Certainly the tutor will have to show that each student must be regarded as, and must accept the role of, expert on the relationship of the training to his own social-educational practice. After all, the tutor is not cast as an 'all-knowing' source of wisdom, but as one person who helps mainly by creating a situation in which other people can really learn.

On many occasions in fact the tutor will be learning with and from the trainees, experiencing with them some or all of the discomforts of learning, and it is important that the students know that this is happening. The fact that the tutor's own education is going on at the same time as the students' does not of course reduce his 'right' to be tutor. For his position is not dependent on superior knowledge and experience of social education: it is justified, and his ability is measured, more by the skill he shows in making others aware of their own knowledge and its limits and in helping them to make more knowledge their own.

At times the tutor may actually need deliberately to make students conscious of his anxieties, his mistakes, his ways of handling situations. His own, as well as the students', foibles and strengths may on occasions be relevant matter for discussion, needing not merely to be lived with and perhaps laughed or grumbled at by trainees, but also to be utilized and exploited by incorporation into the total training process. For if the tutor is intent on developing self-awareness in his students, and if their training is not to become academic and non-personal, then he as well as they must be prepared for self-examination. His own participation in events cannot remain outside the analysis and evaluation in which he wants those he is 'teaching' to engage. Clearly therefore the tutor's understanding of himself will be vital and may on occasions need to be pursued in public.

Once again, the result may sometimes be uncomfortable for the tutor. In the first place students, perhaps educated previously by different methods, may well find it difficult to understand and to use constructively the opportunities presented to them. They may, for example, assume that the tutor is indifferent or incompetent, or that he has formulated some sinister and undeclared plan which is designed to trick them. They may try to force him to act as an authority in areas of study in which he knows he has no special expertise. When he does not fulfil their demands, whether these are justified or not, their own unsureness and confusion may lead them to attack him in ways which may seem very personal.

Tutors will also have to accept that, when they go into a training group, some of its members will almost certainly be more intelligent than they are themselves, some more sensitive to people and some better able, either potentially or actually, to form and develop relationships with young people. This knowledge of the tutor's relative inferiority in some respects will need to be near the surface of his mind and to influence his behaviour throughout the training periods. He will have to be aware that at times it threatens him and makes him defensive, and that, together with more immediate and private moods and feelings, it makes him liable to place the students' training needs second to the preservation of his own self-esteem or peace of mind.

Another requirement on the trainer as tutor is that he make himself deliberately aware of his personal reactions to and feelings about individual trainees. Some of these may seem irrelevant to his training functions since they may simply indicate that he likes some students more than others, would choose to make some of them personal friends but not others. Even so, it is important that he attempt to be conscious of such personal reactions since they can influence his judgment and treatment of the students concerned. Similarly, he needs to make a deliberate effort to acknowledge that individual students will respond to him as a person in a great variety of ways and that his perception of their attitudes to and opinions of him can cause him to modify his contribution to their training. Such a self-conscious search for insight into and control of his own personal feelings is an integral part of his training function.

Yet some of the tutor's interpretations of students' behaviour will be clearly relevant to his work and indeed many of them will need to be made knowingly and deliberately. For he will continually need to be observing and noting how individuals are contributing and reacting even while he is deeply immersed in the mood and arguments of a discussion among trainees, since members of the group will be revealing a great many of their needs by their responses. Bees in bonnets, prejudices, resistances, insecurities, fears, preoccupations, doubts and weaknesses in practice will be displayed during the group's interaction as well as strengths and points of growth and development. The roles which each individual will play at different times – informant, facilitator, saboteur, enquirer, scapegoat, joker, and so on – will all tell something of his personality. The tutor needs of course to interpret what he sees with caution, because he will never be absolutely sure that he is reading the signs aright. But he will need nonetheless to see the experiences he shares with trainees as offering valuable evidence as to how he might help them individually.

However, in playing the role of tutor, a trainer will often have to be prepared to hold back in his relations with students, even though their need seems to be staring him in the face and he is certain he knows the answer. He will have to resist the temptation to solve all their problems for them immediately they arise in order to allow them time to make clear to themselves that these are their problems and that they might solve them more effectively for themselves. He cannot lay all knowledge before the members of his course in an indigestible feast and may have to delay correcting glaring errors, sometimes even of fact, so that students may eventually do these things for themselves if they can. Most of his interventions will be wasted and meaningless unless they are kept until the critical moment when the students can best assimilate them.

Nonetheless, tutorial work may often require the trainer to remind trainees that the course is longer than its current session and to help them to accept that the whole body of knowledge which they want cannot be had at once. They may sometimes need help, too, to realize that an absence of detailed planning does not mean that a group can roam at will each time it meets to study, but that, to maximize the value of its time, limits will need to be set and kept, preferably by the students themselves. For it is unquestionably true that one of the tutor's tasks is to interpret to students the succeeding objectives in the course and to enable them to attain these according to what individually they can and most need to achieve. In fact these two complementary elements in the tutorial function – the refusal to offer ready-made 'answers' with the consequent insistence that students make active and individual responses, and the obligation to play a positive and influential, stimulating role – may not be quickly understood or reconciled by students.

Clearly, however, what all this means in practice is that as often as possible the tutor will have to avoid *spontaneous* introduction of his own opinions and feelings in any group discussion, and consciously and deliberately to ask himself a series of questions about his next intervention. While a group is at work, and also while it is outside its more formal sessions, he will need to judge whether to be passive listener, aggressive contradictor, provider of information, facilitator of one person's contribution or protector of another person's feelings or ideas – or whether to play some other role still. He may on occasion need to change the direction of a discussion, or bring it back to something said earlier. The tutorial function does not entail the trainer in withdrawing from his share in responsibility for the work of the group, nor in leaving unlimited freedom of action to the students: on the contrary, he is at each moment, because he has no procedure laid down in advance, assessing what it is that he should say or do next to aid the progress of the training.

What complicates the picture still further and makes the tutor's job even more taxing is his consciousness that very often there can be no suggestion of reaching a definite conclusion or solution to satisfy everyone. Certainly, the tutor will be continuously alert for confusions of fact with personal opinion and philosophy and he may well exercise a very positive influence either at the time when this occurs or later when the moment is ripe. But he will know that he may not be able to get the group to produce any answers or concrete result from its work, and moreover that coincidence with his own views may be completely irrelevant and certainly not to be desired for its own sake alone. Some, even all, members of the trainee group may reach a conclusion with which the tutor personally profoundly disagrees: they may reject ideas or values which he holds very dear. Where it is opinion and not fact that is being challenged, however, the individual must be sovereign in his own situation and there may be nothing that the tutor could or should do, except perhaps to help the trainee clarify his views.

In particular, when students are working out the underlying sanctions of their practice, deducing from work already done the guiding principles which each believes to be appropriate to his future work with young people, the tutor will need to exercise a special self-discipline. He will need to understand that such principles can legitimately be deduced in this way and that there may emerge honestly held views contrary to his own. It is true that the tutor himself must have a sure grasp of his own principles, and he must feel free to reveal these, particularly if the adults for whose training he is responsible appear to be ignoring, implicitly or explicitly, what he believes to be an inescapable sanction on the work they have elected to do. But the principles he believes in are no dogma received from an unchallengeable source and it would be pointless for him to 'insist' upon their endorsement by unsympathetic students. Even if the students paid lip-service to them in this way, the principles would certainly not serve their only justifying purpose, which is to guide the future actions of those who really accept them.

If the tutor *presented* his students at any stage with principles deduced from past practice, and implied that they *must* work according to these in the future, he would in effect be saying, 'I (and perhaps some co-workers) have behaved in the past in ways which make the following statements accurate generalizations about what *we* did and why we did it. Therefore *you* must in the future behave in such a way that these same statements can be accurately used to generalize about your actions'. Few tutors would take up a position which denies so blatantly their students' independence of thought and judgment. Nonetheless, some tutors are guilty at times of dogmatic assertion on matters where no such authority is possible, and students are properly resentful: equally regrettable is the readiness with which, at other times, students accept distilled experience from a tutor's own past as if it were a potion to cure all the problems of a wider group.

Certainly the experiences of the past, the tutor's no less than those of any other member of the group, need to be offered as bones to chew on – the raw material out of which each trainee's guiding principles can be constructed. Again the tutor must be quick to show inconsistencies if no student draws attention to them. It is for the tutor, too, in this process of hammering out principles, to highlight here as elsewhere any areas of behaviour which are left uncovered or uncharted. By the verbalization of his own assumptions about work with young people; by comparing the purposes and methods of different organizations; by drawing together the views of different members of the group; and by pointing to ideas and values which students, when discussing their practice, ignore or take for granted and so often never consciously encounter – by all these means the tutor can enable students to develop for themselves a body of principles to which they can refer while they are actually at work in social education.

There is another, especially demanding, task which the tutor must in some way fulfil, and that is to find an effective way of incorporating into the course the accumulated wisdom, the facts, the empirically determined data which traditionally are conveyed by some didactic method or by use of enquiry projects. For the students must not only come into contact with this information, they must also face its implications and absorb it so that it influences their future practice. As we have seen, adults learn comparatively quickly and most profitably if they can put words to concepts themselves, if they can link a fact (or an idea) to their own existing schemata of attitudes and assumptions. To help them to do this, the tutor can ask for reactions to what he or others have stated, or say things in such a way that considered responses are forthcoming. Even the commonest words may need public definition by group members if a language is to be evolved which really ensures effective communication. Even the plainest facts may need to be given meaning by their recipient if they are to help him to learn, since little is gained in practice if accurate information is stated without its significance to personal needs and circumstances being seen. Certainly the tutor is using his time wastefully if he merely succeeds in passing across a body of information which students cannot relate to their experience or their special requirements.

In addition the tutor may find himself interpreting to a group or to individuals, or encouraging them to interpret for themselves, the significance of their own group or personal behaviour. He may have to persuade trainees to assess their own progress by asking questions too searching for them to ask themselves, by reminding them of past events and statements in their own shared experience, by pointing to omissions and evasions, by indicating where needs are being fulfilled and where they remain unsatisfied. This task of interpretation, or of stimulating others to interpret, is one of the most important the tutor is called upon to undertake. In fact it reveals what is the essence of the tutor's role. For continually he will find himself acting as a catalyst, making no apparent direct contribution himself but making the contributions of many others possible and effective. The frankness and depth of the discussions, the detachment or emotional involvement of members of a group, the social skills developed, the growth of individual self-awareness made possible as well as the trainees' subsequent disciplined social-educational practice, will all very much depend on the quality, precision and deployment of the tutor's skill and stimulus.

The Experience of Training

The sort of training processes described above can in the long run ensure that the adults concerned in them are much better equipped to fulfil their roles as social educators. By participation in a real and living human relations experience, by having to become conscious of the processes and interaction which this experience embodies, by acknowledging many facets of their own personalities and philosophies, by being brought into contact with broader areas of knowledge and understanding in ways which touch them personally, students are likely to be prepared much more adequately for the commitment and challenges inherent in many of the relationships they will form with young people. Such an operation will not allow them to treat what they meet simply as interesting but irrelevant academic knowledge, or as pleasant play-acting which has no connection with the 'real' job of the social educator. Their encounter with themselves and with others and their common search for principles and understanding must ultimately make them better practitioners.

Such a training, to be effective, should be exciting and enjoyable. There should be a growing recognition by the participants that they are on a course of discovery and self-discovery rather than of instruction, and that they are expected to be directly involved from the outset in the learning processes. This feeling will create an active concern in the minds of the 'trainees' to make the best possible use of the time and opportunities available since as free and responsible people they have so much to gain from the experience. Through this form of training individuals can come to realize that they are capable of achieving much more than they envisaged or admitted before, and qualities, abilities and interests can be stirred and released which previously had lain unsuspected or latent. In consequence almost all of those who undergo it ought to be able to feel that they have derived a great sense of attainment and self-expression and so of pleasure and fulfilment.

Nonetheless such training, with its particular purposes and methods of work, will often prove uncomfortable for all those involved in it. Some of the more disturbing effects on the tutor have already been mentioned. On students, certainly at the start, the impact may prove to be equally unsettling and even for a time painful. Training for any form of human relations work must affect the person being trained in an intimate way. While some of what he may learn as this goes on will certainly be enriching and exciting, some other experiences may prove disquieting.

For, in the first place, self-awareness, as has already been indicated, cannot be achieved unless the trainee seeks out and faces aspects of his personality which previously he has allowed to remain, or has kept, hidden from himself. Traits, feelings, ideas, attitudes which he may never have consciously acknowledged before may on occasions have to be admitted, at least to himself. The student's own immediate reaction may even be one of depression in the face of the apparent criticisms which such self-discovery seems to bring. He may feel that it is rather like holding himself up to a mirror which reflects the psychological rather than the physical, and being shocked by some of the images. Though students often exaggerate the seriousness of what is thus revealed to them, the discomfort, especially at first, may be considerable.

Secondly, students' re-examination of personal beliefs and of their approach to young people may at times be disturbing. Some of them may lack a deep-down assurance about their work and position, while others may have formed their habits, especially in their social-educational work, many years before and may consequently find reappraisal and restatement difficult. The continual questioning may appear to them to threaten or even to deny completely what they stand for and hold dear. They may feel, perhaps unconsciously, that too much probing is likely to expose uncertainties, prejudices and blank spots, and that any attempt to relate what they believe personally to what client-centred, disciplined social education requires of them is contradictory and confusing and so better avoided. For, as training increases their consciousness of the principles relating to their work, they will quickly become more aware of where these conflict with each other and possibly with their own beliefs, and of how difficult the resolution of such conflict can be.

Thirdly, they may feel strongly challenged as they try to put these principles into the context of the human sciences. For, if the latter are approached as practical studies to be applied to the human relationships and behaviour which a trainee encounters in his life and practice, he will almost certainly apply them also to himself and his own behaviour. A growing acquaintance with these sciences, therefore, cannot be simply an objective non-personal process. It is pointless, for example, in training for work of a practical nature among people, to 'learn about' prejudice as an intellectual exercise, to 'know' all there is to know about prejudices, and yet never truly to consider the prejudices one has oneself. To attempt such a consideration, however, to involve oneself personally once more, can sometimes be very disturbing. In a similar way there is little justification, in training for social-educational work with adolescents, to talk of members of a club or class or troop *only* in an objective way, or of 'young people' as if they were a race apart. It is much more profitable, but again much more searching, to speak of adolescent experiences in one's own past and to see young people now as fellows in a comparable existence.

Of course, no adult *need* allow himself to become deeply embroiled in the training process if he does not want to do so. There is a whole host of defences which he can and will construct if he prefers to avoid the pain of involvement. Moreover it needs to be stated categorically that it is not for the trainer to assume that these defences have to be broken down. Almost certainly at some point or other the trainer will have to withdraw, to admit that he should not go or cannot go further, even though the adult's training will seem to him to be incomplete as a result. This is perhaps particularly important in the training of part-time youth workers, since the trainer may meet the students briefly or infrequently and thus have only limited opportunities to follow up and help to resolve any uncertainties created by training. Only the individual trainer can judge in relation to each trainee how far he should go in pursuing his training aims.

Notwithstanding the defences and resistances, however, if training is to be effective and personal it is likely to cause at least some disturbance. For, however much the trainee tries to protect himself or to contain the effects of his training experience, at least some personal confusion is likely to follow from deeper self-understanding, from the re-examination of personal ideals, from the deliberate acknowledgment of the sanctions which circumscribe practice and from the growing contact with the human sciences. Questioning, searching, discovering and applying personally are an integral part of social educators' training.

The long-term and practical results of training, however, are likely to be strengthening, not just to the student's practice as a social educator, but also to him or her as a mature human being. This will not of course occur in any straightforward or direct way. All the answers to the problems of life in general are not suddenly going to become apparent, nor are all the 'gains' of training going to be immediately and obviously available on the job. For training for work involving human relationships is not like training for a mechanical or physical skill. Because the social educator works, not through something external to himself, but through himself as a person, his training cannot be effective in his work until it has touched his own attitudes and assumptions about many areas of life as a whole. It is for this reason that training for social education demands opportunity to think and reflect, to adjust and reorientate. The emphasis in supervision is clearly on reflection and examination, at leisure, and away from the scene of the work. Similarly much of the discussion advocated above has to be carried on in a falsely protected atmosphere, and the crises, problems and happenings of social-educational practice are dealt with in a withdrawn and unhurried way. The student who in the initial stages of training especially must begin to develop self-understanding and the other parts of the discipline relevant to his work will thus be much aided by opportunities to examine with detachment what was done, why it was done, what resulted from it and what action might be needed.

But consideration and discussion of past practice will often in initial training affect the personality of the trainee more than they will affect his immediately ensuing work as a social educator. Only slowly will the beginner be able actually to apply the principles, only gradually will the effects of the structured discussions of the training periods be seen directly and immediately in his actual practice. It is only in the long run that practice is affected by the withdrawal, the reflection, the discussion of basic principles and ideals, the reappraisal of personal viewpoint, and the appreciation of a broader social context. Initially human relations training must help people prepare for later demands. Through their training students should have the chance to work out criteria for rapid action, to build up their personal resources in order that later they can face and overcome crises, to develop existing ideas and traits as well as new values and attributes so that they will not be left without guidance when they are working under pressure. This kind of training does not turn social educators into men and women of thought rather than action. Instead it helps them to respond more surely and with greater precision: with less panic in face of the incomprehensible and with less emotional hastiness. When emergencies occur, and also in the undramatic events of social-educational practice, training of this kind has its justification in greater consistency of good work and in greater transferability of skill. For a worker's performance is no longer made to depend on a particular factor in any situation – be it agency, clients, colleagues or organization – but on a discipline which gives him flexibility and adaptability in the face of a variety of complex circumstances.

What happens in fact is less that the student 'picks up' or 'attaches to himself' techniques and habits and ideas to put into immediate operation. It is much more that over time and especially with experience, he *internalizes* lessons about himself, about others in the reality of their situations, about what is expected of him as a social educator, and about how this is likely to be best achieved. The use to which lessons will be put will not simply or even mainly be by the selection of bits of them for direct application in some mechanical way. They will be used in influencing, often unconsciously, his own actual visible behaviour, in modifying it and in making it more appropriate to the need. The social educator's problems will be no fewer and no less acute, but he will face them with a greater sense of perspective, detachment and self-assurance. The strain of being continually exposed and likely to be challenged, of meeting repeated rebuff and apparently personal denial, will be more easily carried. Inner resources ought to have grown.

What all this implies, what the trainer and trainee need to face as far as possible before the training process ever begins, is that training for social education is likely to *change* people. The change will not be radical: no one will become completely unrecognizable to those who knew him or her before. Nor will the change be in any way sinister, since it will not occur without the trainee's knowledge, making him into something unbeknown to himself. After all, the trainer will have, like the social educator himself, a set of principles to guide his work which will ensure, among other things, that he respects the integrity of each individual client. What arises out of training, however, may well be an undeniable development of the personality which embarked on it. Spots are unlikely ever to be completely changed, but their shading may alter. A trainee's fundamental values and philosophy, his most integral characteristics and his idiosyncrasies may remain unmodified; but less deep-seated patterns of behaviour, more peripheral expressions of personality, more lightly-held assumptions and attitudes, more superficially ingrained habits and customs may be noticeably different. And since human behaviour does not keep to watertight compartments, these changes will often be evident in other areas of the trainee's life than his social-educational practice.

Many adults may have misgivings about such change, either because they fear it or because they feel that in some way it is unethical. Yet it is clear that the vast majority of those who have experienced this kind of training look back on it with pleasure and feel greatly strengthened by it. Moreover if real training for work with people – rather than a superficial accretion of techniques – is to take place, a degree of change is unavoidable. Training for work in the field of human relations necessarily stimulates changes in attitude, since its most important effect is not what it gives to people but what it does to them.

The adult then is likely to emerge from the experience of training with greater assurance and personal strength. If training has been effective, he will have begun the key process of understanding himself and his relationships, and will have begun to develop the discipline relevant to his social-educational practice with young people.

Index